𝔐EDIEVAL 𝔈UROPE: A Short History

Medieval Europe:

A Short History

C. Warren Hollister

John Wiley & Sons, Inc., New York · London · Sydney

SECOND PRINTING, AUGUST, 1965

Copyright © 1964 by John Wiley & Sons, Inc.
All Rights Reserved. This book or any part
thereof must not be reproduced in any form
without the written permission of the publisher.

Library of Congress Catalog Card Number: 64-25888
Printed in the United States of America

TO MY PARENTS

Preface

This brief survey of medieval Western Europe is intended for the beginning college student or for the general reader who wishes a compact summary of the period. When used in college or university courses in Western Civilization or World History, its brevity will allow ample time for collateral readings in the sources or in the more advanced and interpretive secondary literature. It was written to meet a need that I have encountered in my own teaching: for a core book around which diverse supplementary readings could be clustered—a review of the medieval period that is neither a bare outline nor a small encyclopedia.

It is my conviction that such a book must be trustworthy, literate, and brief. The student must be able to depend on the interpretations in the book as representing sound conclusions or modern scholarship rather than brilliant but untested hypotheses of the author. The student should, if at all possible, enjoy the book—drawing from it a lucid organization of the historical data and a sense of liveliness and excitement as well. Finally, he should not be obliged to spend the bulk of his reading time on a narrative survey. The book must be sufficiently long to present a coherent overview of a great historical epoch and to suggest its economic, intellectual, and cultural achievements as well as its political developments, but it must be sufficiently short to permit the student to read widely in supplementary works—to explore special topics in depth, to become familiar with the controversial literature on great historical issues, and to examine some of the contemporary sources. A good sampling of appropriate collateral readings, many of them in paperback, is provided in the annotated bibliographies at the ends of each of the three sections of this book.

For the sake of brevity, much has been omitted. I have seldom been able to probe very far beneath the surface of events. Had I done so consistently, the book would have been far too long to serve the purpose for which it is intended. Historians will inevitably disagree as to what should be included and what excluded in a compact summary of this sort, and the final choice must always rest on the judgment of the individual author. In particular, the careful reader will notice two major omissions in the present book: (1) Eastern Europe has been treated only sketchily, because I believe that its evolution in the Middle Ages was less essential to the making of Western Civilization than was the development of medieval culture in Germany, Italy, France, and England. (2) The narrative closes early in the fourteenth century, thereby excluding the period commonly known as the Late Middle Ages. I have chosen to leave this period to historians of the Renaissance, who quite rightly lay claim to the era of Petrarch and Boccaccio. The teacher of Western Civilization might wish to supplement this book with one of several excellent brief surveys of the Renaissance Age that are available in paperback, for example, Wallace K. Ferguson's splendid volume in the Berkshire Series.

To the several anonymous readers who were selected to evaluate and criticize the present work, I express my thanks. All these readers are well-known historians whose styles clearly betray their identities, but I am not permitted to mention them here by name as I would wish. I also thank Professors Brian Tierney and Richard C. Dales, who provided perceptive suggestions on Chapters 14 and 15, respectively. I am indebted to my wife and my parents, who read the manuscript in full, pruning it of many infelicities and ambiguities. More objective readers could be found, but none more devoted.

Santa Barbara, California   C. WARREN HOLLISTER
August 1964

Contents

List of Maps

List of Plates

MEDIEVAL EUROPE: A Short History

Introduction

A hundred years ago the medieval centuries of European history were widely regarded as "The Dark Ages." Western man was thought to have dropped into a deep slumber at the fall of the Western Roman Empire in A.D. 476, awakening at length, like Rip Van Winkle, in the bright dawn of the Italian Renaissance. Indeed, it was the humanists of fifteenth-century Renaissance Italy who first created this dismal image of their medieval forebears, and the condemnation was echoed by the sixteenth-century Protestant reformers and by the philosophers of the eighteenth-century French enlightenment. The term "Middle Ages" was coined to denote a prolonged era of spiritual and cultural intermission separating classical antiquity from the Renaissance and unworthy of a name of its own. It was an age whose art was barbaric or "Gothic"—a millennium of darkness—a thousand years without a bath.

Today this ungenerous point of view stands discredited, although it persists among the half-educated. Several generations of rigorous historical scholarship have demonstrated clearly that the medieval period was an epoch of immense vitality and profound creativity. The age that produced Thomas Aquinas and Dante, Notre Dame de Paris and Chartres, Parliament and the university, can hardly be described as "dark" or "barbaric."

Still, one is reminded endlessly in textbooks that life in medieval Europe was vastly different from life in modern America and that the medieval intellectual climate was far removed from our own. Countless students have been taught to contrast feudalism with democracy, the medieval mind with the modern mind, the "Age of Faith" with our own age of technology, or doubt, or cybernetics, or whatever it might be. These are truths that few would be in-

1

clined to doubt, and it seems unnecessary to belabor the point that the political and cultural leaders of today are not very much like St. Bernard or Pope Gregory VII. The chief pitfall in understanding medieval Europe is not a failure to recognize its all too obvious contrasts with modern society. Rather, it is the danger that in dwelling too intently upon these alien qualities we may overlook the all-important fact that the Middle Ages constituted the earliest phase of our own civilization. One of the great benefits in the study of medieval history is the opportunity it affords to examine the birth, youth, and early maturity of Western European society. As we investigate the Middle Ages we are scrutinizing our own cultural origins. By the twelfth and thirteenth centuries Western Civilization had succeeded in attaining a cultural level comparable to that of the great civilizations of the past, but it also possessed an enormous potential for further development. It was destined, in later centuries, to transcend by far the achievements of the past and, for good or ill, to transform the world.

Western Civilization was born in the Early Middle Ages, but its ancestry runs far back into classical and preclassical antiquity. Like the two great neighboring civilizations of Byzantium and Islam, which influenced it in so many ways, medieval Europe was an offspring of the mighty Mediterranean civilization that had preceded it—a child of Greece and Rome. But the classical past was by no means the only ingredient that went into the making of Europe. Medieval civilization arose from a synthesis of three powerful, disparate cultural traditions: the Greco-Roman, the Judaeo-Christian, and the Germanic. The process of cultural fusion which underlay the development of medieval Europe was both gradual and uneven, and in order to trace its evolution we must begin our story long before the collapse of Roman authority in the West. We must turn, first of all, to the Roman Empire at the zenith of its power.

Part 1

ROME: Greatness and Decline

1

The Roman Empire at Its Height

THE FIRST TWO CENTURIES

During the two centuries from the rise of Augustus to the death of Marcus Aurelius (*c.* 31 B.C.–A.D. 180), the Roman Empire expanded gradually to include a vast area from the Euphrates to the Atlantic—from the Sahara to the Danube, the Rhine, and the Cheviot Hills of northern Britain.

The burden of defending the far-flung frontiers rested on an army of some 300,000 to 500,000 men, organized on principles laid down by Augustus. Infantry legions manned by Roman citizens on long-term enlistments were supplemented by auxiliary forces, both infantry and light cavalry, made up of non-Romans who were granted citizenship at the end of their extended terms of service. The army was concentrated along the frontiers except for the small and highly privileged Praetorian Guard which served the emperor in Rome itself. A high degree of mobility was ensured by the superb system of roads which connected the city of Rome with her most remote provinces. Paved with stones fitted closely together, these roads were nearly as eternal as the city they served. They eased the flow of commerce as well as the movement of troops and remained in use many centuries after the Roman Peace was shattered by anarchy and barbarian invasions.

Map I.   The Roman Empire at its height: early second century.

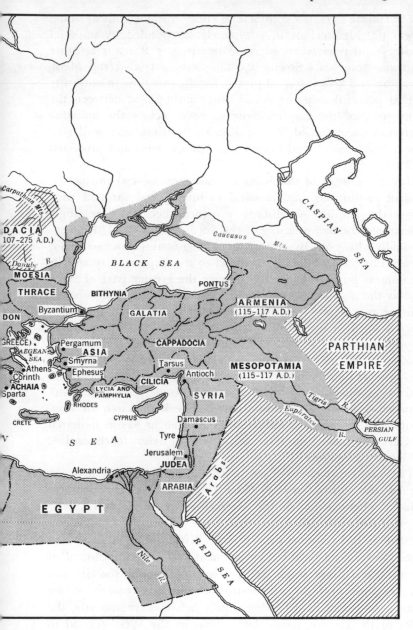

Carpathian Mts.

DACIA
107–275 A.D.)

Danube R.

MOESIA

THRACE

DON

GREECE)

AEGEAN
SEA

Athens

Corinth

ACHAIA

Sparta

CRETE

V

S E A

Byzantium

Pergamum

ASIA

Smyrna

Ephesus

RHODES

LYCIA AND
PAMPHYLIA

CYPRUS

BLACK   SEA

BITHYNIA

PONTUS

GALATIA

CAPPADOCIA

CILICIA

Tarsus

Antioch

SYRIA

Damascus

Tyre

Jerusalem

JUDEA

Alexandria

ARABIA

EGYPT

Nile R.

Caucasus   Mts.

CASPIAN

SEA

ARMENIA
(115–117 A.D.)

PARTHIAN
EMPIRE

MESOPOTAMIA
(115–117 A.D.)

Tigris R.

Euphrates

R.

PERSIAN
GULF

Arabs

RED   SEA

The empire's greatest commercial artery was not built of stone; it was the Mediterranean, completely surrounded by imperial territory and referred to affectionately by the Romans as *Mare Nostrum*—"our sea." Strong Roman fleets patrolled the Mediterranean and kept it free of pirates for the first time in antiquity so that peaceful shipping could move unimpeded between the many parts of the empire. Now as never before the immense territories encompassed by the Roman frontiers were well governed, well policed, and bound together by roads and protected seaways.

Under the aegis of the Roman Peace, commercial prosperity, Roman institutions, and classical culture spread far and wide across the empire. As distant provinces became increasingly Romanized the very meaning of the words "Rome" and "Roman" gradually changed. By the time of Augustus (31 B.C.–A.D. 14) these terms were no longer confined to the imperial city and its inhabitants but had come to embrace the greater part of Italy. And as the decades of the Roman Peace followed one another, citizenship was progressively extended to more and more provincials until finally, in A.D. 212, every free inhabitant of the empire was made a citizen. Emperors themselves now tended, as often as not, to be provincials: Trajan and Hadrian, perhaps the two greatest emperors of the second century, were both natives of Spain. In time the terms "Rome" and "Roman" acquired a universal connotation: a Greek monarch in Constantinople, a Frankish monarch at Aachen, a Saxon monarch in Germany, could, in later centuries, all refer to themselves as "Roman Emperors."

The most conspicuous effect of Romanization was the urbanizing of the entire empire. The city-state, the characteristic political phenomenon of the Greco-Roman world, now spread through the outer provinces—into Gaul, Spain, the lands along the Rhine and Danube, even remote Britain. The city retained a good measure of local self-government and normally controlled the rural territories in its vicinity. In other words, the city was the key unit of local administration; the government of the Roman state remained fundamentally urban. Paradoxically, the cities of the empire, particularly those in the West, tended to be of relatively minor importance as commercial and manufacturing centers. Rome experienced no industrial revolution and, although small-scale urban industry often flourished, especially in the East, the economy of the empire remained fundamentally agrarian. Many of the western cities—most notably Rome itself—consumed far more than they produced. Unlike the cities of medieval and modern Europe they were not economically self-sufficient but instead acted as parasites on the imperial economy. Basically they were administrative and military centers whose mercantile significance was secondary. During the first two centuries of the empire the economy was prosperous enough to support them, but this would not always be the case. In time the cities would decline and with them the whole political organization of the Greco-Roman world.

In the opening years of the empire, as in the late republic, slaves played a crucial role in the economy, particularly in agriculture. But as the frontiers gradually ceased to expand and the flow of captives diminished, the chief source of slaves was cut off. Large landholders now tended to lease great portions of their estates to free sharecroppers called *coloni,* who tended to fall more and more under the control of their landlords and sank slowly to a semifree servile status akin to that of the medieval serfs. The *coloni,* like the impoverished masses which continued to crowd the larger cities, enjoyed very little of the buoyant prosperity of the early empire. The second century A.D. was, by ancient standards, an epoch of remarkable material well-being, but it would be absurd to compare it to the abundance of the advanced industrial states of today. Roman society always included, beneath its imposing veneer, a vast, wretched substratum of half-starved peasants and paupers.

The condition of the lower classes would have been still worse but for the enlightened humanitarian policies of the imperial government. It was particularly among the great second-century emperors that Stoic attitudes of human brotherhood, compassion, and social and political responsibility took hold. Emperors such as Hadrian and Marcus Aurelius regarded their authority as a trust, a profound responsibility to govern in the interests of the people whether rich or poor, privileged or lowly. The empire of the second century is ornamented by its sensitive social conscience no less than by its wise and vigorous leadership in military and administrative affairs.

ROMAN LITERATURE AND THOUGHT

Roman literature, building on its magnificent Greek heritage yet drawing also from its own cultural resources, was to exert a powerful impact on the medieval and modern West. Few medieval scholars and poets knew Greek, but virtually all of them knew Latin. And although Latin translations of important Greek philosophical and scientific works began to flood into the medieval West in the twelfth and thirteenth centuries, Western Europe did not feel the full impact of the Greek tradition in *belles lettres* until the time of the Italian Renaissance. Hence Roman literature influenced the Middle Ages far more deeply than did Greek literature.

Roman writers were not, as a rule, particularly interested in scientific theory or in profound philosophical speculation; as a result they fell far short of the Greeks in these areas. But they succeeded in making the Latin language a superb literary vehicle for their moral and political ideas and their epic and lyric poetry. During the turbulent closing decades of the Roman Republic, Rome produced an impressive group of authors and poets, the most notable of whom was the great senatorial orator, Cicero. His consummate mastery of Latin style, both in his orations and his writings, earned Cicero a lofty position in the field of Roman literature, even though his political career ended in disaster and his desperate efforts to save the tottering republic failed completely.

With the establishment of a strong imperial government under Augustus in the years following 31 B.C., Latin letters entered a new phase. The achievement of political stability after decades of turmoil, the promise of enduring peace, the imperial policy of "careers open to talents," and the inspiring leadership of Augustus himself combined to evoke a powerful surge of optimism, patriotism, and creative originality. The "Augustan Age" constitutes the climax of Roman creative genius, surpassing even the literary brilliance of the troubled late republic. Under Augustus, Roman artists and poets achieved a powerful synthesis of Greek and Roman elements. Roman architecture was obviously modeled on the Greek, but it was just as obviously an expression of a distinctively Roman spirit. Roman temples rose much higher than those of classical Greece and conveyed a feeling that was less serene—more imposing and dynamic, less horizontal—more vertical.

Great Augustan poetry—the urbane and faultless lyrics of Horace, the worldly, erotic verses of Ovid, the majestic cadences of Virgil—employed Greek models and ideas in original and characteristically Roman ways. Rome's supreme poem, Virgil's *Aeneid,* was cast in the epic form of Homer and dealt, as Homer's *Odyssey* did, with the voyage of an important figure in the Trojan War. But Aeneas, Virgil's hero, was also the legendary founder of Rome, and the poem is shot through with lofty patriotic prophecies regarding the great destiny of the state which Aeneas was to found. Indeed, some readers have seen in Aeneas a symbol of Augustus himself. The *Aeneid* also contains, surprisingly, a compassionate, humanitarian strain quite lacking in Homer but evident in the enlightened policies of Augustus and his successors, particularly the emperors of the second century. Above all, there is the feeling of hope that the Roman state, founded by Aeneas, and now led by the great peacemaker Augustus, has at last fulfilled its mission to bring enduring concord and justice to the long-tormented world:

> But Rome! tis thine alone, with awful sway,
> To rule mankind, and make the world obey,
> Disposing peace and war thy own majestic way;
> To tame the proud, the fetter'd slave to free:
> These are imperial arts, and worthy thee.*

The cultural epoch from approximately the death of Augustus to the death of Marcus Aurelius is known as the Silver Age. Less illustrious than the golden Augustan Age, it nevertheless witnessed literary, intellectual, and artistic accomplishments of the first order. Some observers have seen in Silver Age writers, such as the Stoic Seneca, the satirist Lucian, and the biographer

* *Aeneid,* Book VI (tr. John Dryden).

Plutarch, a certain falling off in creative genius. They have stressed the stale conformity of second-century Roman art and literature resulting from the absence of real freedom, the uniformity of culture, and the very dullness of peace and security. Such judgments are necessarily relative, and many sensitive spirits down through the centuries have regarded writers of the Silver Age with enormous admiration. But whatever one may think of the originality and excellence of Silver Age literature, there can be no question but that culture and learning spread significantly both outward and downward. Remote provincial cities boasted impressive temples and baths, theatres and triumphal arches, built in the Roman style. Libraries and schools were scattered abundantly across the empire, and the extent of urban literacy is demonstrated by the many irreverent and obscene scribblings and campaign slogans discovered by modern excavators on the buildings of Pompeii, buried and preserved by a disastrous eruption of Vesuvius in A.D. 79.

Alexandria, the great metropolis of Hellenistic times, retained its commercial and intellectual importance throughout the early empire, producing some of the most brilliant early Christian theologians as well as several distinguished scientists who developed and synthesized the achievements of earlier Hellenistic science and, at the same time, added greatly to the intellectual lustre of the second-century empire. Greek and Hellenistic astronomical thought, for example, was developed into a sophisticated and comprehensive model of the universe by Ptolemy of Alexandria (d. about A.D. 180), who expanded the work of his predecessors into a geocentric world-system which accounted, with remarkable precision, for the observed motions of the sun, moon, and planets among the stars. The Ptolemaic system remained mankind's most far-reaching and successful attempt to explain the movements of the heavenly bodies until the appearance of Copernicus in the sixteenth century. Ptolemy also wrote the most complete geography of antiquity, and Galen (A.D. 131–201), a great medical scientist from Hellenistic Pergamum, produced a magnificent series of works on biology and medicine which dominated these fields for more than a thousand years. And the *Meditations* of Marcus Aurelius, the last of the great second-century emperors, is one of antiquity's most profound and moving expressions of the Stoic philosophy which deepened and humanized so much of the best thought of the era. In literature and art, science and philosophy, the Silver Age produced an effortless fusion of Greek and Roman traditions. The rich legacies of Greece, Rome, and the ancient Orient were summarized and synthesized, to the immense benefit of future civilization.

Of all the achievements of this epoch perhaps the greatest—certainly the most distinctively Roman—was the development of imperial law. The primitive code of the Twelve Tables (c. 450 B.C.) was gradually broadened and humanized by the magistrates of the later republic and early empire, by the great legists of the second and third centuries A.D., and by the enlightened intervention of the emperors themselves. As the Romans became acquainted with more and more peoples, each with its unique set of laws and customs, they gradually emancipated themselves from the peculiarities of their own law and strove to replace it by a body of fundamental principles drawn from the laws of all people.

The *Jus Gentium* or "law of peoples" slowly transformed the Roman code into a legal system suitable to a vast, heterogeneous empire. The evolution was influenced by the Greek concept of the *Jus Naturale*—the "law of nature"— which has played a prominent role in the history of Western thought. More abstract than the *Jus Gentium*, the "law of nature" or "natural law" is based on the belief that in a divinely ordered world there are certain universal norms of human behavior which all people, regardless of their own individual customs and traditions, ought to follow. These norms, based on lofty considerations of political and social justice, served to rationalize and humanize the law of the empire and to provide it with a powerful philosophical foundation. Accordingly, Roman law, a product of the Latin practical political genius influenced by Greek speculative thought, gave substance to the Augustan ideal of justice. Codified at enormous effort by the sixth-century emperor Justinian, it has become a crucial part of the Western heritage, the basis of many legal systems to this day in Europe and in the lands that were once her colonies.

2

Christianity:

Background, Growth, and Victory

ROMAN RELIGION

Roman religion is an immensely complex subject, for the Romans recognized not only many gods but also numerous separate cults. Like the Greek city-states, Rome had its official civic deities, Jupiter and Juno, Minerva and Mars, and many others, who by the later republic had become identified with parallel gods of the Greek Olympic religion. Jupiter was the Greek Zeus, Minerva was the Greek Athena, and so on. Besides these Roman state deities there were innumerable local gods of the myriad cities and districts of the empire. And in Rome itself as well as throughout the empire there were countless unofficial cults which normally enjoyed the toleration of the Roman state. None of these pagan cults was exclusive; none claimed a monopoly on truth, and a single individual might without compromise associate himself with several of them.

With the coming of the Principate* an important new element was added to the state religion: the cult of the emperor. Augustus, like Julius Caesar before him, had been honored by the deification and worship of his "genius" (the spirit of his family), and both

---

* The term given to the imperial government of the first two centuries A.D. It derives from the title *princeps* or "first citizen" which was given to the emperors from Augustus onward.

Augustus and his successors, with a few notorious exceptions, were deified by the Senate after their deaths. In those provinces where god-kings were traditional the *princeps* was regarded as a deity while still alive, and it soon became customary for Romans and provincials alike to participate in formal religious observances to the deified emperors as well as to the major deities of the city of Rome. These observances were at heart more patriotic than religious. They were exceedingly useful in encouraging the allegiance of diverse peoples and, in accordance with the religious attitudes of the day, very few objected to the addition of a handful of new deities to the divine crowd which they already worshiped. To the Jews, and later the Christians, these religio-patriotic observances were quite another matter, for the Jealous God of the Jews permitted the worship of no other. But Rome recognized the Jews as a people apart and usually excused them from participation in the official cults. The Christians, on the other hand, suffered gravely from their refusal to worship the emperors and gods of Rome. To the Romans such intransigence savored of both atheism and treason. It is no accident that Christianity alone of all the religions of the Empire was the object of Roman persecution.

THE MYSTERY CULTS

The centuries after Augustus witnessed a slow but fundamental shift in Roman religious attitudes, from the veneration of the traditional gods of household, clan, and city to the worship of transcendental deities imported from the Near East. The gods of Old Rome, like those of the Greek Olympus, had safeguarded the welfare of social and political groups; the new gods cared little for such things but offered instead the hope of individual redemption, salvation, and eternal life. As the Roman imperial age progressed, the allegiance of the people shifted slowly but inexorably from Jupiter and Minerva to the Egyptian Isis, the Persian Mithras, the Phrygian Great Mother, the Syrian sun god, and other exotic deities who offered solace and eternal joy to people for whom the world was not enough—even the world of the Roman Peace.

This powerful upsurge of mysticism was actually a continuation and expansion of a trend that had been in evidence long before among the Hellenistic Greeks. The very forces that had encouraged the widespread rootlessness and disorientation of the Hellenistic world were now at work throughout the Roman Empire—cosmopolitanism, gradually increasing autocracy, and, among the underprivileged masses, grinding poverty and loss of hope. The shift from civic god to savior god, from this world to the next, constitutes a profound transformation in mood, a repudiation of traditional Greco-Roman humanism. As the peace of the second century gave way to the anarchy of the third, the high hopes of classical humanism—the dream of a rational universe, an ideal republic, a good life—were beginning to seem like cruel illusions, and the movement toward the mystery cults gained enormous momentum.

NEO-PLATONISM

The older pagan cults were by no means completely supplanted, but they were profoundly altered by the powerful upsurge of otherworldliness which accompanied the third-century anarchy. This trend toward a transcendental outlook is particularly conspicuous in the leading philosophical movement of the century, Neo-Platonism. One of the deepest and subtlest minds of the third century, Plotinus, popularized this doctrine of a single god, infinite and beyond reason, unknowable and unapproachable except through an ecstatic trance. Plotinus taught that God was the source of reality and existence. All being, both physical and spiritual, radiated outward from him like concentric ripples in a pool. Greek rationalism was an empty thing indeed for those who believed with Plotinus that the only truth worth knowing lay outside the scope of human reason.

In the later empire all that was vital in pagan religion was incorporated into a vast Neo-Platonic synthesis. The Neo-Platonists taught that the gods of the pagan cults were all symbols of the one unknowable god, and that each pagan cult therefore had validity. Paganism became increasingly monotheistic: Zeus, Jupiter, and Mithras were simply different aspects of a single transcendent deity. In this atmosphere the distinction between the traditional pagan cults and the mystery religions faded. By the fourth century Greek rationalism and humanism had been superseded almost entirely by a spirit of otherworldliness, divine revelation, and yearning for eternal life. Neo-Platonic philosophy and Near Eastern religion were accompanied by a vast upsurge of astrology, magic, charlatanism, and other dark practices which had never been absent from Greco-Roman society but which now dominated popular thinking as never before. It was in this supernatural environment that Christianity won its final victories.

THE EMERGENCE OF CHRISTIANITY

Two fundamental trends characterized religious development in the Roman Empire—the growing impulse toward mysticism which we have just examined, and the interpenetration and fusion of doctrines and practices between one cult and another, a process known as *syncretism*. The syncretic quality of Christianity itself has often been observed, for in numerous instances its beliefs and rituals were similar to those of various earlier religions. Obviously, Christianity drew heavily from Judaism—all the earliest Christians were Jews—but it was also anticipated in various particulars by salvation cults from Persia, Egypt, Asia Minor, and Greece. Many Christian doctrines had long pre-Christian histories, the concept of death and resurrection, the sacramental meal, baptism, personal salvation, and the brotherhood of man under the fatherhood of God, to name but a few. Yet Christianity was far more than a new configuration of old ideas, and it would be profoundly misleading to think of it as merely another of the oriental mystery religions. It differed from them above all in two basic ways. (1) Its god was the Jealous God of the Hebrews, unique in all antiquity in his claims to exclusiveness and omnipotence, and now released by Christianity from his association with a particular chosen people and universalized as the God of all mankind; (2) Christianity's founder and Savior was a vivid historic personality, Jesus.

Jesus, a younger contemporary of Augustus, was a figure in the Hebrew prophetic tradition whose life and teachings show little if any Greek influence. He is depicted in the Gospels as an intensely warm, attractive, magnetic leader who miraculously healed the sick, raised the dead, and stilled the winds. His miracles were regarded as credentials of divine authority. His ministry was chiefly to the poor and outcast, and in Christianity's early decades it was these classes that accepted the faith most readily. He preached a doctrine of love, compassion, and humility; like the Hebrew prophets he scorned empty formalism in religion and stressed the sober, unprepossessing life of generosity toward both friend and enemy and devotion to God. He does not seem to have objected to ritual as such, but only to ritual infected with pride and complacency and divorced from charity and upright conduct. His uncompromising criticism of the moral shortcomings of the established Jewish priesthoods, combined apparently with claims to speak with divine authority, resulted in his crucifixion as a subversive.

According to the Gospels, Jesus's greatest miracle was his resurrection—his return to life three days after he died on the Cross. He is said to have remained on earth for a short period after his resurrection giving solace and inspiration to his disciples and then to have "ascended" into heaven with the promise that he would return in glory to judge all souls and bring the world to an end. The first generations of Christians expected this second coming to occur very quickly, and it is for that reason among others that formal organization was not stressed in the primitive Church.

The early Christians not only accepted Christ's lofty ethical precepts but also worshiped Christ himself as the divine incarnation of the omnipotent God. The Christ of the Gospels distinguishes repeatedly between himself—"the Son of Man"—and God —"the Father"—but he also makes the statement, "I and the Father are One," and he enjoins his disciples to baptize all persons "in the Name of the Father and the Son and the Holy Spirit." Hence Christianity became committed to the notion of a triune deity with Christ as the "Son" or "Second Person" in a Trinity that was nevertheless one God. The doctrine of the Trinity gave Christianity the unique advantage of a single, infinite, philosophically respectable God who could be worshiped and adored in the person of the charismatic, lovable, tragic Jesus. The Christian deity was both transcendent and concrete.

THE EARLY CHURCH

The first generation of Christianity witnessed the beginning of a profound development whereby the Judaeo-Christian heritage was modified and enriched by contact with the main currents of Greco-Roman culture. Christ's own Apostles were no more influenced by Hellenism than their Master, and some of them sought to keep Christianity strictly within the ritualistic framework of Judaism. But St. Paul, a Hellenized Jew and early convert, succeeded in orienting the Church according to his own vision of a universal brotherhood, free of the strict Jewish dietary laws and the requirements of circumcision—which was bound to discourage the conversion of non-Jews—open to all men everywhere who would accept Jesus as God and Savior and open also to the bracing winds of Hellenistic thought. St. Paul traveled far and wide in the empire preaching the message of Christ as he interpreted it, winning converts and establishing Christian communities in many towns and cities of the Mediterranean world. Other Christian missionaries, among them St. Peter and his fellow Apostles, who had been Christ's immediate followers, devoted their lives as St. Paul did to traveling, preaching, and organizing, often at the cost of ridicule and persecution. Tradition has it that St. Paul and all the Apostles died as martyrs. Their work was exceedingly fruitful, for by the end of the apostolic generation Christianity had become a ponderable force among the underprivileged masses of Italy and the East. Within another century it had spread throughout the greater part of the empire.

From the first, the Christians regularly engaged in a sacramental meal which came to be called the *eucharist* or "Holy Communion" and was regarded as an indispensable avenue of divine grace through which the Christian was infused with the spirit of Christ. By means of another important sacrament, baptism, the postulate was initiated into the brotherhood of the Church, had his sins forgiven, and received the grace of the Holy Spirit. A person could be baptized only once, and baptized persons alone could consider themselves true Christians, but in the early Church baptism was frequently delayed until adulthood. Hence many unbaptized persons were associated with the Christian communities without being Christians in the full sense of the word.

As Christian historical sources become more abundant in the second and third centuries A.D., the organization of the Church begins to emerge more sharply than before. The documents of this period disclose an important distinction between the clergy, who governed the Church and administered the sacraments, and the laymen, who played a more passive role. The clergy itself was divided into several classes, the most important of which were the bishops, who served as rulers and pastors over the various urban communities, and the priests, who led the services and administered the sacraments under the jurisdiction of the bishops. And the bishops themselves were of various degrees of eminence. Above the common bishops were the metropolitans or archbishops, who resided in cities of particular importance and exercised control over an extensive surrounding area. At the top of the hierarchy were the bishops of the three or four greatest cities of the Empire, Rome, Alexandria, Antioch, and later Constantinople, who were known as patriarchs and who enjoyed a spiritual hegemony, often more theoretical than real, over vast areas of the Mediterranean world. As time went on, the bishop of Rome— the pope—came to be regarded more and more as the highest of the patriarchs, but the actual establishment of papal authority over even the Western Church was to require the efforts of many centuries.

CHRISTIANITY AND HELLENISM

Medieval and modern Christianity is a product of both the Hebrew and the Greek traditions. The synthesis of these two intellectual worlds began not among the Christians but among the Jews themselves, particularly those who had migrated in large numbers to Alexandria. Here Jewish scholars, in particular a profound religious philosopher of the early first century A.D. named Philo Judaeus, worked toward the reconciliation of Jewish revelation and Greek philosophy, drawing heavily from Aristotle, the Stoics, and particularly Plato, and developing a symbolic interpretation of the Old Testament, which was to influence Christian thought enormously over the centuries.

Following many of the fruitful leads of Philo, Christian theologians strove to demonstrate that their religion was more than merely an immensely appealing myth—that it could hold its own in the highest intellectual circles. The Savior Christ, for example, as true God and true man, constituted a unique synthesis of the material and spiritual worlds. In Greek terms, Christ reconciled the dualism of matter and spirit inherent in Plato's philosophy, for Christ was at once material and spiritual. Christianity differed from most of the Near Eastern mystery religions, particularly those emanating from Persia, in its refusal to reject the material world. Matter could not be evil of itself, so the Christians believed, for it was the handiwork of God; the human body could not be wholly corrupt, for Christ himself was a human in the fullest physical sense. Christianity was therefore not so directly at odds with Greek humanism as was a radically antimaterialistic religion such as Mithraism, although the Christian concept of sin and the fall of man through the disobedience of Adam were obviously far removed from the traditional humanistic point of view of the Greeks.

The fusion of matter and spirit which is so fundamental to orthodox Christianity did not escape challenge among the early Christians. Once the expectation of an immediate second coming began to fade, many Christians began to examine their faith more philosophically than before and to raise difficult questions regarding the nature of Christ and the Trinity. A diversity of opinions emerged, some apparently so inconsistent with the majority view that they were condemned as heresies. As questions were raised and orthodox solutions agreed on, the Christian faith became increasingly precise, increasingly elaborate. The early heresies sought to simplify the nature of Christ and the Trinity by insisting either that Christ was not really human—only a divine phantom— or that Christ was not fully divine—not an equal member of the triune Godhead. The latter position was taken up by the fourth-century Arians whom we shall meet in the next chapter. The orthodox position lay midway between these two views: Christ was fully human and fully divine, a co-equal member of the Holy Trinity who had always existed and always would, but who was incarnate in human form at a particular moment in time and who walked the earth, taught, suffered, and died, as the man Jesus. Thus the synthesis of matter and spirit was strictly preserved, and Christ remained the bridge between the two worlds.

The Christian apologists, the defenders of orthodoxy against pagan attacks from without and heterodox attacks from within, played a crucial role in formulating and elaborating Christian doctrine, coping with problems that had not even occurred to the apostolic generation. It is of the highest significance that the great majority of the apologists worked within the framework of the Greek philosophical tradition. This is particularly true of the great Alexandrian theologian Origen (d. 254) who created a coherent, all-inclusive Christian philosophical system on Platonic foundations. Origen was one of the loftiest thinkers of his age and is widely regarded as one of the supreme minds in the entire history of the Church. His religious system did not win over the pagan intellectual world at a blow—indeed, several of his conclusions were rejected by later Christian orthodoxy—but he and his fellow theologians succeeded in making Christianity meaningful and intellectually attractive to men whose thinking was cast in the Greco-Roman philosophical tradition. The greatest of the Greek philosophers, so the apologists said, had been led toward truth by the inspiration of the Christian God.

CHRISTIANITY AND THE EMPIRE

At the very time that Christian theology was being Hellenized, pagan thought itself was shifting increasingly toward otherworldliness. It must not be forgotten that Origen's greatest pagan contemporary was the Neo-Platonist Plotinus. Indeed, the two had even been schoolmates for a time. The growth of a transcendental outlook throughout the ancient world created an atmosphere that was highly nourishing to a salvation religion such as Christianity. The Christian point of view was becoming increasingly in tune with the times; it appealed to an age hungry for a profound and consoling doctrine of personal redemption. Yet its triumph was by no means assured, for it faced other salvation religions, such as Mithraism and the Isis cult, and traditional Greco-Roman paganism in its new, otherworldly, Neo-Platonic guise. Against these rivals Christianity could offer the immense appeal of the historic Jesus, the ever-increasing profundity of its theology, the infinite majesty of its God, and the compassion and universalism of its message, preserved and dramatized in its canonical books—the Old and New Testaments. Few social groups were immune to its attraction. The poor, humble, and underprivileged made up the bulk of its early converts, and it was to them that Jesus directed much of his message. Intellectuals were drawn by its Hellenized theology, men of feeling were captivated by its mysticism, and men of affairs were attracted by the ever-increasing effectiveness and logic of its administrative hierarchy. For in administration no less than in theology the Church was learning from the Greco-Roman world.

Before the collapse of the Roman Empire in the West, Christianity had absorbed and turned to its own purposes much of Rome's heritage in political organization and law, carrying on the Roman administrative and legal tradition into the medieval and modern world. Roman civil law was paralleled by the canon law of the Church. The secular leadership of the Roman Empire gave way to the spiritual leadership of the Roman pope, who assumed the old republican and imperial title of *pontifex maximus*—supreme pontiff—and preserved much of the imperial ceremonial of the later empire. As imperial governors and local officials gradually disappeared in the West, their traditions were carried on, in a new spiritual dimension, by metropolitans and bishops. Indeed, the *diocese*, the traditional unit of a bishop's jurisdiction, was originally an imperial administrative district. In this organizational sense, the medieval Church has been described as a ghost of the old Roman Empire. Yet it was far more than that, for the Church reached its people as Rome never had, giving the impoverished masses a sense of participation and involvement that the empire had failed to provide.

From the beginning the Christians of the empire were a people apart, convinced that they alone possessed the truth and that the truth would one day triumph, eager to win new converts to their faith, uncompromising in their rejection of all other religions, willing to learn from the pagan world but unwilling ever to submit to it. Their stark seriousness of purpose, their cohesiveness, which doubtless appeared to their enemies as clannishness, their sense of destiny, and their refusal to worship the state gods proved

exceedingly aggravating to their pagan contemporaries. Consequently, the Christians were often objects of suspicion, hatred, and
persecution. The emperors themselves followed a rather inconsistent policy toward them. Violent persecutions, such as those
under Nero and Marcus Aurelius, alternated with long periods
of inaction. On the whole, the Church throve on the blood of its
martyrs; the persecutions were neither sufficiently ruthless nor
sufficiently lengthy to come near wiping out the entire Christian
community. The pagan emperors of Rome might have learned
much from the Christian inquisitors of sixteenth-century Spain
on the subject of liquidating troublesome religious minorities.

Most of the emperors, if they persecuted Christians at all, did
so reluctantly. The great second-century emperor Trajan instructed a provincial governor neither to seek Christians out nor
to heed anonymous accusations. Such a procedure, Trajan observed, was inconsistent with "the spirit of the age." Only if a man
should be denounced as a Christian, tried and found guilty, and
then should persist in his refusal to worship the imperial gods,
was he to be punished. One can admire the Christian who would
face death rather than worship false gods, but one can also sympa-
thize with emperors such as Trajan who hesitated to apply their
traditional policy of religious toleration to a people who seemed
bent on subverting the empire by their blatantly un-Roman
activities.

The greatest imperial persecution—and the last—occurred at
the opening of the fourth century under the emperor Diocletian.
By then Christianity was too strong to be destroyed, and the failure
of Diocletian's persecution must have made it evident that the
empire had no choice but to accommodate itself to the Church.
A decade after the outbreak of this last persecution, Constantine,
the first Christian emperor, undertook a dramatic reversal of religious policy. Thereafter the empire endorsed Christianity instead
of fighting it, and by the close of the fourth century the majority
of the inhabitants of the empire had been brought into the Christian fold. Rome and Jerusalem had come to terms at last.

3

The Late Empire

THE THIRD CENTURY

The turbulent third century, the era of Origen and Plotinus, brought catastrophic changes to the Roman Empire. The age of the great second-century emperors (A.D. 96–180) was followed by a hundred troubled years during which anarchy alternated with military despotism. The army, now fully conscious of its strength, made and unmade emperors. One military group fought against another for control of the imperial title—a man might be a general one day, emperor the next, and dead the third. No fewer than nineteen emperors reigned during the calamitous half-century between 235 and 285, not to mention innumerable usurpers and pretenders whose plots and machinations contributed to the general chaos. In this fifty-year period every emperor save one died violently, either by assassination or in battle. The Silver Age had given way to what one observer described as an age "of iron and rust."

A crucial factor in the chaos of the third century was the abandonment of the "adoption principle" which had worked so splendidly in the previous epoch. The second-century emperors selected and "adopted" their successors from among the most talented and dedicated younger statesmen of the empire. But in the third century the imperial succession was all too often determined by the whims of the legions. Perhaps the most successful emperor of the period, Septimius Severus (193–211), maintained his power by expanding and pampering the army, opening its highest offices to every class, and broadening its recruitment. A military career was now the logical avenue to high civil office, and the bureaucracy began to display an increasingly military cast of mind. The old ideals of republic and Principate were less and less meaningful to the new governing class, many of whom rose from the dregs of society through successful army careers to positions of high political responsibility. These new administrators were often men of strength and ability, but they were not the sort who could be expected to cherish the old Roman political traditions. Septimius Severus tightened imperial taxes to fatten his treasury and appease his troops. Soldiers prospered at the expense of an increasingly impoverished civilian population as the empire drifted more and more toward military absolutism. Septimius' dying words to his sons are characteristic of his reign and his times: "Enrich the soldiers and scorn the world."

Rome's troubles in the third century cannot be ascribed entirely to the problem of imperial succession. As early as the reign of Marcus Aurelius (161–180) the empire had been struck by a devastating plague which lingered on for a generation and by an ominous irruption of Germanic barbarians who spilled across the northern and eastern frontiers as far as Italy itself. Marcus Aurelius, the philosopher-emperor, was obliged to spend the greater part of his reign campaigning against the invaders, and it was only at enormous effort that he was able to drive them out of the empire. During the third century the Germans attacked with renewed fury, penetrating the frontiers time and again, forcing the cities of the empire to erect protective walls, and threatening for a time to submerge the state under a barbarian flood. The Germanic onslaught was accompanied by furious attacks from the East by the recently reconstituted Persian Empire led by able and dedicated kings of its new Sassanid dynasty.

Rome's real problems, however, were internal ones. During the third century, political disintegration was accompanied by social and economic breakdown. The ever-rising fiscal demands of the mushrooming bureaucracy and the insatiable army placed an intolerable burden on the inhabitants of town and country alike. Peasants began to flee their fields to escape the ubiquitous tax collector, and the urban middle classes became shrunken and demoralized. The self-governing town, the bedrock of imperial administration and, indeed, of Greco-Roman civilization itself, was beginning to experience serious financial difficulties; as one city after another turned to the emperor for financial aid, civic autonomy declined. These problems arose in part from the parasitical nature of many of the Roman cities, in part from rising imperial taxes, and in part from the economic stagnation that was slowly gripping the empire. Long before the death of Marcus Aurelius, Rome had abandoned her career of conquest in favor of a defensive policy of consolidation. The flow of booty from conquered lands had ceased, and the empire as a whole was thrown back on its own resources and forced to become economically self-sufficient. For a time all seemed well, but as administrative and military expenses mounted without a corresponding growth in commerce and industry, the imperial economy began to suffer. The army, once a source of riches from conquered lands, was now an unproductive encumbrance.

By the third century, if not before, the Roman economy was shrinking. Plagues, hunger, and a sense of hopelessness resulted in a gradual decline in population. At the very time when imperial expenses and imperial taxes were rising, the tax base was contracting. Prosperity gave way to depression and desperation, and the flight of peasants from their farms was accompanied by the flight of the savagely taxed middle classes from their cities. The empire was now clogged with beggars and brigands, and those who remained at their jobs were taxed all the more heavily. It was the western half of the empire that suffered most. What industry there was had always been centered in the East, and money was gradually flowing eastward to productive centers in Syria and Asia Minor and beyond, to pay for luxury goods, some of which came from outside the empire altogether—from Persia, India, and China. In short, the empire as a whole, and the Western Empire in particular, suffered from an unfavorable balance of trade which resulted in a steady reduction in Rome's supply of precious metals.

The increasingly desperate financial circumstances of the third-century empire forced the emperors to experiment in the devaluation of coinage, adulterating the precious metals in their coins with baser metals. This policy provided only temporary relief. In the long run it resulted in runaway inflation which further undermined the economy. Between A.D. 256 and 280 the cost of living rose 1000 per cent.

The third-century anarchy reached its climax during the 260s. By then the Roman economy was virtually in ruins. Barbarian armies were rampaging across the frontiers. Gaul and Britain in the West and a large district in the East had broken loose from imperial control and were pursuing independent courses. The population was speedily shrinking, and countless cities were in an advanced state of decay. Rome's demise seemed imminent. As it turned out, however, the empire was saved by the relentless efforts of a series of stern, dedicated leaders who rose to power in the later third century. The Roman state survived in the West for another two centuries and in the East for more than a millennium. But the agonies of the third century left an indelible mark on the reformed empire. The new imperial structure which brought order out of chaos was profoundly different from the government of the Principate: it was a naked autocracy of the most thoroughgoing sort.

THE REFORMS OF DIOCLETIAN

Even at the height of the anarchy there were emperors who strove desperately to defend the Roman state. After A.D. 268 a series of able, rough-hewn emperor-generals from the Danubian provinces managed to turn the tide, restoring the frontiers, smashing the invading armies of Germanic barbarians and Persians, and recovering the alienated provinces in Gaul and the East. At the same time measures were undertaken to arrest the social and economic decay that was debilitating the empire. These policies were expanded and brought to fruition by Diocletian (284–305) and Constantine (306–337) to whom belong the credit—and responsibility—for reconstituting the empire along authoritarian lines. No longer merely a *princeps* or "first citizen", the emperor was now *dominus et deus*—lord and god—and it is appropriate that this new despotic regime which replaced the Principate should be called the Dominate.

In the days of Augustus it had been necessary, in order not to offend republican sensibilities, to disguise the power of the emperor. In Diocletian's day the imperial title had for so long been dishonored and abused that it was necessary to exalt it. Diocletian and his successors glorified the office in every way imaginable. The emperor became a lofty, remote, unapproachable figure clothed in magnificent garments, a diadem on his head. An elaborate court ceremonial was introduced, much of it borrowed from Persia, which included the custom of prostration in the emperor's sacred presence.

Diocletian's most immediate task was to bring to a close the turbulent era of short-lived "barracks emperors" and military usurpers. In order to stabilize the succession and share the ever-growing burden of governing the empire, he decreed that there would thenceforth be two emperors, one in the East, the other in the West, who would work together harmoniously for the welfare and defense of the state. Each would be known by the title of *Augustus*, and each would adopt a younger colleague, with the title *Caesar*, to share his rule and ultimately to succeed him. The empire was now divided into four parts, each supervised by an Augustus or a Caesar. Well aware of the increasing importance of the eastern over the western half of the empire, Diocletian made his own capital in the East and did not set foot in Rome until the close of his reign. A usurper would now, presumably, be faced with the perplexing task of overcoming four widely scattered personages instead of one. The chances of military takeover were further reduced by Diocletian's rigorous separation of civil and military authority. The army was considerably enlarged, chiefly by the incorporation of barbarian forces which now assumed much of the burden of guarding the frontiers, but it was reorganized in such a way that the emperor—or emperors—could control it far more effectively than before.

Imperial control was the keynote of this new, paternalistic regime. The Senate, which had traditionally performed the function of advising the emperor, was now merely ornamental. The emperor ruled through his obedient and ever-expanding bureaucracy, issuing edict after edict to regulate, systematize, and regiment the state. The money shortage was circumvented by a new land tax to be collected in kind, and the widespread flight from productive labor was halted by new laws freezing peasants, artisans, and businessmen to their jobs. Quickly there developed a vast hereditary caste system; the law required sons to take up the careers and tax burdens of their fathers. Peasants were bound to the land, city dwellers to their urban professions. Workers in the mines and quarries were literally branded. By these harsh means economic collapse was temporarily averted but at the cost of social petrification and loss of hope. The once-autonomous cities now lay under the iron hand of the imperial government, and commitment to the empire was rapidly waning among the tax-ridden middle classes which had formerly been among its most enthusiastic supporters. To many citizens the cure must have seemed worse than the disease.

It was Diocletian's mission to save the empire whatever the cost, and it may well be that authoritarian measures were the only ones possible under the circumstances. For every problem Diocletian offered a solution—often autocratic and heavy handed —but a solution nevertheless. A thoroughgoing currency reform had retarded inflation but had not stopped it altogether; consequently Diocletian issued an edict fixing the prices of most commodities by law. To the growing challenge of Christianity, Diocletian responded, regretfully, by inaugurating a persecution of unprecedented severity. As it turned out, neither the imperial price controls nor the imperial persecution achieved their purposes, but the very fact that they were attempted illustrates the length to which the emperor would go in his effort to preserve—by force—the unity and stability of the state.

The division of the empire among the two Augusti and the two adopted Caesars worked satisfactorily only so long as Diocletian himself was in power. Once his firm hand was removed, there was a struggle for power which brought renewed civil strife. Everyone wanted to be an Augustus; no one was satisfied to be a Caesar. Moreover, the principle of adoption, which the sonless Diocletian had revived without serious difficulty, was challenged by the sons of his successors. The era of chaos ran from the end of Diocletian's reign in 305 to the victory of Constantine over the last of his rivals in 312 at the battle of the Milvian Bridge near Rome.

THE REIGN OF CONSTANTINE (306–337)

Constantine's triumph at the Milvian Bridge marked the return of political stability and the consummation of Diocletian's economic and political reforms. Imperial ceremonial was further elaborated, authoritarianism grew, and the hereditary caste system persisted. In certain respects, however, Constantine's policies took radical new directions. In place of Diocletian's abortive principle of adoption, Constantine founded an imperial dynasty of his own. For a time he shared his authority with an imperial colleague, but in 324 he conquered his co-emperor and thereafter ruled alone. Nevertheless, the joint rule of an eastern and a western emperor became common in the years after Constantine's death; he himself contributed to the division of the empire by building the magnificent eastern capital of Constantinople on the site of the ancient Greek town of Byzantium.

Constantinople was a second Rome. It had its own Senate, its own imposing temples, palaces, and public buildings, its own Christian Patriarch, even its own hungry proletariat fed by a bread dole and amused by chariot races in its enormous Hippodrome. Constantine plundered the Greco-Roman world of its artistic treasures to adorn his new city and lavished his vast resources on its construction. Founded in A.D. 330, Constantinople was to remain the capital of the Eastern Empire for well over a thousand years, impregnable behind its great walls, protected on three sides by the sea, perpetually renewing itself through its control of the rich commerce flowing between the Black Sea and the Mediterranean. The age-long survival of the Eastern Empire owes much to the superb strategic location of its capital.

Even more momentous than the building of Constantinople was Constantine's conversion to Christianity and his concomitant reversal of imperial policy toward the Church. Although he put off baptism until his dying moments, Constantine had been committed to Christianity ever since his triumph in 312. From that time onward he issued a continuous series of pro-Christian edicts insuring full toleration, legalizing bequests to the Church, which accumulated prodigiously over the subsequent centuries, and granting a variety of other privileges. Christianity was now an official religion of the empire. It was not yet *the* official religion, but it would become so before the fourth century was ended.

Several explanations have been offered for Constantine's conversion. He has even been portrayed as an irreligious political schemer bent on harnessing the vitality of the Church to the failing state. But there seems no reason to doubt that in fact his conversion was sincere if somewhat superficial. Strictly speaking, there were no irreligious men in the fourth century.

THE CHRISTIAN EMPIRE

The respite gained by Diocletian's reforms and the subsequent conversion of Constantine made it possible for the Church to develop rapidly under the benevolent protection of the empire. The years between Constantine's victory at the Milvian Bridge in 312 and the final suppression of the Western Empire in 476 were momentous ones in the evolution of Christianity. For one thing, the fourth century witnessed mass conversions to the Christian fold. Perhaps 10 per cent of the inhabitants of the Western Empire were Christians in 312—in the East the figure would have been considerably higher—whereas by the century's end the now-respectable Christians were in the majority. But, as is so often the case, triumph evoked internal dissension, and the fourth century witnessed a violent struggle between orthodoxy and heresy. Here, too, the Christian emperors played a determining role, and it was with strong imperial support that the greatest of the fourth-century heresies, Arianism, was at length suppressed within the empire.

The Arians maintained that the purity of Christian monotheism was compromised by the orthodox doctrine of the Trinity. Their solution to this conflict was the doctrine that God the Father was the only true God, that Christ the Son was not fully divine. The orthodox Trinitarians regarded this doctrine as subversive to one of their most fundamental beliefs—the equality and codivinity of Father, Son, and Holy Spirit. Constantine sought to heal the Arian-Trinitarian dispute by summoning a universal or ecumenical council of Christian bishops at Nicaea in A.D. 325. The emperor's own presence was the decisive factor at Nicaea; his Trinitarian leanings resulted in the almost unanimous adoption of an anti-Arian creed in which the three divine Persons of the Trinity were declared equal: Jesus Christ was "of one substance with the Father."

Constantine, however, was no theologian. In afteryears he vacillated, sometimes favoring Arians, sometimes condemning them, and the same ambiguity characterized imperial policy throughout the greater part of the fourth century. At length the uncompromisingly orthodox Theodosius I (378–395) broke the power of the Arians by condemning and proscribing them. It was under Theodosius and his successors that Christianity became the one legal religion of the empire. Paganism itself was now banned and persecuted and quickly disappeared as an organized force.

Orthodox Christianity now dominated the empire, but its triumph, won with the aid of political force, was far from complete. For one thing, the mass conversions of the fourth century tended to be superficial, even nominal. Conversion to Christianity was the path of least resistance, and the new converts were on the whole a far cry from the earlier society of saints and martyrs. It was at this time that many ardent Christians, discontented with mere membership in a safe, respectable, work-a-day Church, began taking to the desert as hermits or flocking into monastic communities.

Moreover, the imperial program of enforced orthodoxy proved exceedingly difficult to carry out. Old heresies lingered on and vigorous new ones arose in the fifth century and thereafter. Even Arianism survived, not among the citizens of the empire but among the Germanic barbarians. For during the mid-fourth century, at a time when Arianism was still strong in the empire, large numbers of barbarians had been converted to Christianity in its Arian form, and the Trinitarian policies of Theodosius I had no effect on them whatever. Accordingly, when the barbarians ultimately formed their kingdoms on the ruins on the Western Empire, most were separated from their Old-Roman subjects not only by language and custom but by a deep religious chasm as well.

Finally, in accepting imperial support against paganism and heresy, the Church sacrificed much of its earlier independence. The Christians of Constantine's day were so overwhelmed by the emperor's conversion that they tended to glorify him excessively. As a Christian Constantine could no longer claim divinity, but contemporary Christian writers such as the historian Eusebius allowed him a status that was almost quasi-divine. To Eusebius and his contemporaries Constantine was the thirteenth Apostle, his office was commissioned by God, he was above the Church. His commanding position in ecclesiastical affairs was illustrated dramatically by his domination of the Council of Nicaea, and the ups and downs of Arianism in the following decades depended largely on the whims of his successors. In the East this glorification of the imperial office ripened into the doctrine known as *Caesaropapism*—that the emperor is the real master of both Church and state, that he is both Caesar and pope—and Caesaropapism remained a dominant theme in the politics and religion of the Eastern or Byzantine Empire throughout its long history. Church and state tended to merge under the sacred authority of the emperor. Indeed, the Christianization and sanctification of the imperial office were potent forces in winning for the eastern emperors the allegiance and commitment of the masses of their Christian subjects. Religious loyalty to the Christian emperor provided indispensable nourishment to the East Roman state over the ensuing centuries. Conversely, widespread hostility toward imperial orthodoxy in districts dominated by heretical groups resulted in the alienation and eventual loss to the Byzantine Empire of several of its fairest provinces.

Caesaropapism was far less influential in the West, for as the fifth century dawned the Western Empire was visibly failing. Western churchmen were beginning to realize that Christian civilization was not irrevocably bound to the fortunes of Rome. Gradually the Western Church began to assert its independence of state control with the result that Church and state in medieval Western Europe were never fused but remained always in a state of tension.

THE DOCTORS OF THE LATIN CHURCH

During the later fourth and early fifth centuries, at a time when the Christianization of the Roman state was far advanced but before the Western Empire had lost all its vitality, the long-developing synthesis of Judaeo-Christian and Greco-Roman culture reached its climax in the West with the work of three immensely gifted scholar-saints: Ambrose, Jerome, and Augustine. These men are justly regarded as "Doctors of the Latin Church," for their voluminous and wide-ranging writings dominated medieval thought. Each of the three was thoroughly trained in the Greco-Roman intellectual tradition; each devoted his learning and his life to the service of Christianity; each was at once an intellectual and a man of affairs.

Ambrose (c. 340–397) was bishop of the great city of Milan, which by the later fourth century had replaced Rome as the western imperial capital. He was famed for his eloquence and administrative skill, for his vigor in defending Trinitarian orthodoxy against Arianism, and for the ease and mastery with which he adapted the literary traditions of Cicero and Virgil and the philosophy of Plato to his own Christian purposes. Above all, he was the first churchman to assert, in the teeth of a great Christian emperor, the independence and superiority of Church over state in spiritual affairs. When the powerful Emperor Theodosius I ruthlessly massacred the inhabitants of rebellious Thessalonica, Ambrose barred him from the Church of Milan until he had formally and publicly repented. Ambrose's bold stand and Theodosius' humble submission constituted a stunning setback for the principle of Caesaropapism and a dramatic prelude to the long struggle between Church and state in the Christian West.

Jerome (c. 340–420) was a masterly scholar and a restless, inquisitive reformer with a touch of acid in his personality. He once remarked to an opponent. "You have the will to lie, good sir, but not the skill to lie." Wandering far and wide through the empire, he founded a monastery in Bethlehem where he set his monks to work copying manuscripts, thereby instituting a custom which throughout the Middle Ages preserved the tradition of Latin letters and transmitted it to the modern world. Like other Christian intellectuals he feared that his love of pagan literature might dilute his Christian fervor, and he tells of a dream in which Jesus banished him from heaven with the words, "Thou art a Ciceronian, not a Christian." But in the end he managed to reconcile pagan culture and Christian faith by using the former only in the service of the latter. His greatest contribution to Christian thought was in the field of biblical translation and

commentary—above all, in his monumental and scholarly translation of the scriptures from Hebrew and Greek into Latin. Jerome's
Latin Vulgate Bible has been used ever since by Roman Catholics
and has served as the basis of innumerable translations into modern languages (English-speaking Catholics use the Douay translation of Jerome's Vulgate). It was an achievement of incalculable
significance to Western Civilization.

The most profound of the Latin Doctors was Augustine (354–
430), who spent his final forty years as bishop of the North African
city of Hippo. Like Jerome, Augustine worried about the dangers
of pagan culture to the Christian soul, finally concluding, much
as Jerome did, that Greco-Roman learning, although not to be
enjoyed for its own sake, might properly be used to elucidate
the Faith. Augustine was the chief architect of medieval theology.
Even more than his contemporaries he succeeded in fusing Christian doctrine with Greek thought, particularly the philosophy of
Plato and the Neo-Platonists. It has been said that Augustine
baptized Plato. As a Platonist he stressed the importance of ideas
or archetypes over tangible things, but instead of locating his
archetypes in the abstract Platonic "heaven" he placed them in
the mind of God. The human mind had access to the archetypes
only through the grace of "divine illumination."

As a bishop Augustine was occupied with the day-to-day cares
of his diocese and his flock. His immense contribution to religious
thought arises not from the dispassionate working-out of an abstract system of theology but rather from his responses to the
burning issues of the moment. His thought is a fascinating mixture
of profundity and immediacy, of the abstract and the human.
His *Confessions*, the first psychologically sensitive autobiography
ever written, tell of his own spiritual journey through various
pagan and heretical cults to Christian orthodoxy. Implicit in this
great book is the hope that others as misguided as he once was
might also be led by God's grace to the truth in Christ.

Against the several heretical doctrines that threatened Christian
orthodoxy in his day Augustine wrote clearly and persuasively
on the nature of the Trinity, the problem of evil in a world created
by God, the special character of the Christian priesthood, and
the nature of free will and predestination. His most influential

work, the *City of God*, was prompted by a barbarian sack of Rome in A.D. 410 which the pagans ascribed to Rome's desertion of her old gods. Augustine responded by developing a Christian theory of history which interpreted human development not in political or economic terms but in moral terms. As the first Christian philosopher of history, Augustine drew heavily on the profound historical insights of the ancient Hebrews. Like the Hebrew prophets of old, he asserted that kingdoms and empires rose and fell according to a divine plan, but he insisted that this plan lay forever beyond human comprehension. Augustine rejected the Hebrew notion of tribal salvation, putting in its place the Christian notion of *individual* salvation. The ultimate units of history were not tribes and empires but individual immortal souls. The salvation of souls, Augustine stated, depends not on the fortunes of Rome but on the grace of God. Christ is not dependent on Caesar. And if we look at history from the moral standpoint—from the standpoint of souls—we see not the clash of armies or the rivalry of states but a far more fundamental struggle between good and evil which has raged through history and which rages even now within each soul. Humanity is divided into two classes, those who live in God's grace and those who do not. The former belong to what Augustine called the "City of God," the latter to the "City of Evil." The members of the two cities are hopelessly intermixed in this world, but they will be separated at death by eternal salvation or damnation. It is from this transcendental standpoint, Augustine believed, that the Christian must view history. Only God could know what effect Rome's decline would have on the City of God. Perhaps the effect would be beneficial, perhaps even irrelevant.

Augustine is one of the two or three seminal minds in Christian history. His Christian Platonism governed medieval theology down into the twelfth century and remains exceedingly influential in Christian thought even today. His emphasis on the special sacramental power inherent in the priestly office became and remains a keystone of Catholic theology. His emphasis on divine grace and predestination, although softened considerably by the medieval Church, re-emerged in the sixteenth century to dominate early Protestant doctrine. And his theory of the two cities, although often in oversimplified and debased form, had an enormous influence on Western historical and political thought over the next millennium.

Ambrose, Jerome, and Augustine were at once synthesizers and innovators. The last great minds of the Western Empire, they operated at a level of intellectual sophistication that the Christian West would not reach again for seven hundred years. The strength of the classical tradition that underlies medieval Christianity and Western Civilization owes much to the fact that these men, and others like them, found it possible to be both Christians and Ciceronians.

4

The Decline of Rome
and the Germanic Invasions

DECLINE AND FALL

The catastrophe of Rome's decline and fall has always fascinated historians, for it involves not only the collapse of mankind's most impressive and enduring universal state but also the demise of Greco-Roman Civilization itself. The reasons are far too complex to be explained satisfactorily by any single cause—Christianity, disease, slavery, soil exhaustion, or any of the other master keys which have been proposed from time to time. One must always bear in mind that the Roman Empire "fell" only in the West. It endured in the East, although there, too, Greco-Roman Civilization was changed significantly. The civilization of the Eastern Empire during the medieval centuries is normally described not as "Roman" or even "Greco-Roman" but as "Byzantine," and the change in name betokens a profound alteration in mood. In other words, Greco-Roman culture was gradually transformed in both East and West, but its transformation in the West was accompanied by the dismemberment of the Roman state, whereas its transformation in the East occurred despite an underlying political continuity in which emperor followed emperor in unbroken succession.

In the West, then, we are faced with two separate phenomena—political breakdown and cultural transformation. The political

39

collapse culminated in the deposition of the last western emperor
in A.D. 476, but the real period of crisis was the chaotic third century. The recovery under Diocletian and Constantine was merely
partial and temporary; the impending death of the body politic
was delayed but the disease remained uncured. The impoverished
masses in town and countryside had never participated meaning-
fully in Roman civilization, and the third-century anarchy resulted in the spiritual disengagement of the middle classes as well.
Initiative and commitment ebbed in the atmosphere of economic
and political upheaval and were stifled by the autocracy that followed. Fourth-century Rome was a totalitarian police state which
robbed its subjects of their independence and watched over them
by means of a vast network of informers and secret agents. The
collapse of such a state cannot be regarded as an unmitigated
disaster. To many it must have seemed a blessing.

The West had always been poorer and less urbanized than the
East, and its economy, badly shaken by the political chaos of the
third century, began to break down under the growing burden
of imperial government and the defense of hard-pressed frontiers.
Perhaps the fatal flaw in the western economy was its inability to
compensate for the cessation of imperial expansion by more inten-
sive internal development. There was no large-scale industry,
no mass production; the majority of the population was far too
poor to provide a mass market. Industrial production was exceedingly inefficient and technology progressed at a snail's pace. The
economy remained fundamentally agrarian, and farming techniques advanced very little during the centuries of the empire.
The Roman plow was rudimentary and inefficient; windmills
were unknown and water mills exceptional. The horse could not
be used as a draught animal because the Roman harness crossed
the horse's windpipe and tended to strangle him under a heavy
load. Consequently, Roman agriculture was based on the less
efficient oxen and on the muscles of slaves and *coloni*.

Economic exhaustion brought with it the twin evils of population decline and creeping poverty; and at the very time that the
manpower shortage was becoming acute and impoverishment was
paralyzing the middle classes, the expenses of government were
soaring. The army and bureaucracy steadily expanded until at
length the state payroll contained more names than the tax rolls.

One result of these processes was the deurbanization of the West. By the fifth century the once vigorous cities were becoming ghosts of their former selves, drained of their wealth and much of their population. Only the small class of great landowners managed to prosper in the economic atmosphere of the late Western Empire, and these men now abandoned their town houses, withdrew from civic affairs, and retired to their estates where they often assembled sizable private armies and defied the tax collector. The aristocracy, having now fled the city, would remain an agrarian class for the next thousand years. The rural nobility of the Middle Ages had come into being.

The decline of the city was fatal to the urbanized administrative structure of the Western Empire. More than that, it brought an end to the urban-oriented culture of Greco-Roman antiquity. The civilization of Athens, Alexandria, and Rome could not survive in the fields. It is in the decay of urban society that we find the crucial connecting link between political collapse and cultural transformation. In a very real sense Greco-Roman culture was dead long before the final demise of the Western Empire; the deposition of the last emperor in 476 was merely the faint postscript to a process that had been completed long before. By then the cities were moribund. The rational, humanist outlook had given way completely to transcendentalism and mysticism. The army and even the civil government had become barbarized as the desperate emperors, faced with a growing shortage of manpower and resources, turned more and more to Germanic peoples to defend their frontiers and keep order in their state. In the end barbarians abounded in the army, entire tribes were hired to defend the frontiers, and Germanic military leaders came to hold positions of high authority in the Western Empire. Survival had actually come to depend on the success of half-hearted Germanic defenders against plunder-hungry Germanic invaders.

Despite the deurbanization, the mysticism, the barbarism of the late empire, it is nevertheless true that in a certain sense Greco-Roman culture never died in the West. It exerted a profound influence, as we have seen, on the Fathers of the Latin Church and, through them, on the mind of the Middle Ages. It was the basis of repeated cultural revivals, great and small, down through the centuries—in the era of Charlemagne, in the High Middle

Ages, in the Italian Renaissance, and in the neoclassical eighteenth century. And if in one sense the Roman state was dead long before the line of western emperors ended in 476, in another it survived long thereafter—in the ecclesiastical organization of the Roman Catholic Church and in the medieval Holy Roman Empire. Roman law endured to inspire western jurisprudence; the Latin tongue remained the language of educated Europeans for more than a millennium while evolving in the lower levels of society into the Romance languages, Italian, French, Spanish, Portuguese, and Roumanian. In countless forms the rich legacy of classical antiquity was passed on to the Middle Ages; Europeans for centuries to come would be nourished by Greek thought and haunted by the memory of Rome.

THE GERMANIC PEOPLES

Medieval civilization owed much to its Greco-Roman heritage, but it drew sustenance also from the Judaeo-Christian and the Germanic cultural traditions. We have already observed the fusion of Greco-Roman and Christian culture in the Roman Empire, beginning with the early Christian apologists and culminating in the work of Ambrose, Jerome, and Augustine. By the fifth century the fusion of these two traditions was essentially complete, but their integration with Germanic culture had only begun. Throughout the turbulent centuries of the Early Middle Ages the Greco-Roman-Christian tradition was preserved by the Church, while the Germanic tradition dominated the political and military organization of the barbarian states which established themselves on the carcass of the Western Empire. The Germanic invaders soon became at least nominal Christians, but for centuries a cultural gulf remained between the Church, with its Greco-Roman-Christian heritage, and the Germanic kingdoms with their primitive, war-oriented culture. The Church of the Early Middle Ages was able to preserve ancient culture only in a simplified and debased form, for as time went on ecclesiastical leaders and aristocratic laymen came more and more to be drawn from the same social milieu. Still, it remained the great task of the early medieval Church to civilize and Christianize the Germanic peoples. In the end the Classical-Christian-Germanic synthesis was achieved, and a new Western European Civilization came into being.

Most of the tribes that invaded the Western Empire seem to have come originally from the Scandinavian area, the homeland of the later Vikings. Gradually they migrated into Eastern and Southeastern Europe and began to press against the Rhine and Danube frontiers. It is hazardous to make broad generalizations regarding their culture and institutions, for customs varied considerably from tribe to tribe. The Franks, the Angles, and the Saxons, for example, were agrarian peoples whose movements were slow but who, once settled, were difficult to displace. Little influenced by Roman civilization they came into the empire as heathens. The Visigoths, Ostrogoths, and Vandals, on the other hand, were at once more mobile and more rootless. All three had absorbed Roman culture to some degree before they crossed the frontiers, and all had been converted in the fourth century to Arian Christianity.

A good contemporary account of early Germanic institutions is to be found in a short book entitled *Germania* written by the Roman historian Tacitus in A.D. 98. This work is not entirely trustworthy; it is a morality piece written with the intention of criticizing the "degeneracy" of the Romans by comparing them unfavorably with the simple and upright barbarians. Nevertheless, it is an invaluable source of information on early Germanic customs and institutions. We can certainly accept Tacitus' description of the Germans as large men with reddish-blond hair and blue eyes, living in simple villages, but his eulogy of their virtue and chastity is a gross exaggeration. On the whole they appear to have been drunks, liars, and lechers, whose vices were certainly no less numerous than those of the Romans, only cruder. Their standards of personal hygiene are suggested by the observation of a fifth-century Roman gentleman: "Happy the nose that cannot smell a barbarian."*

Although the Germans used iron tools and weapons, their social and economic organization was in many ways reminiscent

---

* The author, some of whose best friends are of Frankish and Anglo-Saxon descent, disclaims any sort of ethnic bias. The crudeness of the barbarians was due entirely to their lack of social and educational opportunities.

of the Neolithic culture stage. Their chief activities were tending crops or herds and fighting wars. The key social unit within the tribe had traditionally been the kindred group or clan, which protected the welfare of its members by means of the blood feud. When a man was killed, his clan was bound to avenge his death by conducting a feud—declaring war, as it were—against the killer and his clan. In the boisterous atmosphere of the tribe, killings were only too common, and in order to keep the social fabric from being torn asunder by blood feuds it became customary for the tribe to establish a *wergeld,* a sum of money which the killer might pay to the relatives of his victim to appease their vengeance. Wergeld schedules became quite elaborate, the amount of money to be paid by the killer varying in accordance with the social status of his victim. Smaller wergelds were established for lesser injuries such as the cutting off of a victim's arm, leg, thumb, or finger. There was no guarantee, however, that the man who did the killing or maiming would agree to pay the wergeld, or that the victim or his clan would agree to accept it. In spite of the wergeld system, blood feuds continued far into the Middle Ages.

The ties of kinship were strong among the early Germans, but they were rivaled by those of another social unit, the war band or *comitatus.* Kinship played no part in this institution; it consisted rather of a group of warriors bound together by their loyalty to a chief or king. The comitatus was a kind of military brotherhood based on honor, fidelity, courage, and mutual respect between the leader and his men. In warfare the leader was expected to excel his men in courage and prowess, and should the leader be killed, his men were honor-bound to fight to the death even if their cause should appear hopeless. The heroic virtues of the comitatus persisted throughout the Early Middle Ages as the characteristic ideology of the European warrior nobility.

The comitatus and the clan were subdivisions of a larger unit, the tribe, whose members were bound together by their allegiance to a king and by their recognition of a body of customary law. Germanic law was arbitrary and childish compared with the majestic legal edifice of Rome. Procedural formalities were all important, and guilt or innocence was often determined by requiring the accused to grasp a bar of red-hot iron or to plunge his hand into a cauldron of boiling water. Nevertheless, throughout the Early Middle Ages the legal structure of the Western European states was Germanic rather than Roman. It was not until the twelfth century that Roman law was revived in the West and began to make its influence felt once again. In the meantime, Germanic law, for all its crudeness, implanted one singularly fruitful idea in the Western mind: that law was a product not of the royal will but of the immemorial customs of the people. And if law could not be altered by the king, then royal authority could not be absolute. In the Early Middle Ages a number of Germanic kings had the customs of their people put into writing, but they rarely claimed the power to legislate on their own. Out of this Germanic background there emerged in the High Middle Ages the constitutional principle of government under the law.

The centuries immediately preceding the invasions witnessed the development of relatively stable royal dynasties among many of the Germanic tribes. Perhaps an unusually gifted warrior with a particularly large comitatus might start such a dynasty, but before many generations had gone by the kings were claiming descent from some divine ancestor. When a king died, the assembly of the tribe chose as his successor the ablest member of his family. This might or might not be his eldest son, for the tribal assembly was given considerable latitude in its power to elect. The custom of election persisted in most Germanic kingdoms far into the Middle Ages. Its chief consequence during the fifth-century invasions was to insure that the barbarian tribes were normally led by clever, battle-worthy kings or chieftains at a time when the Western Empire was ruled by weaklings and fools.

Historians of previous centuries made much of the fact that certain Germanic institutions seemed to contain the seeds of constitutionalism and popular sovereignty. Democracy, so it was said, had its genesis in the forests of Germany. It should be obvious, however, that the veneration of a customary "law of the folk" or the political prominence of a tribal assembly is not uniquely Germanic but is common to many primitive peoples. The surprising thing about these institutions is not their existence among the Germanic barbarians but their endurance and development in the centuries that followed.

The Germanic peoples had long been a threat to the empire. They had defeated a Roman army in the reign of Augustus; they had probed deeply into the empire under Marcus Aurelius and again in the mid-third century. But until the later fourth century the Romans had always managed eventually to drive the invaders out. Beginning in the mid-370s, however, an exhausted empire was confronted by renewed barbarian pressures of an unprecedented magnitude. Lured by the relative wealth, the good soil, and the sunny climate of the Mediterranean world, the barbarians tended to regard the empire not as something to destroy but as something to enjoy. Their age-long yearning for the fair lands across the Roman frontier was suddenly transformed into an urgent need by the westward thrust of a ferocious tribe of Asiatic nomads known as the Huns. These fierce horsemen conquered one Germanic tribe after another and turned them into satellites. The Ostrogoths fell before their might and became a subject people. The other great Gothic tribe, the Visigoths, sought to avoid a similar fate by appealing for sanctuary behind the Roman Danube frontier. The eastern emperor Valens, a fervent Arian, sympathized with the Arian Visigoths, and in 376 the entire tribe crossed peacefully into the empire.

There was trouble almost immediately. Corrupt imperial officials cheated and abused the Visigoths, and the hot-tempered tribesmen retaliated by going on a rampage. At length Emperor Valens himself took the field against them, but the emperor's military incapacity cost him his army and his life at the battle of Adrianople in 378. Adrianople was a military debacle of the first order. Valens' successor, the able Theodosius I, managed to pacify the Visigoths but he could not expel them. When Theodosius died in 395 the Roman Empire was split among his two incompetent sons, and, as it happened, the eastern and western halves were never again rejoined. A vigorous new Visigothic leader named Alaric now led his people on a second campaign of pillage and destruction that threatened Italy itself. In 406 the desperate Western Empire recalled most of its troops from the Rhine frontier to block Alaric's advance, with the disastrous consequence that the Vandals and a number of other tribes swept across the unguarded Rhine into Gaul. Shortly thereafter the Roman legions abandoned distant Britain, and the defenseless island was gradually overrun by Angles, Saxons, and Jutes. In 408 the only able general in the West was executed by the frantic, incompetent Emperor Honorius who then abandoned Rome and took refuge behind the marshes of Ravenna. The Visigoths entered Rome unopposed in 410 and Alaric permitted them to plunder the city for three days.

The sack of Rome had a devastating impact on imperial morale, but in historical perspective it appears as a mere incident in the disintegration of the Western Empire. The Visigoths soon left the city to its feeble emperor and turned northward into Southern Gaul and Spain, where they established a kingdom that endured until the Moslem conquests of the eighth century. Meanwhile other tribes were carving out kingdoms of their own. The Vandals swept through Gaul and Spain and across the Straits of Gibraltar into Africa. In 430, the very year of St. Augustine's death, they took his city of Hippo. A new Vandal kingdom arose in North Africa, centering on ancient Carthage. Almost immediately the Vandals began taking to the sea as buccaneers, devastating Mediterranean shipping and sacking one coastal city after another. Vandal piracy shattered the age-long peace of the Mediterranean and dealt a crippling blow to the waning commerce of the Western Empire.

Midway through the fifth century the Huns themselves moved against the West, led by their brilliant and pitiless leader Attila, the "Scourge of God." Defeated by a Roman-Visigothic army in Gaul in 451, they returned the following year, hurling themselves toward Rome and leaving a path of unimaginable devastation behind them. The western emperor abandoned Rome to Attila's mercies, but the Roman bishop, Pope Leo I, traveled northward from the city to negotiate with the Huns on the wild chance that they might be persuaded to turn back, Oddly enough, Pope Leo succeeded in his mission. Perhaps because the health of the Hunnish army was adversely affected by the Italian climate, perhaps because the majestic Pope Leo was able to overawe the superstitious Attila, the Huns retired from Italy. Shortly afterward Attila died, the Hunnish empire collapsed, and the Huns themselves vanished from history. They were not mourned.

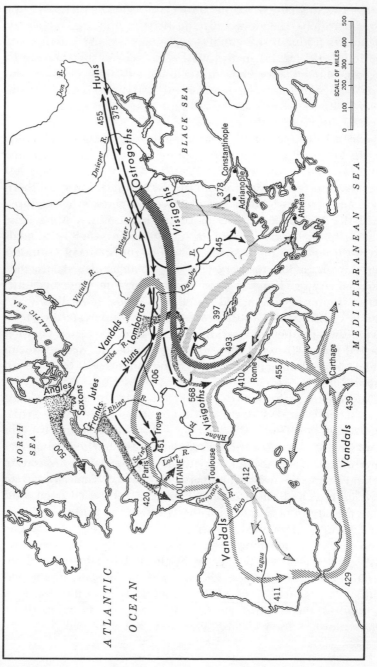

Map II.   The Germanic invasions.

In its final years the Western Empire, whose jurisdiction now scarcely extended beyond Italy, fell under the control of hard-bitten military adventures of Germanic birth. The emperors continued to reign for a time, but their Germanic generals were the powers behind the throne. In 476 the barbarian general Odo-vacar, who saw no point in perpetuating the farce, deposed the last emperor, sent the imperial trappings to Constantinople, and asserted his sovereignty over Italy by confiscating a good deal of farmland for the use of his Germanic troops. Odovacar claimed to rule as an agent of the Eastern Empire but in fact he was on his own. A few years later the Ostrogoths, now free of Hunnish control and led by a brilliant king named Theodoric, advanced into Italy, conquered Odovacar, and established a strong state of their own.

Theodoric ruled Italy from 493 to 526. More than any other barbarian king he appreciated and respected Roman culture, and in his kingdom the Arian Ostrogoths and the orthodox Romans lived and worked together in relative harmony, repairing aque-ducts, erecting impressive new buildings, and bringing a degree of prosperity to the long-troubled peninsula. The improving polit-ical and economic climate gave rise to a minor intellectual revival that contributed to the transmission of Greco-Roman culture into the Middle Ages. The philosopher Boethius, a high official in Theodoric's regime, produced philosophical works and translations which served as fundamental texts in western schools for the next five hundred years. His *Consolation of Philosophy*, an interesting mixture of Platonism and Stoicism, was immensely popular throughout the Middle Ages. Theodoric's own secretary, Cassiodorus, was another scholar of considerable distinction. Cas-siodorus spent his later years as abbot of a monastery and set his monks to the invaluable task of copying and preserving the great literary works of antiquity, both Christian and pagan.

During the years of Theodoric's beneficent rule in Ostrogothic Italy, another famous barbarian king, Clovis (481–511), was creat-ing a Frankish kingdom in Gaul. Clovis was far less Romanized, far less enlightened, far crueler than Theodoric, but his kingdom proved to be the most enduring of all the barbarian successor states. The Franks were good farmers as well as good soldiers, and they established deep roots in the soil of Gaul. Moreover,

the Frankish regime was buttressed by the enthusiastic support
of the Catholic Church. For Clovis, who had been untouched by
Arianism, was converted directly from heathenism to Catholic
Christianity. He remained a savage barbarian to the end, yet the
Church came to regard him as another Constantine, a defender
of orthodoxy in a sea of Arianism. As the centuries went by the
royal name "Clovis" was softened to "Louis" and the "Franks"
became the "French." And the friendship between the Frankish
monarchy and the Church developed into one of the great determining elements in European politics.

EUROPE IN A.D. 500

As the sixth century dawned, the Western Empire was only a
memory. In its place were a group of barbarian successor states
that foreshadowed in certain respects the nations of modern
Western Europe. Theodoric headed a tolerant and relatively en-
lightened Ostrogothic-Arian regime in Italy. The barbaric but
orthodox Clovis was completing the Frankish conquest of Gaul.
The Vandal monarchy, Arian in religion and increasingly corrupt
and intolerant, lorded it over the restive population of North
Africa. The Arian Visigoths were being driven out of southern
Gaul by the Franks, but their regime continued to dominate
Spain for the next two centuries. And the Angles, Saxons, and
Jutes were in the process of establishing a group of small heathen
kingdoms in Britain which would one day coalesce into "Angle-
land" or England.

At the very time that the Germanic kingdoms were establishing
themselves in the West the Roman papacy was beginning to play
an important independent role in European society. We have
seen how the great mid-fifth century pope, Leo I (440–461),
assumed the task of protecting the city of Rome from the Huns,
thereby winning for himself the moral leadership of the West.
Leo and his successors declared that the papacy was the highest
authority in the Church, and, following the example of St. Ambrose, they insisted on the supremacy of Church over state in
spiritual matters. In proclaiming its doctrines of papal supremacy
in the Church and ecclesiastical independence from state control,
the papacy was hurling a direct challenge at Byzantine Caesaro-

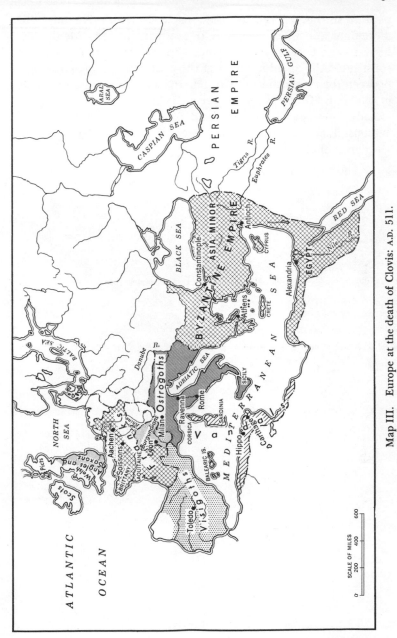

Map III.   Europe at the death of Clovis: A.D. 511.

papism. In the fifth century these papal doctrines remained little more than words, but they were to result in an ever widening gulf between the Eastern and Western Church. More than that, they constituted the opening phase of the prolonged medieval struggle between the rival claims of Church and state. The mighty papacy of the High Middle Ages was yet many centuries away, but it was already foreshadowed in the bold independence of Leo I. The Western Empire was dead, but eternal Rome still claimed the allegiance of the world.

CHRONOLOGY OF THE LATER EMPIRE

All Dates A.D.

180–192: Reign of Commodus
96–180: The age of the great second-century emperors
193–211: Reign of Septimius Severus
235–284: Height of the anarchy; "barracks emperors"
185–254: Origen
205–270: Plotinus
284–305: Reign of Diocletian
306–337: Reign of Constantine
325:     Council of Nicaea
330:     Founding of Constantinople
354–430: St. Augustine of Hippo
376:     Visigoths cross Danube
378:     Battle of Adrianople
378–395: Reign of Theodosius I
395:     Final division of Eastern and Western Empires
410:     Alaric sacks Rome
430:     Vandals capture Hippo
451–452: Huns invade Western Europe
440–461: Pontificate of Leo I
476:     Last western emperor deposed by Odovacar
493–526: Theodoric the Ostrogoth rules Italy
481–511: Clovis rules Franks, conquers Gaul

Suggested Readings

The asterisk indicates a paperback edition.

GENERAL HISTORIES OF ROME

Max Cary, *A History of Rome* (2nd ed., St. Martin's Press). The best single-volume text.

M. Rostovtzeff, *Rome* (*Oxford Galaxy). A reprint of Vol. II of Rostovtzeff's *History of the Ancient World* first published in 1927; a scholarly masterpiece which stresses social history and perhaps overestimates class antagonisms.

Among the several other general accounts of Roman civilization are

R. H. Barrow, *The Romans* (*Penguin).

Donald R. Dudley, *The Civilization of Rome* (*Mentor).

Michael Grant, *The World of Rome* (*Mentor). 133 B.C.–A.D. 217.

THE MYSTERY RELIGIONS AND CHRISTIANITY

F. Cumont, *The Mysteries of Mithra* (*Dover), and *Oriental Religions in Roman Paganism* (*Dover). Two fundamental studies by a great scholar, outdated in details but still useful.

R. Bultmann, *Primitive Christianity in its Contemporary Setting* (*Meridian). Readable and authoritative.

Michael Gough, *The Early Christians* (Praeger). A good popular account with fine illustrations.

E. R. Goodenough, *The Church in the Roman Empire* (*Henry Holt). A brief, lucid survey.

V. Latourette, *History of Christianity* (Harper). One of the best short histories of the Christian Church.

H. O. Taylor, *The Emergence of Christian Culture in the West* (*Harper). An ageless study by one of the masters of medieval intellectual history.

C. N. Cochrane, *Christianity and Classical Culture* (*Oxford Galaxy). An intellectual tour de force, sympathetic to the rise of the mystical point of view.

THE LATER EMPIRE AND THE GERMANIC INVASIONS

J. B. Bury, *History of the Later Roman Empire* (*2 vols., Dover). The standard account, full and authoritative, by one of the distinguished historians of this century.

F. Lot, *The End of the Ancient World and the Beginnings of the Middle Ages* (*Harper). A masterly study which places stress on the economic factors in the decline. A valuable introduction by Glanville Downey summarizes recent scholarship on the problem of "decline and fall."

Mortimer Chambers (Ed.), *The Fall of Rome* (*Holt, Rinehart, and Winston). Well-chosen excerpts from historical writings dealing with the decline of Rome provide a compact, illuminating survey of historical opinion on the subject.

Solomon Katz, *The Decline of Rome* (*Cornell). A brief, perceptive, well-written survey.

Samuel Dill, *Roman Society in the Last Century of the Western Empire* (*Meridian). A brilliant older work.

Edward Gibbon, *The Triumph of Christendom in the Roman Empire* (*Harper). Chapters XV–XX from Gibbon's masterpiece, *The Decline and Fall of the Roman Empire*. The entire work is available in a three-volume Modern Library edition.

SOURCES

B. Davenport (Ed.), *The Portable Roman Reader* (*Viking). One of several good anthologies now available in paperback.

There are numerous available editions of the works of Cicero, Caesar, Virgil, Horace, Plutarch, Tacitus, Suetonius, and other important Roman writers, many of them in paperback, which enable the student to experience Roman civilization first hand. For early Christianity the New Testament is the ideal source. Modern paperback editions of the four Gospels and the Acts of the Apostles are readily available. St. Augustine's *Confessions* has been published in several paperback editions. For the *City of God*, see Vernon J. Bourke, (Ed.), *St. Augustine's City of God* (Doubleday Image). An intelligent abridgment.

Gregory of Tours, *History of the Franks*, tr. O. M. Dalton (Oxford). Provides an interesting account of Clovis and the early Franks in Gaul.

Part 2

THE Early Middle Ages:
The Genesis of Western Civilization

5

Byzantium Endures

By the opening of the sixth century the Western Empire had dissolved into a group of barbarian successor states, but the Eastern Empire continued to hold sway over a vast territory stretching from the Balkans to Asia Minor, Syria, Palestine, and Egypt. Many of the same forces that had weakened and demoralized the West operated in the East as well, yet imperial authority collapsed in the West and survived in the East. Why was this so?

For one thing, the East had always been more populous than the West. Its civilization was far older and more deeply rooted; its cities were larger and more numerous. The East had remained the commercial and industrial center of the empire even in the great days of Rome, and when disaster struck it proved to be far more resilient than the West.

Asia Minor was the Eastern Empire's great reservoir of manpower and revenues (see map, p. 51). For many centuries it was to remain the chief recruiting ground for the Byzantine army and the most dependable source of imperial taxes. During the cataclysmic fifth century, while barbarians were conquering the western provinces, Asia Minor was a bulwark of the empire. Its tough loyal troops provided the eastern emperors with an invaluable alternative to the ruinous policy of complete dependence on hired Germanic armies.

Asia Minor was protected against the Germanic onslaught by impenetrable Constantinople. This great city, the New Rome, was the heart of the Eastern Empire. So long as it remained inviolate behind its great landward and seaward walls the empire lived on. In later centuries enemies would sweep across the empire to the very gates of Constantinople only to fall back in rage and frustration. In the seventh century Constantinople withstood a great Persian siege; in the eighth century it repelled the full fury of the all-conquering Moslems. Little wonder that the Germanic barbarians preferred the more vulnerable West. More than once, the East Roman government relieved itself of Germanic pressure by suggesting to the barbarians that if they moved West they might have better luck and easier conquests. Doubtless cynical, this suggestion was also true.

The Eastern Empire had the further advantage during the crucial fifth century of being much better governed than the Western Empire. A series of able eastern emperors carefully husbanded their resources, fattened their treasury, and strengthened the fortifications of Constantinople while the Western Empire was collapsing. Superior leadership undoubtedly helped the East weather the storm, but its emperors could have accomplished little had it not been for the superb strategic location of their capital and the enduring commercial and human resources of the lands they ruled. The cradle of ancient civilizations had the strength to survive the barbarian flood that submerged the more recently civilized West.

BYZANTINE GOVERNMENT

The civilization of the Byzantine Empire was a synthesis of three elements: Roman government, Christian religion, and Greco-Oriental culture. From Rome the Eastern Empire drew its legal system, its bureaucracy, and its principles of administration. Indeed, Byzantine government was a direct offspring of the third- and fourth- century Dominate: Byzantine autocracy had its roots in Diocletian's glorification of the emperor; Byzantine Caesaropapism evolved out of the Christian Empire of Constantine and Theodosius I. The heavy taxation of the Dominate continued, and life in the Byzantine Empire remained burdensome and insecure.

The prevailing Byzantine mood was defensive and conservative. The state, oppressive though it was, had to be preserved at all costs. The swollen, tradition-bound bureaucracy abhorred novelty. It took no risks, resisted the bold policies of imaginative emperors, yet held the state together in eras of anarchy and incompetent rule. Corrupt and wasteful, the bureaucracy nevertheless contributed to the empire's remarkable stability and endurance.

More efficient than the bureaucracy, the army was a relatively small but highly effective force, thoroughly trained and usually well led. In many wars the very survival of the empire was at stake, and Byzantine generals, like Byzantine bureaucrats, took few risks. They preferred caution to daring, cunning to brute force. War was both an art and a science to the Byzantines, and although frequently outnumbered in the field they were seldom outmaneuvered or outfought. Still, the empire often chose to pacify its enemies with tribute rather than take its chances against them in battle.

BYZANTINE CHRISTIANITY

It was Christianity that created the widespread dedication to the state so essential to Byzantium's age-long endurance. The orthodox Christians of the empire, although taxed to the ears and tormented by the arbitrary tyranny of the government, remained fervently committed to the sacred emperor. No mere secular sovereign, the emperor was the viceroy of God, and his state was the province of Christ. When Constantine founded his New Rome in 330 he dedicated the city to the Holy Trinity and the Blessed Virgin Mary, and the Byzantine Empire throughout its long history regarded itself as under their special protection. As the state went, so went the Church of Christ, or so the Byzantines believed. Their armies fought not merely for the empire but for Almighty God; every war was a crusade. The fires of patriotism, nourished by the Christian Faith, burned more fiercely in Christian Byzantium than they ever had in pagan Rome.

The Byzantine emperors continued the tradition of Caesaropapism which began with Constantine. The Eastern Church worked in close partnership with the state, and the patriarch of Constantinople often took his orders from the sacred emperor. Even the decisions of general councils of the Church required imperial approval. But although the emperor's control of the Church magnified his power and earned for him the allegiance of the orthodox, it also multiplied his problems and responsibilities. Religious disputes became matters of imperial concern, and heresy was a threat to the state.

As it happened, the Eastern Church of the fifth and sixth centuries was torn by doctrinal controversies. The most prominent heresy of the age was a doctrine known as *Monophysitism* which arose in Egypt, spread to Syria and Palestine, and created in these regions a feeling of bitter hostility toward the orthodox emperors whose policies ranged from ineffective attempts at conciliation to naked persecution. The Monophysites were concerned above all with the nature of Christ. It had already been established that Christ was fully human and fully divine, but the question remained, what precisely was the relationship between Christ's humanity and Christ's divinity? Was Christ in fact two persons, was he a single person with two natures, or was he one person with one nature in which humanity and divinity were blended? Each of these views had its adherents among the Christians of the fifth and sixth centuries. Orthodoxy was represented by the middle view—that Christ was one person with two natures—whereas the Monophysites clung passionately to the doctrine of a unified Christ with a single, blended nature. The Monophysites tended to regard Christ as more divine than human, and their doctrine has therefore been interpreted as a swing toward the spiritualism of the ancient Orient, which scorned human nature and the physical universe. These "Christological" disputes may seem remote and meaningless to the twentieth-century mind, but they were enormously important in their day, and they created insoluble difficulties for the eastern emperors. Religious unity was essential to the survival of their state, and as masters of the Eastern Church they were responsible for achieving and maintaining it. Several emperors sought to work out a compromise doctrine that would satisfy everyone—for example, that Christ had two natures but one *will*—but in fact they satisfied no one.

The West, which the emperors hoped one day to reconquer, was firmly orthodox and refused to accept any doctrinal formula that smelled even slightly of Monophysitism. In 451 a general council of the Church was held at Chalcedon which fell under

the influence of the great Roman pope, Leo I, and declared firmly in favor of the orthodox view of Christ as one person with two natures. As a result, the Monophysites in Egypt formed a separate Church with its own hierarchy, traces of which exist to this day. In the years that followed, the emperors sought to win back the Monophysites, sometimes by compromise, sometimes by persecution. But Monophysitism remained an anti-imperial nucleus—a rallying point for nationalist separatism. When, in the seventh century, Moslem armies swept into the empire they were welcomed by the Monophysites of Syria and Egypt, who preferred the relative tolerance of Arab rulers to the militant orthodoxy of the Christian emperors. Only when these rich but troublesome provinces were lost forever to the empire could a final doctrinal settlement be made.

BYZANTINE CULTURE

From Rome the Eastern Empire drew its principles of law and government; from the hellenized Christianity of the fourth-century empire it drew its theology, its popular faith, its Caesaropapism; and from Greece it drew its language and its philosophical and literary inspiration. To the end, the Byzantines preserved and cherished their Greek heritage, but their enduring Hellenism was strongly modified by Christian and Oriental influences, particularly in the field of art, where they achieved a brilliant fusion of Hellenistic and Near-Eastern styles. The classical ideal of Greek and Roman antiquity—the massive, straightforward, marvelously proportioned buildings, the muscular, realistic sculpture—had been profoundly modified by the spiritual transformation of the third and fourth centuries. Throughout the fourth-century Roman Empire the new mood of otherworldliness gave rise to new artistic values which de-emphasized the earthly and the concrete, stressing instead religious symbolism and spiritual exaltation. The hero of the new age was the saint, and the artistic representation of human beings stressed their holiness rather than their physiological perfection. Typical of the new Christian art was the heavily robed, emaciated figure with slender, solemn face and deep eyes. Lost or ignored were the traditional Greco-Roman techniques of perspective, but in

(a)

(b)

Plate I. (a) Detail from a mosaic of Justinian and his Courtiers that adorns the interior of S. Vitale in Ravenna, built 526–547. (b) Mosaic of Theodora and her Attendants from S. Vitale.

their place the Christian artists employed glittering, exuberant colors to convey a feeling of transcendental radiance akin to the glory of paradise.

This new art, with its oriental splendor and solemn grandeur, was ideally suited to the Byzantine spirit, and it dominated the Eastern Empire for the remainder of its history. Magnificent, domed churches adorned the cities of the empire, their interiors aglow with richly colored mosaic decorations worked on backgrounds of gold. The Byzantine artist strove not to portray nature but to transcend it, and even to this day a visitor stepping inside one of the great Byzantine churches—Sancta Sophia in Constantinople, St. Mark's in Venice—is struck with the feeling that he has suddenly stepped beyond this world altogether and into another. In short, the art of Byzantium was just as successful in achieving its objectives as was the very different art of Periclean Athens or Augustan Rome.

THE AGE OF JUSTINIAN

In the preceding pages we have been using the terms "Byzantine" and "East Roman" more or less interchangeably. It might well be asked, when did the empire cease to be "East Roman" and become "Byzantine"? The question is impossible to answer since, as we have seen, the key elements of Byzantine civilization developed gradually out of the fourth-century Dominate. In general, the "Byzantinization" of the Eastern Empire involved a slow but steady shift from a westward to an eastward outlook, from Latin to Greek, and from classical to Oriental. Yet Byzantine art was orientalized from the beginning and retained elements of Greco-Roman classicism to the end. The Byzantines never forgot their Greco-Roman heritage, nor did they forget that their ruler was a "Roman emperor." But as time progressed they became increasingly involved in their struggles with eastern enemies—the Persians, the Moslems, and various tribes of Asiatic nomads. They forgot their Latin. They ceased to be seriously concerned with the Roman pope or the lost western provinces. They turned their backs on Europe and their faces toward Asia.

In many respects the Emperor Justinian (527–565) was Constantinople's last Roman. Although his reign marks the first Golden Age of Byzantine art and the apogee of Byzantine Caesaro-

Historical Pictures Service — Chicago

Plate II.   Engraving of St. Mark's in Venice, the largest remaining church of the Second Golden Age of Byzantium, begun in 1063.

Italian Cultural Institute

Plate III.   Interior of St. Mark's in Venice, showing some of the art work for which the church is famous.

papism, Justinian was nevertheless a Latin-speaking emperor who was driven by the dream of reconstructing the old Roman Empire in all its former grandeur. The two great missions of his life were the codification of Roman law and the reconquest of the West.

When Justinian came to the throne in 527 the Eastern Empire was stronger than it had been for many decades. His predecessors had weathered the worst of the Germanic invasions and had accumulated a sizable financial reserve in the imperial treasury. Theodoric, the able ruler of Ostrogothic Italy, had died the year before, and several of the barbarian successor states in the West seemed to be losing their early vigor. A man of iron convictions, boundless energy, and intellectual distinction, Justinian renounced traditional Byzantine conservatism for a policy of bold resolution and audacity. The accomplishments of his reign were spectacular—and his empire almost died from the strain.

Justinian received invaluable support and encouragement in the realization of his plans from his brilliant and beautiful wife—the ex-prostitute Theodora—and from a remarkable group of talented subordinates in the fields of law, administration, architecture, and warfare. But Justinian himself was the consummate genius of his age, the tireless executor of imperial policy, the "Emperor who never sleeps." He was a learned theologian who grappled energetically but vainly with the insoluble problem of reconciling orthodoxy and Monophysitism. He administered the *coup de grace* to dying paganism by closing the pagan schools at Athens, which had been in operation ever since the days of Aristotle and Plato. He was a great builder who lavished his resources on the beautification of Constantinople. Under his direction the most gifted architects of the age produced Byzantium's greatest artistic triumph—the Church of Sancta Sophia (the Holy Wisdom) in Constantinople. The interior of this magnificent structure, opulent with gold, silver, ivory, blazing mosaics, and precious gems, was crowned by a vast dome, an architectural marvel that seemed to float on air. The total effect was indescribable. Justinian is reported to have exclaimed at Sancta Sophia's dedication, "Glory to God who has judged me worthy of accomplishing such a work as this! O Solomon, I have outdone thee!"

Plate IV. Drawing of Sancta Sophia (The Church of Holy Wisdom) in Constantinople which was built during Justinian's reign (532-537).

Justinian was also one of the great creative figures in the history of jurisprudence. He ordered that the vast body of precedents, juridical opinions, and imperial edicts of the Roman legal tradition be brought together into a single definitive body of civil law—the *Corpus Juris Civilis*. This monumental work, the product of a prodigious collective effort, thenceforth governed Byzantine jurisprudence. More than that, it was the vehicle through which Roman law was revived in twelfth-century Western Europe to inspire the legal systems of the European states. In Justinian's hands, Roman law became more rational and systematic than ever before, but it also took on an autocratic tone characteristic of his own age which would one day contribute to the growth of authoritarianism in the nations of the West. The monarchs of late medieval and early modern Europe were able to challenge the medieval Germanic notion of government under the law by turning from the legal crudities of Germanic custom to the sophisticated but autocratic principles of Justinian's great codification. For in the *Corpus Juris Civilis*, the collective legal wisdom of ancient Rome was colored by Justinian's own doctrine that law was the product of the ruler's will.

Obsessed with the glories of the Roman past, Justinian almost inevitably turned his attention to the reconquest of the West. He sent a small but well-trained army into North Africa, which, under the brilliant leadership of his general Belisarius, crushed the rotting Vandal regime in two quick battles. In 534 Belisarius occupied the former Vandal capital of Carthage, and two years later he led his forces into Italy hoping for an equally easy victory over the Ostrogothic kingdom. But Ostrogothic resistance proved unexpectedly tenacious. Only after an agonizing struggle of twenty years (535–555) were the Ostrogoths crushed and Italy returned to the empire. Ironically, the devastation wrought by these "Gothic Wars" virtually annihilated the old civilization of Italy. The peninsula had thrived under the Ostrogoth Theodoric; now it was a desert. Rome had changed hands again and again during the long struggle and was now depopulated and demolished. Justinian, hoping to recapture the past, had only succeeded in destroying it.

Justinian's forces enjoyed some success against Visigothic Spain, occupying a large strip of land along the Mediterranean shore,

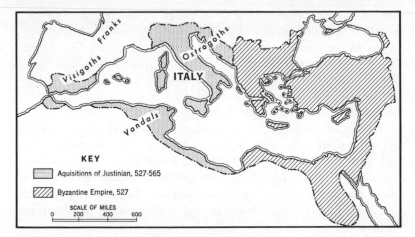

Map. IV.   The Conquests of Justinian.

but they were powerless to push back the entrenched Frankish regime in Gaul. In the end Justinian won control of most of the Mediterranean coastline but at tremendous cost. The conquered lands were too exhausted and impoverished to pay the heavy taxes necessary to support the protracted wars, and the imperial treasury was soon depleted. Justinian's greatest shortcoming was his inability to match ambitions to resources, and he left his empire overextended and exhausted. In retrospect the reconquest of the West was a momentous blunder, yet it would be fatuous to criticize Justinian for seeking to re-establish Mediterranean unity and to recapture Rome. As a Roman emperor in the tradition of Augustus and Diocletian he was bound to make the attempt.

THE EASTWARD ORIENTATION

Justinian's later years were darkened by the increasing economic exhaustion of his empire, the onslaught of a devastating plague, and growing bitterness between the orthodox and the Monophysites. The decades following his death in 565 saw a gradual transformation of imperial policy as the tottering empire abandoned many of its newly conquered western territories and summoned its remaining strength to ward off dangerous enemies from the north and east. Latin gave way to Greek as the language of the imperial administration, and the emperors were thenceforth known by the Greek title *Basileus* rather than *Caesar* or *Augustus*. The dream of a reconstituted Western Empire slowly dissolved. Three years after Justinian died, a savage Germanic tribe, the Lombards, broke into Italy and brought renewed devastation to the tormented Roman homeland. The Byzantines continued to hold much of southern Italy and a few coastal cities to the north, including their provincial capital of Ravenna, but elsewhere the Lombards raged unchecked. Within a few decades of Justinian's death the Visigoths had destroyed Byzantine power in southern Spain. North Africa remained in Byzantine hands for well over a century but fell eventually to the wide-ranging Moslems in the 690s.

In the meantime, Justinian's beleagured successors were faced with the task of restoring the treasury and coming to grips with eastern problems. Persia, relatively quiescent under Justinian, reasserted its dangerous pressure on the eastern frontier, and from the seventh century onward Slavic tribes were pouring into the Balkans. A new tribe of Asiatic nomads, the Avars, looked hungrily at the comparative wealth of Byzantium, and only heavy tribute payments succeeded in keeping them at bay. The preoccupation with the East and gradual abandonment of the West, the disappearance of Latin from the court, and the increasing orientalization of Byzantine culture and the Byzantine outlook mark the beginning of a new era.

CRISIS AND SURVIVAL

The threat from the East reached its climax in the reign of the able warrior-emperor Heraclius (610–641). For years Heraclius fought desperately against powerful Persian armies bent on the empire's destruction, and at one point (626) Constantinople withstood a ferocious double siege of Persians and Avars. Ultimately Heraclius destroyed the Persian army and forced the Persian Empire to conclude a humiliating peace. No sooner had the Persians been crushed then the Moslems, fired by the new faith of Mohammed (d.632), burst into Palestine, Syria, and Egypt detaching these rich provinces permanently from the rule of Constantinople. Heraclius died exhausted and broken, and the Byzantine Empire was reduced to Asia Minor, the Balkans, and a few scarcely defensible territories far to the west, which would be lost during the next century or so.

With the indispensable resources of Asia Minor still at its disposal Byzantium survived. Constantinople underwent a fierce Moslem siege in 717–18 but held firm. Indeed, in later centuries the Byzantines recovered their balance and extended their influence. They converted the Slavs and the Russians to Christianity and brought them into the fold of the Eastern Church. They fought the Arabs to a standstill and drove the nomads from the Balkans. They experienced new Golden Ages of art and learning. Indeed, at the very moment of Constantinople's fall to the Turks in 1453 the empire was undergoing a great classical-humanist revival which made a significant impact on the culture of the Italian Renaissance.

THE BYZANTINE LEGACY

Throughout the Middle Ages Constantinople remained Europe's eastern bastion against the Moslems. Its impregnable walls protected not only the Byzantine Empire but Western Europe as well from the ravages of Asiatic invaders. And the West was indebted to Byzantium for far more than its soldiers and its walls. The Eastern Empire served Western Europe and the world as a custodian of classical culture. The writings of the Greek philosophers, for example, were with a few exceptions unknown in the early medieval West but were preserved and studied in Constantinople. The Byzantines systematized and perpetuated the great Roman legal heritage. Byzantine art influenced the work of medieval and Renaissance painters. Byzantine missionaries Christianized and civilized the Slavs and laid the political and theological foundation for Czarist Russia. Indeed, when Constantinople fell in 1453, Moscow became the third Rome: its rulers assumed the Byzantine mantle as Caesars or Czars, lording it over both Church and state just as their Byzantine predecessors had. It has even been suggested that the present rulers of Russia, with their control of both the State and the Communist ideological apparatus, are carrying on the tradition of Byzantine Caesaropapism in a secularized form.

Yet the Byzantine achievement had its limitations. Byzantium remained an autocracy to the end, and its creative genius was stunted by its profound conservatism. Its originality was limited largely to the realms of art and heresy. For most of its long history it was a society under siege, and so much of its energy was devoted to its own survival that little was left for social, political, or technological experimentation or bold philosophical speculation. It performed the priceless service of preserving the thought and letters of Greco-Roman antiquity, but to this magnificent legacy it added little of its own. Perhaps its heritage from classical antiquity was too complete; perhaps the Byzantines were so awed by the achievements of their Greco-Roman forebears that they were psychologically incapable of surpassing them or striking out in new directions. In this sense the Byzantines were prisoners of their own past. The sophistication of Constantinople stands in sharp contrast to the ignorance and barbarism of the early medieval West, but the West, for all its barbarism, had the inestimable advantage of a fresh start. Its relapse into intellectual twilight and semisavagery resulted ultimately in its liberation from the dead hand of the past. The spirit of Greco-Roman antiquity inspired and enriched Western Christendom but did not shackle it.

6

The Barbarian West

THE "DARK AGES"

Between about A.D. 500 and 700, Roman culture in the West was in an advanced state of rot and the new civilization of Western Europe was just beginning to develop. The most obvious characteristics of sixth- and seventh-century Europe were ignorance, savagery, and semianarchy. In many respects, early medieval Europe was what would be described today as an "underdeveloped society."

The intellectual level of the period can best be appreciated by looking briefly at a few of its leading scholars. Bishop Gregory of Tours (d. 594), whose *History of the Franks* is our best source for the reigns of Clovis and his successors, wrote in barbaric, ungrammatical Latin and filled his history with outrageous and silly miracles. His was a world of savage cruelty and naked force beclouded by magic and superstitious fantasy.

Pope Gregory the Great (d. 604) was awarded a place alongside Ambrose, Jerome, and Augustine as one of the four Doctors of the Latin Church. But his writings, although marked by profound practical wisdom and psychological insight, had the effect of popularizing and oversimplifying Augustinian theology. The lofty theological issues with which Augustine grappled are overshadowed in Pope Gregory's thought by his concentration on such other matters as angels, demons, and relics.

75

Bishop Isidore of Seville (d. 636) was known as the greatest intellectual of the age. His most impressive work, the *Etymologies,* was intended to be an encyclopedia of all knowledge, but its value was vastly diminished by Isidore's remarkable lack of critical powers. He included every scrap of information that he could find, true or false, profound or absurd. On the subject of monsters, for example, he writes as follows:

> The Cynocephali are so called because they have dogs' heads and their very barking betrays them as beasts rather than men. These are born in India. The Cyclopses, too, hail from India, and they are so named because they have a single eye in the midst of the forehead. . . The Blemmyes, born in Lybia, are believed to be headless trunks, having mouth and eyes in the breast; others are born without necks, with eyes in their shoulders. . . . . They say the Panotii in Sythia have ears of so large a size that they cover the whole body with them. . . . The race of the Sciopodes is said to live in Ethiopia. They have one leg apiece, and are of a marvelous swiftness, and. . . in summertime they lie on the ground on their backs and are shaded by the greatness of their feet.

Finally, in a burst of skepticism, Isidore concludes:

> Other fabulous monstrosities of the human race are said to exist, but they do not; they are imaginary.

Isidore's discussion of numbers is also instructive. Twenty-two is a magic number because "God in the beginning made twenty-two works." There are therefore twenty-two sextarii in the bushel, twenty-two letters in the Hebrew alphabet, twenty-two generations from Adam to Jacob, and—presumably the clincher—twenty-two books in the Old Testament—as far as Esther.

In fairness to Isidore it should be stressed that the foregoing passages do not show him to best advantage. Moreover, much of Isidore's sense and nonsense was drawn from the writings of antiquity. But he combined and synthesized these ancient materials with a credulity typical of his times. His significance lies in the fact not that he was naive and uncritical, but that he was the best his age could produce.

ECONOMIC AND SOCIAL CHANGE

Significantly, all three of these leading Dark-Age intellectuals were bishops, and all three came from towns—Tours, Rome, Seville. The towns of the West had been declining ever since the beginning of the third century, and by about 600 they were shrunken phantoms. North of the Alps, the municipal governments of antiquity had disappeared without a trace. Still, many of the towns managed to survive after a fashion as centers of ecclesiastical administration. They remained the headquarters of important bishops and the sites of cathedral churches.* Often these cathedrals possessed the relics of important saints and thereby became pilgrimage centers. Tours, for example, owned the bones of the famous wonder worker St. Martin, whose miracles were so heavily emphasized in Bishop Gregory's *History of the Franks* that one might almost suspect the good bishop of striving to increase the pilgrim trade of the city.

Although many towns survived as episcopal centers they played only a peripheral role in the culture and economy of the barbarian states. The typical institutions of the age were the monastery, the peasant village, and the great farm or villa owned by some wealthy Roman or Germanic aristocrat and divided into small plots worked by semifree tenant farmers. A small-scale international luxury trade persisted, but by and large the sixth and seventh centuries were characterized by economic localism. Small agrarian communities produced most of their own needs and came close to being economically self-sufficient.

Except in Britain and northeastern Gaul, the barbarians tended to be absorbed into the older indigenous population, and free Germanic farmers often sank to the level of semiservile *coloni*. But the barbarian warrior nobility set the pattern of aristocratic life, and the civility of the Roman villa gradually disappeared. The Roman and barbarian nobility were fused through intermarriage into a single class, hard-bitten, rough, and warlike—far more Germanic than Roman.

---

* Technically, the term *cathedral* denotes the seat of a bishopric. A church, whether large or small, is a "cathedral" if it serves as a bishop's headquarters.

The barbarian kings, with the exception of Theodoric, proved themselves utterly incapable of carrying on the Roman administrative traditions which they inherited. The Roman tax system broke down almost completely, the privilege of minting coins fell into private hands, and the power and wealth of the government declined accordingly, not because the kings were generous but because they were ignorant. They lacked the slightest conception of responsible government and regarded their kingdoms as private estates to be exploited or alienated according to their whims. They made reckless gifts of land and political authority to the nobility and the Church, and considered what was left as their personal property, to be governed for the sole purpose of their own enrichment. In short, they managed to combine the worst features of anarchy and tyranny. In the words of a recent French historian, "Never in our history has the conception of the state known so complete an eclipse."*

Western Europe was doubtless overgoverned during the Dominate; now it was radically undergoverned. The Germanic kings did absolutely nothing to enliven the economy or ameliorate the general impoverishment. The Church strove bravely to fill the vacuum by dispensing charity and glamorizing the virtue of resignation, but even the Church was ill-equipped to cope with the chaos of the barbarian West. Ecclesiastical organization was confined largely to the defunct towns and the walled monasteries. Only gradually were rural parishes organized to meet the needs of the countryside. Indeed, it was not until the eighth century that the country parish became a characteristic feature of the Western Church. Until then a peasant was fortunate if he saw a priest once a year. The monarchy and the Church, the two greatest landholders in the barbarian kingdoms, were better known among the peasantry as acquisitive landlords than as fountains of justice and divine grace. The countryside was politically and spiritually adrift, and rural life was harsh, brutish, and short.

WESTERN EUROPE IN A.D. 600

We last surveyed Europe in A.D. 500 on the morrow of the

* Robert Latouche, *The Birth of Western Economy*, tr. E. M. Wilkinson (London, 1961), p. 129.

Western Empire's collapse. At that time Theodoric's Ostrogothic regime dominated Italy, the Vandals ruled North Africa, the Visigoths governed Spain, Clovis and his Franks were conquering Gaul, and the Anglo-Saxons were beginning their settlements in Britain. A century later, two of these states had been destroyed by Justinian's armies; North Africa was now Byzantine rather than Vandal, and the Ostrogothic kingdom of Italy had collapsed.

By 600 the Anglo-Saxon tribes had occupied much of Britain, enslaving many of the indigenous Celtic inhabitants and driving the rest into the western mountains of Wales. Anglo-Saxon Britain was now a confused medley of small, independent, heathen kingdoms in which the process of Christian conversion was just beginning.

To the south, the Franks dominated Gaul under the cruel and incompetent dynasty of Clovis—the *Merovingian* dynasty, named after Clovis' half-mythical ancestor, Merovech. The Frankish Merovingian dynasty followed the Germanic custom of dividing the kingdom among the sons of a deceased ruler. The sons then usually engaged in bitter civil war until, as it sometimes happened, one emerged as sole monarch of the Franks. He then died, dividing the kingdom among *his* sons, and the bitter comedy was repeated. Merovingian government was predatory and unenlightened, and the Merovingian Church was becoming disorganized and corrupt.

Corruption was also paralyzing Church and state in Visigothic Spain. The monarchy, converted in 589 from Arianism to Catholicism, was able at length to reconquer its Mediterranean shore from feeble Byzantium (c. 624), but the inept Visigothic kings allowed their power to slip little by little into the hands of a greedy and oppressive landed aristocracy. The worm-eaten regime was an easy prey for the conquering Moslems in the early 700s.

Italy had declined phenomenally in the century since Theodoric. The horrors of Justinian's Gothic wars were followed by the invasion of the savage Lombards. By 600 the decimated peninsula was divided between the Byzantines in Ravenna and the south, and the Lombards in the north. The papacy, under nominal Byzantine jurisdiction, dominated the lands around Rome and sought to preserve its fragile independence by playing Lombard against Byzantine.

Map V.   Europe around 600.

THE DYNAMISM OF THE DARK AGES

Such was the condition of Western Europe in 600. At first glance one can see little to hope for in the all-prevailing gloom. Yet this was the society out of which Western Civilization was born. This was the formative epoch—the age of genesis—in which apparently minor trends would one day broaden into the powerful traditions that would govern the course of European history. Even in 600 there were glimmerings of light in the darkness. Classical culture still survived, if only in profoundly vulgarized form. Isidore of Seville was no Augustine, but he was far more than a mere barbarian. The Church, although tainted by the ignorance and corruption of its environment, still retained something of its power to inspire, to enlighten, and to civilize.

Far to the north, Ireland had been won for Christianity by St. Patrick in the fifth century, and by 600 it had developed an astonishingly creative Celtic-Christian culture. Irish scholars mastered both Greek and Latin literature at a time when Greek was unknown elsewhere in the West, and Irish artists produced magnificent illuminated manuscripts in a flowing, curvilinear Celtic style. Irish Christianity, isolated from the continental Church by the heathen Anglo-Saxon kingdoms, developed distinctive customs of its own. It was organized around the monastery rather than the diocese, and its leaders were abbots rather than bishops. Irish monks were famous for their learning, the austere severity of their lives, and the vast scope of their missionary activities. They converted large portions of Scotland to their own form of Christianity and by the early 600s were conducting missionary activities on the Continent itself.

EARLY CHRISTIAN MONASTICISM

Monasticism was the most dynamic and significant institution in the Early Middle Ages. The impulse toward monastic life is not peculiar to Christianity but is found in many religions—Buddhism and Judaism, to name but two. The Essenes, for example, whose cult may have produced the famous Dead Sea Scrolls, constituted a kind of Jewish monastic order.

There have always been religious souls who longed to withdraw from the sinful world and devote their lives to uninterrupted communion with God, but among Christians this impulse was particularly strong. Monasticism came to be regarded as the most perfect form of the Christian life—the consummate embodiment of Christ's own words: "And every man that has forsaken home, or brothers, or sisters, or father, or mother, or wife, or children, or lands for my name's sake, shall receive his reward a hundredfold, and obtain everlasting life" (Matt., 19:29).

The impulse toward withdrawal and renunciation first affected Christianity in the later third century when the Egyptian St.

Anthony retired to the desert to live the ascetic life of a godly hermit. In time the fame of his sanctity spread, and a colony of would-be ascetics gathered around him to draw inspiration from his holiness. St. Anthony then organized a community of hermits who lived together but had no communication with one another, like apartment dwellers in a large American city. Similar hermit communities soon arose throughout Egypt and spread into other regions of the empire. Hermit saints abounded in the fourth and fifth centuries. One of them, St. Simeon Stylites, achieved the necessary isolation by living atop a sixty-foot pillar for thirty years, evoking widespread admiration and imitation.

In the meantime a more down-to-earth type of monasticism was developing, based on a cooperative communal life. Beginning in early fourth-century Eygpt and expanding quickly throughout the Roman Empire, these early monastic communities attracted numerous fervent Christians who found insufficient challenge in the increasingly complacent post-Constantine Church. The holy individualism of the desert and pillar saints gave way to a more ordered monastic life, but the early communities remained loosely organized and continued to emphasize the ascetic practices of severe fasting, hair shirts, and purifying lashings, which had been pioneered by the hermits.

BENEDICTINE MONASTICISM

St. Benedict of Nursia (c. 480–c. 544) changed the course of western monasticism, tempering its flamboyant holiness with common sense and realistic principles of organization. As a youth St. Benedict fled corrupt Rome and took up the hermit life in a cave near the ruins of Nero's country palace. In time word of his saintliness circulated and disciples gathered around him. As it turned out, Benedict was more than a mere ascetic; he was a man of keen psychological insight—a superb organizer, who slowly learned, from the varied monastic experiences of his youth, how the monastic life might best be lived. Born of a Roman aristocratic family, he brought to his task a practical genius and a sense of order and discipline that were typically Roman. He founded a number of monasteries which drew not only prospective saints but ordinary people as well, even the sons of wealthy Roman families. At length he established his great monastery of Monte Cassino atop a mountain midway between Rome and Naples. For centuries thereafter Monte Cassino was one of the chief centers of religious life in Western Europe. At Monte Cassino, Benedict created a model monastery, governed by a comprehensive, practical, compassionate rule. In the midst of Justinian's Gothic Wars St. Benedict died, but his rule survived him to inspire and transform Western Europe.

Pope Gregory the Great described the Rule of St. Benedict as "conspicuous for its discretion." It provided for a busy, closely regulated life, simple but not violently ascetic. Benedictine monks were decently clothed, adequately fed, and seldom left to their own devices. Theirs was a life dedicated to God and to the attainment of personal sanctity, yet it was also a life that was available to any dedicated Christian and was rendered all the more attractive by the increasing brutality of the outside world. The monastic day was filled with carefully arranged activities: communal prayer, devotional reading, and work—field work, household work, manuscript copying, etc., according to the needs of the monastery and the ability of the monk. The fundamental obligations were chastity, poverty, and obedience; the monk must be celibate; he must discard all personal possessions; he must obey his abbot. The abbot, elected by the monks for life, was unquestioned master of the monastery, but he was to consult the monks in all his decisions. He was strictly responsible to God and was instructed to govern justly in accordance with the Rule. He was cautioned not to sadden or "overdrive" his monks or give them cause for "just murmuring." Here especially is the quality of discretion to which Pope Gregory alludes and which doubtless has been the major factor in the Rule's success.

Within two centuries of Benedict's death the Rule had spread throughout Western Christendom. The result was not a vast hierarchical monastic organization but rather a host of individual, autonomous monasteries sharing a single Rule and way of life but administratively unrelated. Benedict had visualized his monasteries as spiritual sanctuaries into which pious men might withdraw from the world, but the chaotic and illiterate society of the barbarian West, desperately in need of the discipline and learning of the Benedictines, could not permit them to abdicate from secular affairs. As it turned out, the Benedictines had enormous impact on the world they renounced. Their schools produced the vast majority of literate Europeans during the Early Middle Ages. They served as a cultural bridge, transcribing and preserving the writings of Latin antiquity. They spearheaded the penetration of Christianity into the forests of heathen Germany and later into Scandinavia, Poland, and Hungary. They served as scribes and advisers to kings and were drafted into high ecclesiastical offices. As recipients of gifts of land from pious donors over many generations they held and managed vast estates which became models for their age of intelligent agricultural organization and technological innovation. With the coming of feudalism, Benedictine abbots became great vassals, responsible for political and legal administration and military recruitment over the large areas under their control. Above all, as islands of peace, security, and learning in an ocean of barbarism, the Benedictine monasteries were the spiritual and intellectual centers of the developing Classical-Christian-Germanic synthesis that underlay European Civilization. In short, Benedictine monasticism was the supreme civilizing influence in the barbarian West.

POPE GREGORY THE GREAT (590–604)

The Benedictines carried out their great civilizing mission with the enthusiastic and invaluable support of the papacy. The alliance between these two institutions was consummated by the first Benedictine pope, Gregory the Great, who recognized immediately how effective the Benedictines might be in spreading the Catholic Faith and extending papal leadership far and wide across Christendom.

We have already encountered Pope Gregory as a Dark Age scholar—a popularizer of Augustinian thought. His theology, although highly influential in subsequent centuries, failed to rise much above the intellectual level of his age. His real genius lay in his keen understanding of human nature and his ability as an administrator and organizer. His *Pastoral Care*, a treatise on the duties and obligations of a bishop, is filled with practical wisdom and common sense. It answered a great need of the times and became one of the most widely read books in the Middle Ages.

Gregory loved the monastic life and ascended the papal throne with genuine regret. On hearing of his election he went into hiding and had to be dragged into the Roman basilica of St. Peters to be consecrated. But once resigned to his new responsibilities, Gregory bent every energy to the extension of papal authority. Following in the tradition of Pope Leo I, Gregory the Great believed fervently that the pope, as successor of St. Peter, was the rightful ruler of the Church. He reorganized the financial structure of the papal estates and used the increased revenues for charitable works to ameliorate the wretched poverty of his age. His integrity, wisdom, and administrative ability won for him an almost regal position in Rome and central Italy, towering over the contemporary Lombards and Byzantines who were then struggling for control of the peninsula. The reform of the Frankish Church was beyond his immediate powers, but he set in motion a process that would one day bring both France and Germany into the papal fold when he dispatched a group of Benedictine monks to convert heathen England.

THE CONVERSION OF ENGLAND

The mission to England was led by the Benedictine St. Augustine (not to be confused with the great theologian of an earlier day, St. Augustine of Hippo). In 597 Augustine and his followers arrived in the English kingdom of Kent and began their momentous work. England was then divided into a number of independent barbarian kingdoms of which Kent was momentarily the most powerful, and Augustine was assured a friendly reception by the fact that the king of Kent had a Christian wife. The conversion progressed speedily, and on Whitsunday, 597, the king and thousands of his subjects were baptized. The chief town of the realm, "Kent City" or Canterbury, became the headquarters of the new Church, and Augustine himself became the first archbishop of Canterbury.

During the decades that followed, the fortunes of English Benedictine Christianity rose and fell with the varying fortunes of the barbarian kingdoms. Kent declined, and by the mid-600s political power had shifted to the northernmost of the Anglo-Saxon states, Northumbria. This remote outpost became the scene of a deeply significant encounter and struggle between the two great creative forces of the age: Irish-Celtic Christianity, moving southward from its monasteries in Scotland, and Roman-Benedictine Christianity, moving northward from Kent.

The two movements shared a common faith but had different cultural backgrounds, different notions of monastic life and ecclesiastical organization, and even different systems for calculating the date of Easter. At stake was England's future relationship with the Continent and the papacy; a Celtic victory would probably have resulted in the isolation of England from the main course of Western Christian development. But at the Synod of Whitby in 663, King Oswy of Northumbria decided in favor of Roman-Benedictine Christianity and papal influence in England was assured. Six years later, in 669, the papacy sent the scholarly Theodore of Tarsus to assume the archbishopric of Canterbury and reorganize the English church into a coherent hierarchical system. As a consequence of Northumbria's conversion and Archbishop Theodore's tireless efforts, England, only a century out of naked heathenism, became Europe's most vigorous and creative Christian society.

The Irish-Benedictine encounter in seventh-century Northumbria produced a significant cultural surge known as the Northumbrian Renaissance. The two traditions influenced and inspired one another to such an extent that the evolving civilization of the barbarian West reached its pinnacle in this remote land. Boldly executed illuminated manuscripts in the Celtic curvilinear style (see Plate V), a new script, a vigorous vernacular epic poetry, and an impressive architecture all contributed to the luster of Northumbrian civilization in the late 600s and early 700s. The Northumbrian Renaissance centered in the great monasteries founded by Irish and Benedictine missionaries, particularly in the Benedictine monastery of Jarrow. Here, the supreme scholar of the age, St. Bede the Venerable, spent his life.

Bede entered Jarrow as a child and remained there until his death in 735. The best known of his many works is his *Ecclesiastical History of England,* a study that displays a keen critical sense far superior to that of Bede's medieval predecessors and contemporaries. The *Ecclesiastical History* is our chief source for early English history. It reflects a remarkable cultural breadth

(a)

(b)

Plate V.   (a) Cross Page from the *Lindisfarne Gospels* (c. A.D. 700), illustrating the artistic illuminations typical of the North-umbrian Renaissance.   (b) Detail of the Cross Page.

and a penetrating mind and establishes Bede as the greatest intellectual figure since Augustine of Hippo.

By Bede's death in 735 the Northumbrian kings had lost their political hegemony and Northumbrian culture was beginning to fade. But the tradition of learning was carried from England back to the Continent during the eighth century by a group of intrepid Anglo-Saxon Benedictine missionaries. In the 740s the English monk St. Boniface reformed the Church in Frankland, infusing it with Benedictine idealism and binding it more closely to the papacy. Pope Gregory had now been in his grave for 140 years, but his spirit was still at work. St. Boniface and other English missionaries founded new Benedictine monasteries among the Germans east of the Rhine and began the long and difficult task of Christianizing and civilizing these savage peoples, just as Augustine and his monks had once Christianized heathen Kent. By the late 700s the cultural center of Christendom had shifted southward again from England to the rapidly rising empire of the Frankish leader Charlemagne, whose career will be traced in a later chapter. Significantly, the leading scholar in Charlemagne's kingdom was Alcuin, a Benedictine monk from Northumbria.

THE CHURCH AND WESTERN CIVILIZATION

The barbarian West differed from the Byzantine East in innumerable ways, the most obvious being its far lower level of civilization. But even more important is the fact that the Western Church was able to reject Byzantine Caesaropapism and to develop more or less independently of the state. The spiritual and secular authorities often worked hand in hand, yet the two were never merged as they were in Constantinople and, indeed, in most ancient civilizations. The early Christian West was marked by a profound dichotomy—a separation between cultural leadership which was ecclesiastical and monastic, and political power which was in the hands of the barbarian kings. This dualism underlay the fluidity and dynamism of Western culture. It produced a creative tension which tended toward change rather than crystalization, toward an uninterrupted series of cultural climaxes, and toward ever-new intellectual and spiritual configurations. Like St. Augustine's two cities, the heroic warrior culture of the Germanic states and the Classical-Christian culture of Church and monastery remained always in the process of fusion yet never completely fused. The interplay between these two worlds governed the development of medieval civilization.

CHRONOLOGY OF SIXTH AND SEVENTH CENTURIES

481–511: Rule of Clovis
493–526: Theodoric rules Italy
527–565: Reign of Justinian
c.544:   Death of St. Benedict
590–604: Pontificate of Gregory the Great
597:      St. Augustine's mission arrives in Kent
632:      Death of Mohammed: Beginning of Arab conquests
636:      Death of St. Isidore of Seville
610–641: Heraclius reigns at Constantinople
663:      Synod of Whitby: Northumbria adopts Roman-Benedictine Christianity
669–690: Theodore of Tarsus is archbishop of Canterbury
717–718: Arabs besiege Constantinople
733:      Battle of Tours: Deepest Arab penetration into Western Europe
735·   Death of Bede

7

The Explosion of Islam

ISLAM, BYZANTIUM, AND WESTERN CHRISTENDOM

During the greater part of the Middle Ages the old Mediterranean empire of the Romans was split into three distinct cultural units: Western Christendom, Byzantine Christendom, and the Moslem world. These three cultures were divided by profound differences in style and mood, yet from our own detached viewpoint they had much in common. Each was an heir of Greco-Roman Civilization. Each had a strongly religious outlook which drew heavily from the Hebrew tradition. Each, indeed, claimed as its own the God of the Old Testament, and each viewed history as a great moral struggle beginning with the Creation and ending with the Last Judgment. There was a great deal of cultural exchange and inter-penetration among the three cultures in medieval times, yet none was influenced decisively by the other two. Although prompted and stimulated by its rivals, each worked out its own destiny.

Until about the twelfth century medieval Western Christendom was the most primitive and underdeveloped of the three cultures and had much to learn from Islam and Byzantium. Its developing synthesis of Classical, Christian, and Germanic traditions was shaped in many ways by the two neighboring civilizations, but the influence of these neighbors on the West was impeded by Europe's profound hostility toward the "infidel" Moslems and the "effete, treacherous" Byzantines. In the eighth and ninth centuries Western Europe's contacts with Islam were limited largely to the

90

battlefield. Only later did the West begin to draw upon the rich legacy of Moslem thought and culture.

MOHAMMED (*c.* 571–632)

Islam made its unexpected debut early in the seventh century and developed with astonishing speed into a great, cohesive civilization extending from India to Spain. The birthplace of this compelling new faith was the Arabian Peninsula—the modern Saudi Arabia—which for countless centuries had harbored fierce nomadic tribes which emerged periodically into the rich civilized districts of Palestine, Syria, and Mesopotamia to the north. The many Semitic invaders of the Ancient Near East seem to have come originally from the Arabian Desert—the Amorites, the Chaldeans, the Canaanites, even the Hebrews. These peoples quickly assimilated the ancient civilization of the Fertile Crescent and developed it in new, creative ways, but their kinsmen who stayed in Arabia remained primitive and disorganized.

In Mohammed's time most Arabians still clung to their nomadic ways and to their crude, polytheistic religion, but by then new civilizing influences were beginning to make themselves felt. A great caravan route running northward from southern Arabia served as an important link in a far-flung commercial network between the Far East and the Byzantine and Persian Empires. Along this route cities developed to serve the caravans, and with city life came a modicum of civilization. Indeed, the greatest of these trading cities, Mecca, became a bustling commercial center which sent its own caravans northward and southward and grew wealthy on its middleman profits. At Mecca and other caravan cities tribal life was beginning to give way to commercial life, and new, foreign ideas were beginning to challenge old ways and old points of view. It was in Mecca, around the year 571, that the prophet Mohammed was born.

At Mohammed's birth, the Emperor Justinian had been in his grave for six years. Mohammed's contemporaries include such men as Emperor Heraclius, Pope Gregory the Great, and Bishop Isidore of Seville. When the Benedictine mission from Rome landed in Kent in 597 to begin the conversion of England,

Mohammed was in his twenties and was as yet unknown outside of his own immediate circle.

He was born of a poor branch of Mecca's leading clan. With little formal education behind him, he became a caravan trader, and his travels brought him into close contact with Judaism, Christianity, and Persian Zoroastrianism. A nervous, sensitive man with a powerful, winning personality, he received God's call while in his late thirties and began to promulgate his new faith by preaching and writing. He won little support in Mecca apart from his wife and relatives and a few converts from the under-privileged classes. The Meccan commercial oligarchy seemed immune to the teaching of this low-born upstart. Perhaps they feared that his new religion would discredit the chief Meccan temple, the *Kaaba,* which housed a sacred meteoritic stone and was a profitable center of pilgrimages. Their belief that Mohammed's faith would ruin Mecca's pilgrim business was an ironic miscalculation, but their hostility to the new teaching forced Mohammed to flee Mecca in 622 and settle in the town of Medina, 280 miles northward on the caravan route.

The flight to Medina, known among the Moslems as the Hegira (He-jī'-ra), was a momentous turning point in the development of Islam and marks the beginning date of the Moslem calendar. Mohammed quickly won the inhabitants of Medina to his faith and became the city's political chief as well as its religious leader. Under Mohammed's direction, religious and civil authority were fused. The sacred community was at once a state and a church, and in this respect it foreshadowed later Islamic Civilization.

The Medinans made war on Mecca, raiding its caravans and blockading its trade. In 630 Medina conquered Mecca and incorporated it into the sacred community, and during the two remaining years of his life Mohammed, now an almost legendary figure in Arabia, received the voluntary submission of many of the tribes in the peninsula. By the time of his death in 632 he had united the Arabians for the first time into a coherent political-religious group, well-organized, well-armed, and inspired by a powerful new monotheistic religion. The violent energies of these desert people were now channeled toward a single lofty goal—the conquest and conversion of the world.

ISLAMIC RELIGION

Faith was the cement with which Mohammed unified Arabia. The new faith was called *Islam,* the Arabic word for "surrender." Mohammed taught that his followers must surrender to the will of Allah, the single, almighty God of the universe. Allah's attributes of love and mercy were overshadowed by those of power and majesty, and the greatest good was therefore not to love God but to submit to his commands. Mohammed was not regarded as divine. Rather, he was the last and greatest of a long line of prophets of whom he was the "seal." Among his predecessors were Moses, the Old Testament prophets, and Jesus.

Islam respected the Old and New Testaments and was relatively tolerant toward Jews and Christians—the "people of the book." But the Moslems had a book of their own, the *Koran,* which superseded its predecessors and was believed to contain the pure essence of divine revelation. The *Koran* is the comprehensive corpus of Mohammed's writings, the bedrock of the Islamic faith: "All men and jinn in collaboration could not produce its like." Moslems regard it as the word of Allah, *dictated* to Mohammed by the angel Gabriel from an original "uncreated" book located in heaven. Accordingly, its inspiration and authority extend not only to its meaning but also to its every letter, of which there are 323,621, and it loses its inspiration in translation. Every good Moslem must therefore read the *Koran* in Arabic, and as Islam spread, the Arabic language necessarily spread with it.

The *Koran* is perhaps the most widely read book ever written. More than a manual of worship, it was the text from which the non-Arabian Moslem learned Arabic. It was the supreme authority not only in religion but also in law, science, and the humanities, and it therefore became the standard text in Moslem schools for every imaginable subject. Mohammed's genius is illustrated vividly by his success in adapting a primitive language such as seventh-century Arabic to the sophisticated religious, legal, and ethical concepts that one encounters in his sacred book.

Mohammed offered his followers the assurance of eternal bliss if they led upright, sober lives and followed the precepts of Islam. Above all, they were bound to a simple confession of faith: "There is no god but Allah, and Mohammed is his prophet." The good

Moslem was also obliged to engage in ritualistic prayers and fasting, to journey as a pilgrim to Mecca at least once in his lifetime, and to work devoutly toward the welfare and expansion of the sacred community. Holy War was the supremely meritorious activity, for service to the faith was identical with service to the state. Public law in Islamic lands had a religious sanction, and the fusion of religion and politics which Mohammed created at Medina remained a fundamental characteristic of Islamic society. There was no Moslem priesthood, no Moslem "Church" apart from the state; Mohammed's political successors, the caliphs, were defenders of the faith and guardians of the faithful. The creative tension between Church and state which proved such a stimulus to medieval Europe was unknown in the Moslem World.

THE EARLY CONQUESTS: 632–655

Immediately after Mohammed's death the explosive energy of the Arabs, harnessed at last by the teachings of the Prophet, broke upon the world. The spectacular conquests that followed resulted in part from the youthful vigor of Islam, in part from the weakness and exhaustion of its enemies. Emperor Heraclius had just defeated the Persians, and both Byzantium and Persia were spent and enfeebled by their long and desperate conflict. And the Monophysites of Syria and Egypt remained deeply hostile to their orthodox Byzantine masters.

The Arabs entered these tired, embittered lands afire with religious zeal, lured by the wealth and luxuries of the civilized world. They had no master plan of conquest—most of their campaigns began as plundering expeditions—but unexpected victories resulted in an ever-accumulating momentum. Moving into Byzantine Syria they annihilated a huge Byzantine army in 636, captured Damascus and Jerusalem, and by 640 had occupied the entire land, detaching it permanently from Byzantine control. In 637 they inflicted an overwhelming defeat on the Persian army and entered the Persian capital of Ctesiphon, gazing in bewilderment at its opulence and wealth. Within another decade they had subdued all Persia and arrived at the borders of India. In later years they penetrated deeply into the Indian subcontinent and laid the foundations of modern Moslem Pakistan. The inhabitants of the

Persian Empire gradually adopted the Islamic faith and the Arab language. They were destined in later years to play a central role in Islamic politics and culture.

Meanwhile the Moslems were pushing westward into Egypt. They captured Alexandria in the 640s thus absorbing the great metropolis which had been a center of Greek culture ever since the Hellenistic Age. With Egypt and Syria in their hands they took to the sea, challenging the long-established Byzantine domination of the eastern Mediterranean. They captured the island of Cyprus, raided ancient Rhodes, and in 655 won a major victory over the Byzantine fleet.

THE CIVIL WAR: 655–661

In 655 Islamic expansion ceased momentarily as the new empire became locked in a savage dynastic struggle. The succession to the caliphate was contested between the Omayyads, a leading family in the old Meccan commercial oligarchy—late to join the Islamic bandwagon but no less ambitious for all that—and Ali, the son-in-law of Mohammed himself. Ali headed a faction that was to become exceedingly powerful in later centuries. His followers insisted that the caliph must be a direct descendant of the Prophet. As it happened, Mohammed had left no surviving sons, and only one daughter, Fatima, who married the Prophet's cousin, Ali.

In 661 the Omayyad forces vanquished those of Ali in battle and initiated an Omayyad dynasty of caliphs that held power for nearly a century. But the legitimist faction that had once supported Ali persisted as a troublesome, dedicated minority, throwing its support behind various of the numerous progeny of Ali and Fatima. In time the political movement evolved into a heresy known as *Shi'ism,* which held that the *true* caliphs—the descendents of Mohammed through Fatima and Ali—were sinless, infallible, and possessed of a body of secret knowledge not contained in the *Koran*. Shi'ism became an occult underground doctrine which occasionally rose to the surface in the form of civil insurrection. In the tenth century it gained control of Egypt and established a "Fatimid" dynasty of caliphs in Cairo. It inspired an infamous band of Moslem desperados known as the "Assassins" and survives to this day in the Ismaili sect led by the Aga Khan.

THE OMAYYAD DYNASTY: 661–750

The intermission in the Moslem expansion ended with the Omayyad victory over Ali in 661. The capital of the growing Islamic Empire, which had been at Medina prior to the civil war, was now moved to Damascus in Syria, but the old Arabian aristocracy exerted a firm control over Islam. Constantinople was now the chief military goal, but the great city on the Dardanelles threw back a series of powerful Moslem attacks between 670 and 680. The Byzantine defense was aided by a remarkable secret weapon known as "Greek Fire," a liquid which ignited on exposure to air and could not be extinguished by water, but only by vinegar or sand. In 717–718 a great Arab fleet and army assaulted Constantinople in vain, and having expended all their energies and resources without success the Moslems abandoned their effort to take the city. Byzantium survived for another seven centuries, and the Moslems were effectively barred from southeastern Europe for the remainder of the Middle Ages.

In the meantime, however, Moslem armies were enjoying spectacular success in the West. From Egypt they moved westward along the North African coast into the old Vandal kingdom, now ruled by distant Byzantium. In 698 the Moslems took Carthage. In 711 they crossed the Straits of Gibraltar into Spain and crushed the tottering Visigothic kingdom at a blow, driving Christianity into the fastness of the Pyrenees Mountains. Next the Moslems moved into southern Gaul and threatened the kingdom of the Merovingian Franks. In 733, 101 years after the Prophet's death, the Moslems were halted at last at the battle of Tours* by a determined Christian army led by the brilliant Frankish aristocrat, Charles Martel. The Christians at Tours were not the sort that one imagines when singing "Onward Christian Soldiers." They were semi-barbarous Franks clad in wolf skins, their tangled hair hanging down to their shoulders. But they managed to halt the momentum of militant Islam in Western Europe, just as the Byzantines had stopped it in the East.

---

* The battle was fought between Tours and Poitiers and is sometimes called the battle of Poitiers. It is traditionally, but incorrectly, dated 732.

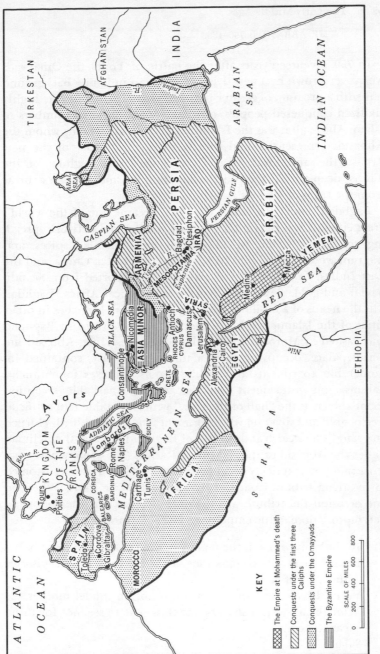

Map VI. The Islamic Empire.

KEY

The Empire at Mohammed's death

Conquests under the first three Caliphs

Conquests under the O'mayyads

The Byzantine Empire

SCALE OF MILES

0   200   400   600   800

THE ABBASIDS: 750–1258

In 750, seventeen years after the battle of Tours, the Omayyads were overthrown by a new dynasty, Arabian in family background but with a program of greater political participation for the highly civilized conquered peoples, now converting in large numbers to Islam. Above all it was the Islamized Persian aristocracy whom the Abbasids represented, and shortly after the victory of the new dynasty the capital was moved from Damascus to Baghdad on the Tigris, deep within the old Persian Empire and a stone's throw from the ruins of ancient Babylon.

Baghdad, under the early Abbasids, became one of the world's great cities. It was the center of a vast commercial network spreading across the Islamic world and far beyond. Silks, spices, and fragrant woods flowed into its wharves from India, China, and the East Indies; furs, honey, and slaves were imported from Scandinavia; and gold, slaves, and ivory from tropical Africa. Baghdad was the nexus of a far-flung banking system with branches in other cities of the Islamic world. A check could be drawn in Baghdad and cashed in Morocco, 4000 miles to the west. The Abbasid imperial palace, occupying fully a third of the city, contained innumerable apartments and public rooms, annexes for eunuchs, harems, and government officials, and a remarkable reception room known as the "hall of the tree," which contained an artificial tree of gold and silver on whose branches mechanical birds chirped and sang. The wealth and culture of Baghdad reached their climax under the Abbasid caliph, Harun-al-Rashid (786–809), whose opulence and power quickly became legendary. Harun was accustomed to receiving tribute from the Byzantine Empire itself. When on one occasion the tribute was discontinued he sent the following peremptory note to the emperor at Constantinople:

> In the name of God, the merciful, the compassionate.
> From Harun, the commander of the faithful, to Nicephorus, the dog of a Roman.
> Verily I have read thy letter, O son of an infidel mother. As for the answer, it shall be for thine eye to see, not for thine ear to hear.
> Salam.

The letter was followed by a successful military campaign which forced the unlucky Byzantines to resume their tribute.

The era of Harun-al-Rashid was an age of notable intellectual activity in which the learned traditions of Greece and Rome and of Persia and India were absorbed and synthesized. Harun's son and successor founded a great intellectual institute in Baghdad—the House of Wisdom—which was at once a library, a university, and a translation center. Thus the Abbasids pushed civilization far beyond the level that it had reached under their Omayyad predecessors. Islamic culture had come of age with remarkable speed. At a time when Charlemagne was struggling desperately to civilize his semibarbaric Franks, Harun reigned over glittering Baghdad.

The rise of the Abbasids marked the breakdown of the Arabian aristocracy's monopoly on political power. Now the government was run by a medley of races and peoples, often of humble origin. As one disgruntled aristocrat observed, "Sons of concubines have become so numerous amongst us; Lead me to a land, O God, where I shall see no bastards." The Abbasid government drew heavily from the administrative techniques of Byzantium and Persia. A sophisticated and complex bureaucracy ran the affairs of state from the capital at Baghdad and kept in touch with the provinces through a multitude of tax-gatherers, judges, couriers, and spies. The government was enlightened up to a point, although no more sensitive to the demands of social justice than other governments of its day. The Abbasid regime undertook extensive irrigation works, drained swamps, and thereby increased the amount of land under cultivation. But the status of the peasant and unskilled laborer was kept low by the competition of vast numbers of slaves. The brilliance of Abbasid culture had little effect on the underprivileged masses, who, aside from their fervent Islamic faith, retained the same primitive way of life that they had known for the last two millennia.

The Abbasid Revolution of 750 was followed by a long process of political disintegration, as one province after another broke free of the control of the caliph of Baghdad. Even in the palmy days of Harun-al-Rashid the extreme western provinces—Spain, Morocco, and Tunisia—were ruled by independent local dynasties. In the later ninth century the trend toward disintegration gained momentum as Egypt, Syria, and eastern Persia (Iran) broke free of Abbasid control. By then, the Abbasids were slowly losing their grip on their own government in Baghdad. Ambitious army commanders gradually usurped power, establishing control over the tax machinery and the other organs of government. The Abbasid dynasty endured until 1258 when Baghdad was ravaged by the Mongols, but by 950 the caliphs had become the pawns of the supreme military commander and the imperial guard.

ISLAMIC CULTURE

Throughout this epoch of political disintegration the Moslem world remained united by a common tongue, a common culture, and a common faith. It continued to struggle vigorously and often successfully with Byzantium for control of the Mediterranean, and managed for a time to occupy the key islands of Crete, Sicily, Sardinia, and Corsica.

By now virtually all the inhabitants of Syria, Egypt, and North Africa had converted to Islam, even though these lands had once supported enthusiastic and well-organized Christian churches. The Moslems did not ordinarily persecute the Christians; they merely taxed them, and it may well be that the prolonged tax burden was a more effective instrument of conversion than ruthless persecutions would have been.

The brilliant intellectual awakening of Harun-al-Rashid's day continued unabated. The untutored Arab from the desert became the cultural heir of Greece, Rome, Persia, and India, and within less than two centuries of the Prophet's death Islamic culture had reached the level of a mature, sophisticated civilization. Its mercurial rise was a consequence of the Arabs' success in absorbing the great civilized traditions of their conquered peoples and employing these traditions in a cultural synthesis both new and unique. Islam borrowed, but never without digesting. What it drew from previous civilizations it transmuted and made its own.

The political disintegration of the ninth and tenth centuries was accompanied by a diffusion of cultural activity throughout the Moslem world. During the tenth century, for example, Cordova, the capital of Islamic Spain, acquired prodigious wealth and became the center of a brilliant cultural flowering. With a population of half a million or more, Cordova was another Baghdad. No other city in Western Europe could even remotely approach it in population, beauty, or municipal organization. Its magnificent mosques, mansions, aqueducts, and baths, its bustling markets and shops, its efficient police force and sanitation service, its street lights, and, above all, its splendid, sprawling palace, flashing with brightly colored tiles and surrounded by graceful minarets and sparkling fountains, made Cordova the wonder of the age.

All across the Islamic world, from Cordova to Baghdad and far to the East, Moslem scholars and artists were developing the fruitful legacy of past civilizations. Architects were molding Greco-Roman forms into a brilliant and distinctive new style. Philosophers were studying and elaborating the writings of Plato and Aristotle despite the hostility of narrowly orthodox Islamic theologians. Physicians were expanding the ancient medical doctrines of Galen and his Greek predecessors, describing new symptoms and identifying new curative drugs. Astronomers were tightening the geocentric system of Ptolemy, preparing accurate tables of planetary motions, and giving Arabic names to the stars, names such as Altair, Deneb, and Aldebaran which are used to this day. The renowned astronomer-poet of Persia, Omar Khayyam, devised a calendar of singular accuracy. Moslem mathematicians borrowed creatively from both Greece and India. From the Greeks they learned geometry and trigonometry, and from the Hindus they appropriated the so-called Arabic numerals, the zero, and algebra, which were ultimately passed on to the West to revolutionize European mathematics.

But the Moslem scholars and scientists, although masters of the knowledge of past cultures and diligent observers of the world around them, were by and large unsuccessful in superseding their predecessors in any basic way. They tightened, they elaborated, they tinkered, but they produced few fundamental hypotheses—they created no new systems of rational thought to replace those of Aristotle, Plato, and Galen. They knew their Ptolemy backward, yet they produced no Copernicus.

This same inability to think creatively in large systematic terms characterizes Islamic literature. Arab prose is fragmentary and episodic; the individual anecdote takes precedence over the extended narrative. Moslem poets endeavored to perfect individual verses rather than to create long coherent poems. The quatrains of Omar Khayyam's *Rubaiyat* actually seem to have been arranged in alphabetical order; the chapters of the *Koran* itself were assembled in order of decreasing length without the slightest thought of structural unity.

Still, there is no gainsaying Islam's immense achievement. The Arabs conquered their vast territories three times over: with their armies, their faith, and their language. In the end, the term "Arab" applied to every Moslem from Spain to India, regardless of his ethnic background. Within its all-encompassing religious and linguistic framework, Arab culture provided a new stimulus and orientation to the long-civilized peoples of former empires. With its manifold ingredients the rich Islamic heritage would one day provide invaluable nourishment to the voracious mind of the re-awakening West.

MOSLEM CHRONOLOGY

c.571–632: Mohammed
622:       The Hegira
632–655: The First Conquests
655–661: Civil War: Omayyads versus Ali
661–750: Omayyad Dynasty: New Conquests
717–718: Arabs besiege Constantinople
733:      Arabs defeated at Tours
750–1258: Abbasid Dynasty at Baghdad
786–809: Harun-al-Rashid; Zenith of Abbasid power

8

Carolingian Europe

THE NEW EUROPE

We have already remarked on the striking contrast between
Harun-al-Rashid's Baghdad and Charlemagne's Frankland. It is
a contrast between a brilliant, opulent, mercantile civilization
and a half-barbarized agrarian people struggling toward political
and intellectual coherence. But eighth-century Western Europe,
although far removed from the civilized level of ancient Rome
or contemporary Baghdad, was undergoing developments of
momentous consequence for the future. For the first time it was
beginning to dawn on a few Europeans that they were a people
apart—participants in a new and distinctive civilization with its
roots in Athens and Jerusalem, Rome and Germany, bound together—much as the Moslems were—by a common faith, a common
scholarly language, and a common heritage. The new Europe
was aroused spiritually by the wide-ranging Benedictines and
united politically by a new dynasty of Frankish monarchs, the
Carolingians, whose family name is derived from that of their
most illustrious representative—Charles the Great, or Charlemagne.

Carolingian Europe differed profoundly from the Western Roman Empire of old. It was a land without large cities, thoroughly
agrarian in economic organization, with its culture centered
on the monastery and the cathedral rather than the forum. Although Charlemagne extended his authority into Italy, his capital

and his heart remained in northern Frankland. In a word, the new Europe no longer faced the Mediterranean; its axis had shifted northward.

AGRICULTURAL TECHNOLOGY

The relative brightness of the age of Charlemagne was the product of creative processes that had been at work during the preceding dark centuries. From the economic standpoint, the most interesting and significant of these processes was the development of a new agrarian technology which increased the productivity of northern European farmlands beyond the level of the old Roman Empire.

By the opening of the eighth century the ineffective scratch plow of Roman times had been superseded throughout the northern districts of the barbarian West by a heavy compound plow with wheels, colter, plowshare, and moldboard, which cut deeply into the soil, pulverized it, and turned it aside, thereby producing ridges and furrows. The development of this heavy plow was complex and gradual; the basic idea may perhaps have been brought into Western Europe by the Slavs in the sixth or seventh centuries. Its introduction into the West opened up vast areas of rich, heavy soil in which the older scratch plow was ineffective, and accentuated the tendency toward dividing fields into long strips cultivated by the eight-ox teams which the heavy plow required. Peasants now pooled their oxen and their labor in order to exploit the new plow; in so doing they laid the foundation for the co-operative agricultural communities of medieval Europe with strong village councils to regulate the division of labor and resources.

The upsurge in productivity brought about by the introduction of the heavy compound plow made possible a fundamental change in the method of rotating crops. By the Carolingian age, much of northern Europe was beginning to adopt the three-field system in place of the two-field system typical of Roman times. Formerly a typical farm had been divided into two fields, one of which was planted each year and allowed to lie fallow the second year. But it was found that the rich northern soils, newly opened by the heavy plow, did not require a full year's rest between crops. Instead, they were often divided into three fields, each of which underwent a three-year cycle of autumn planting, spring planting, and fallow. The shift from two fields to three had an important impact on the European economy, for it increased food production significantly and brought a degree of prosperity to northern Europe. It seems likely that the heavy plow and the three-field system, which could not be employed efficiently in the light, dry soils of the Mediterranean South, contributed to the northward shift in the economic and cultural orientation of Carolingian Europe.

The age of Charlemagne also profited from a trend toward mechanization. The water mill, which was used occasionally in antiquity for grinding grain, had now come into widespread use and was a typical feature of the Carolingian farm. During the centuries following Charlemagne's death the water mill was put to new uses—to power the rising textile industry of the eleventh century, and to drive trip-hammers in forges. Thus the technological progress of Merovingian and Carolingian times continued into the centuries that followed. By A.D. 1000 the development of the horseshoe and a new, efficient horse collar, both apparently imported from Siberia or Central Asia, made possible the very gradual replacement of the ox by the more energetic horse as the chief draught animal on the farms of northwestern Europe. And in the twelfth century the windmill made its debut in the European countryside. These new advances resulted in still greater productivity and underlay the rich and prosperous civilization of northern Europe in the High Middle Ages (c. 1050–1300). Slowly one of the chief economic bases of human slavery was being eroded as human power gave way more and more to animal and machine power.

Carolingian Europe gained much from the earlier phase of this drawn-out revolution in agrarian technology, but even so the peasants of the Carolingian age remained near the level of subsistence. A single bad year could ruin them. During a great famine of 791, for example, the peasants were driven to cannibalism and were even reported to have eaten members of their own family. Conditions were improving, but only very gradually.

THE FRANKISH POLITICAL REVIVAL

The dynasty of Clovis, the Merovingians, had declined over the centuries from bloodthirsty autocrats to crowned fools. By the later

600s all real power had passed to the aristocracy. Meanwhile, as a consequence of the Merovingian policy of dividing royal authority and crown lands among the sons of a deceased king, Frankland had split into several distinct districts, the most important of which were Neustria (Paris and northwestern France), Austrasia (the heavily Germanized northeast including the Rhinelands), and Burgundy in the southeast (see map, p. 111).

During the seventh century a great aristocratic family, later known as the Carolingians, rose to power in Austrasia. The Carolingians became "mayors of the palace," that is, they held the chief administrative post in the Austrasian royal household and made it hereditary. As the Merovingians grew increasingly feeble and inept, the Carolingians became the real masters of Austrasia. The Carolingian mayor of the palace increased his power by gathering around him a considerable number of trained warriors somewhat in the tradition of the old Germanic comitatus (see p. 44). These men became his *vassals*, that is, they placed themselves under his protection and maintenance and swore fealty to him. Other aristocrats also had their private vassalic armies, but the Carolingians with far the greatest number of followers, dominated the scene. In 687 a Carolingian mayor led his Austrasian army to a decisive victory over the Neustrians, and the Carolingians thenceforth were the leading family in all Frankland. With Neustria under their control, Burgundy swung into line, and when the Moslems moved into Gaul in the early 730s they faced a united Frankish people under the able leadership of the vigorous Carolingian mayor, Charles Martel—"the Hammer" (714–741).

This brilliant, ruthless warrior not only turned back the Moslems at the battle of Tours (733); he also won victory after victory over Moslems and Christians alike, consolidating his power over the Franks, and extending the boundaries of the Frankish state. Like the Adams family in American history, the Carolingians of the seventh and eighth centuries had the good fortune to produce exceedingly able representatives over several generations. Martel's father had conquered Neustria; Martel himself defeated the Moslems and, indeed, almost everybody he faced. His son, Pepin the Short, gained the Frankish crown, and his grandson, Charlemagne, won an empire.

Surprisingly, the Carolingians followed the same policy of divided succession among male heirs which had so weakened the Merovingians. Here, too, Carolingian luck placed a crucial role in history, for as it happened the Carolingian mayors—and later kings—over several generations had only one long-surviving heir. Frankish unity was maintained not by policy but in spite of it. When Charles Martel died in 741 his lands and authority were divided among his two sons, Carloman and Pepin the Short. But Carloman ruled only six years, retiring to a Benedictine monastery in 747 and leaving the field to his brother Pepin. Carloman represented a new kind of barbarian ruler, deeply affected by the spiritual currents of his age, whose piety foreshadowed that of numerous saint-kings of later centuries. Christian culture and Germanic power were beginning to draw together.

THE BENEDICTINE REFORM

The synthesis of these two worlds was carried further by Pepin the Short (741–768), who supported a Benedictine Christian revival in Frankland and consummated an alliance of far-reaching consequences between the Frankish monarchy and the Catholic Church. In the early 700s the Frankish Church had been corrupt, disorganized, and ignorant—a product of several centuries of Merovingian misrule. Many areas had no priests at all, and numerous peasants were scarcely removed from heathenism. Priests themselves sacrificed animals to the gods and shared their homes with concubines. During the 740s, a group of dedicated English Benedictines led by St. Boniface devoted themselves to the reform of the Frankish Church. For some years Boniface had been doing evangelical work among the heathen Germans, and it evidently occurred to him that there was work to be done within Christendom as well as outside it. Boniface, like other English Benedictines, was closely associated with the papacy and had been working in Germany under a papal commission. There he and his co-workers had founded several important monasteries which became important spiritual and intellectual centers of the new German Church. In Frankland, Boniface reformed monasteries along the lines of the Benedictine Rule, saw to the establishment of monastic schools, and worked toward the development of an adequate parish system to bring the Gospel to the country folk. This great missionary, a child of the vigorous Anglo-Saxon Benedictine culture of the previous century, laid the groundwork for the revitalized Christian culture of Charlemagne's reign.

THE FRANCO-PAPAL ALLIANCE

It may well have been at Boniface's prompting that Pepin the Short sought papal support for his seizure of the Frankish crown. The Merovingians had long been shadowy, do-nothing kings, yet their family retained the enormous prestige always enjoyed by a Germanic royal dynasty. If the Carolingians hoped to replace the Merovingians on the Frankish throne, they would have to call on the most potent spiritual sanction available to their age: papal consecration. The popes, for their part, had long been seeking a strong and trustworthy ally against the untrustworthy Byzantines and aggressive Lombards of Italy. By 750 the problems of the papacy had come to a head. Their nominal political supporters in Italy, the Byzantine emperors, had embraced a semiheretical doctrine known as *Iconoclasm* which condemned the use of all statues and pictures of Christ and the saints in Christian worship. The Byzantine East was almost torn in two by the Iconoclastic Controversy; the West was unanimously hostile to the new doctrine. Yet the papacy could scarcely turn for help to the still-barbaric Lombards, who in 750 were on the rampage once again, threatening not only the Byzantine holdings in Italy but also the territories of the pope himself. In 751 the Byzantine Italian capital of Ravenna fell to the Lombards at last. The papacy had never been in such desperate need of a champion.

In the very year of Ravenna's fall, the champion was found. Pepin the Short had sent messengers to Rome with the loaded question, "Is it right that a powerless ruler should continue to bear the title of King?" The pope answered in the negative, and the bargain was struck. In 751 Pepin was crowned King of the Franks —by Boniface himself, so tradition has it—and the last Merovingians were packed off to a monastery. In 754 the pope traveled northward to anoint the new sovereign, thereby giving every spiritual sanction at his disposal to the upstart Carolingian monarchy.

In return, Pepin led his armies into Italy, defeated the Lombards, and donated a large portion of central Italy to the papacy. This "Donation of Pepin" relieved the popes of the ominous Lombard pressure and became the basis for the Papal States which were to remain a characteristic feature of Italian politics until the late nineteenth century. For the moment, the papacy had been rescued from its peril. It remained to be seen whether the popes could prevent their new champion from becoming their master.

CHARLEMAGNE: 768–814

Pepin the Short, like all successful monarchs of the Early Middle Ages, was an able general. As the first Carolingian king he followed in the warlike traditions of his father, drove the Moslems from Aquitaine, and left Frankland larger and better organized than he had found it. Pepin was a great king, but he was overshadowed by his even greater son. Charlemagne (768–814) was a phenomenally successful military commander, a statesman of rare ability, a friend of learning, and a monarch possessed of a deep sense of responsibility for the welfare of the society over which he ruled. In this last respect he represents a notable advance over his Merovingian predecessors, whose relationship to their state was that of a leech to his host.

Charlemagne towered over his contemporaries both figuratively and literally. He was 6 ft. 3½ in. tall, thick-necked and pot-bellied yet imposing in appearance for all that. He could be warm and talkative, but he could also be hard, cruel, and violent, and his subjects came to regard him with both admiration and fear. He was possessed of a strong, if superficial, piety which prompted him to build churches, collect relics, and struggle heroically for a Christian cultural revival in Frankland, but did not prevent him from filling his court with concubines and other disreputable characters. In short, Charlemagne, despite his military and political genius, was a man of his age, in tune with its most progressive forces, yet by no means out of touch with its barbaric past.

Above all else Charlemagne was a warrior-king. He led his armies on yearly campaigns as a matter of course. Only gradually did he develop a notion of Christian mission and a program of unifying and systematically expanding the Christian West. At the behest of the papacy, Charlemagne followed his father's footsteps into Italy, where he conquered the Lombards completely in 774 and incorporated them into his growing state. Thenceforth he used the title "King of the Franks and the Lombards." Between 778 and 801 he conducted a series of campaigns against the Spanish Moslems, establishing a frontier district, the "Spanish March," on the Spanish side of the Pyrenees centered in Barcelona. In 787 he conquered and absorbed Bavaria, organizing its easternmost district into a forward defensive barrier against the Slavs. This East March or *Ostmark* became the nucleus of a new state later to be called Austria. In the 790s Charlemagne pushed still further to the southeast, destroying the rich and predatory Avar state which had long tormented Eastern Europe.

But Charlemagne's greatest and most prolonged military effort was directed against the heathen Saxons of northern Germany. With the double purpose of protecting the Frankish Rhinelands and bringing new souls into the Church, Charlemagne campaigned for some thirty years (772–804), conquering the Saxons repeatedly and baptizing them by force, only to have them rebel when his armies withdrew. In a fit of savage exasperation Charlemagne ordered the execution of 4500 unfaithful Saxons in a single bloody day in 782. At length, however, Saxony submitted to the remorseless pressure of Frankish soldiers and Benedictine monks. By about 800 Frankish control of Saxony was well established, and in subsequent decades Christianity seeped gradually into the Saxon soul. A century and a half later, Christian Saxons were governing the most powerful and enlightened state in Europe.

CHARLEMAGNE'S EMPIRE

Charlemagne's armies, by incorporating the great territories of central Germany into the new civilization, had succeeded where the legions of Augustus and his successors had failed. No longer a mere Frankish king, Charlemagne, by 800, was the master of the West. A few small Christian states such as the kingdoms of Anglo-Saxon England remained outside his jurisdiction, but with these relatively minor exceptions Charlemagne's political sway extended throughout Catholic Christendom. He was, in truth, an emperor. On Christmas Day of 800 his immense accomplishment was given

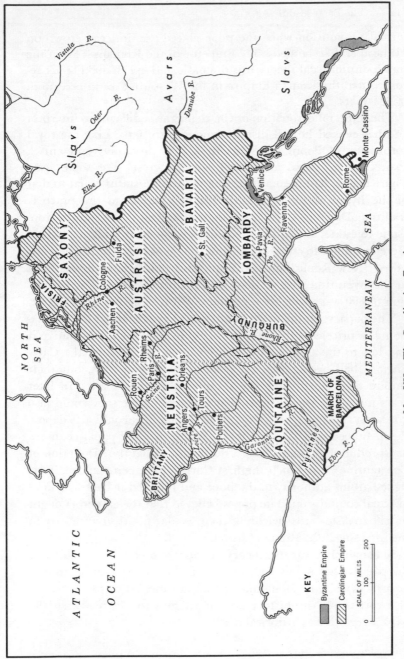

Map VII. The Carolingian Empire.

formal recognition when the pope placed the imperial crown on his head and acclaimed him "Emperor of the Romans." From the standpoint of legal theory this dramatic and epoch-making act reconstituted the Roman Empire in the West after an interregnum of 324 years.

The imperial coronation of Charlemagne is difficult to interpret and has evoked heated dispute among historians. Like the royal coronation of Pepin the Short in 751, it probably represents a coalescence of papal and Carolingian interests. For some years Charlemagne had been attempting to attain a status equal to that of the Byzantine emperors. In 794 he abandoned the practice, traditional among Germanic kings, of traveling constantly from estate to estate, and established his permanent capital at Aachen. Here he sought to create a Constantinople of his own: Aachen was called "New Rome," and an impressive palace church was built in the Byzantine style—a poor man's Sancta Sophia. The coronation of 800 was probably a product of this same imitative policy.

The papacy, on the other hand, must have regarded the coronation as a priceless opportunity to regain some of the initiative it had lost to the all-powerful Charlemagne. To be sure, the Carolingians had been promoted from kings to emperors, but their empire thenceforth bore the stamp, "Made in Rome." In later years the popes would insist that what they gave they could also take away. If the papacy could make emperors, it could also depose them. Indeed, it was only shortly before that the papal chancery had produced a famous forged document called the "Donation of Constantine"* in which the first Christian emperor allegedly resigned all his authority to the pope and received it back as a kind of papal commission. The popes believed that the emperors ought to be papal stewards—wielding their secular political authority in the interests of the Roman Church.

So convincing was this theory of papal supremacy in the eyes of the papacy that it justified the use of any documentation to support its case. The "Donation of Constantine," therefore, was not an effort to rewrite history but an attempt to buttress what the papacy regarded as historical truth.

* Probably sometime in the 740s.

Charlemagne always respected the papacy, but he was unwilling to cast himself in the subordinate role which papal theory demanded of him. He was careful to retain the title, "King of the Franks and the Lombards" alongside his new title of "Emperor," and when the time came to crown his son emperor, Charlemagne excluded the pope from the ceremony and did the crowning himself. In these maneuvers we are witnessing the prologue to a long, bitter struggle over the correct relationship between empire and papacy which reached its crescendo in the eleventh, twelfth, and thirteenth centuries. At stake was the ultimate mastery of Western Christendom.

But during the reign of Charlemagne the struggle remained latent for the most part. Charlemagne's power was unrivaled, and the popes were much too weak to oppose him seriously. Indeed, the warm Carolingian-papal relations of Pepin's day continued, and the papacy was nearly smothered in Charlemagne's affectionate embrace.

CAROLINGIAN THEOCRACY

At no time since has Europe been so nearly united as under Charlemagne, and never again would Western Christendom flirt so seriously with theocracy. The papal anointing of Pepin and Charlemagne gave the Carolingian monarchy a sacred, almost priestly, quality, and Charlemagne used his immense authority to govern not only the body politic but the imperial Church as well. The laws and regulations of his reign, which are known as *capitularies,* dealt with ecclesiastical as well as secular matters. He did not claim to legislate on church doctrine, but he felt a deep sense of responsibility for purifying and systematizing ecclesiastical discipline. He was a far greater force in the Carolingian Church than was the pope. He summoned a number of ecclesiastical synods and even presided over one of them. Indeed, the significant intellectual revival known as the "Carolingian Renaissance" was by and large a product of Charlemagne's concern for the welfare of the Church and the perpetuation of ecclesiastical culture.

The term "Carolingian Renaissance" is dangerously misleading. Charlemagne's age produced no lofty abstract thought, no original philosophical or theological system, no Leonardo da Vinci. If we look for a "renaissance" we are bound to be disappointed. The intellectual task of the Carolingian age was far less exalted—far more rudimentary. Charlemagne assembled scholars from all over Europe who, under the leadership of the Northumbrian Alcuin of York, set about to rescue continental culture from the pit of ignorance into which it was sinking. Alcuin prepared an accurate new edition of the Bible, purged of the scribal errors which had crept into it over the centuries, thereby saving Christian culture from the hopeless confusion arising from the corruption of its most fundamental text. Alcuin and his fellow scholars purified and regularized the liturgy of the Church and encouraged the preaching of sermons. They carried on the monastic reforms begun by Boniface and saw to it that every important monastery had a school. It was a question not of producing new Aristotles and Augustines but of preserving literacy itself. A new, standardized script was developed—the Carolingian minuscule—which replaced the heterogeneous and often illegible scripts previously employed. And throughout the realm monks set about copying manuscripts on an unprecedented scale. Classical-Christian culture was advanced very little by these activities but was at least preserved. Above all, its base was broadened. Carolingian scholars were engaged in a crucial work of cultural salvage. The success of their efforts is demonstrated by the fact that the European mind never again sank to the pre-Carolingian level. It is characteristic of the powerful theocratic tendencies of the age that this significant spiritual-pedagogical achievement was accomplished through royal rather than papal initiative. With the breakdown of European unity after Charlemagne's death the momentary fusion of political and spiritual energies dissolved, yet the intellectual revival continued. In the monasteries and cathedrals of the ninth and tenth centuries, particularly in the recently conquered German districts, documents continued to be copied—schools continued to operate. By the eleventh century Europe was ready to build soaring and original intellectual edifices on her sturdy Carolingian foundations.

THE CAROLINGIAN STATE

Charlemagne held his immense empire together by the strength of his personality. In an era of primitive roads and wretched communications he was obliged to depend heavily on the competence and loyalty of the counts, dukes and margraves who administered his provinces. He kept some control over them by sending pairs of inspectors known as *missi dominici* from his court into the provinces to ensure the implementation of his will, but the allegiance of the counts and dukes was chiefly a product of their respect for Charlemagne himself. They obeyed his commands and submitted to his capitularies not because of their patriotism to his state but because of their devotion to his person. In sum, the administrative institutions of the Carolingian Empire were grossly inadequate to the needs of a great state. Beneath the imposing military and cultural veneer, Carolingian Europe was still semibarbaric. Alcuin was yielding to illusion when he told Charlemagne, "If your intentions are carried out, it may be that a new Athens will arise in Frankland, and an Athens fairer than of old, for our Athens, ennobled by the teachings of Christ, will surpass the wisdom of the Academy." Alcuin's vision was a pathetic mirage; the Carolingian state remained a land of rude, untutored warriors and peasants just emerging from savagery.

Charlemagne's "Roman Empire" was an almost ludicrous parody of Augustus's; yet one can only admire this dogged Carolingian who could do so much with so little—who could make such an effort to transcend his own barbaric past—who as an adult struggled vainly to learn how to write—who sought bravely but hopelessly to master the lofty subtleties of Augustine's *City of God*. The historian Christopher Dawson caught the spirit of Charlemagne's achievement perfectly when he wrote, "The unwieldy empire of Charles the Great did not long survive the death of its founder, and it never really attained the economic and social organization of a civilized state. But, for all that, it marks the first emergence of the European culture from the twilight of pre-natal existence into the consciousness of active life."*

---

* C. Dawson, *The Making of Europe* (Meridian Press, 1957), p. 187.

CAROLINGIAN CHRONOLOGY

687:	Carolingian mayor of Austrasia defeats Neustria Carolingian hegemony established
714–741:	Rule of Charles Martel
733:	Arabs defeated at Tours
741–768:	Rule of Pepin the Short
751:	Pepin crowned king of the Franks Merovingian Dynasty ends
754:	Death of St. Boniface
768–814:	Reign of Charlemagne
772–804:	Charlemagne's Saxon Wars
800:	Charlemagne crowned Roman Emperor

9

The New Invasions

The economic and cultural revival under Charlemagne, tentative though it was, might well have developed steadily in the direction of a prosperous and sophisticated civilization had it not been for the devastating new invasions that followed Charlemagne's death in 814. Until then the Carolingian realm had enjoyed at least relative peace. Intellectual life, although still rudimentary, was in the process of reawakening, and with the stimulus of the sound silver coinage which Charlemagne issued, commerce was quickening. One historian has recently gone so far as to suggest that under the bracing influence of Charlemagne's economic policy towns were beginning to grow and flourish once again. But these hopeful signs proved to be a false dawn. During the ninth and tenth centuries, Europe was obliged to fight for its life against the savage attacks of the seminomadic Hungarians from the East, the piratical Saracens (Moslems) from the South, and the wideranging Vikings from the North. As a result, the coming of high civilization was delayed in Europe for another two centuries.

THE LATER CAROLINGIANS

It would be wrong to ascribe the political fragmentation of the Carolingian Empire entirely to these outside pressures, for Charlemagne himself, in keeping with Frankish tradition, planned to divide his state among his several sons. As it happened, however, Charlemagne outlived all but one. The luck of the Carolingians was still running, and when the great conqueror died in 814 his realm passed intact to his remaining heir, Louis the Pious (814–840).

Louis was by no means incompetent, but his military and political talents were distinctly inferior to those of his father Charlemagne, his grandfather Pepin the Short, and his great-grandfather Charles Martel. Carolingian unity continued but Carolingian leadership was beginning to fail. Louis the Pious was well named. He ran Charlemagne's minstrels and concubines out of the imperial court and replaced them with priests and monks. Far more than his hard-headed father, Louis committed himself to the dream of a unified Christian Empire—a City of God brought down to earth. Yet he was far less suited than Charlemagne to the Herculean task of maintaining unity and cohesion in the immense, heterogeneous empire which the Carolingians had won. He was the first of his line to conceive the notion of bequeathing supreme political authority to his eldest son and thereby making the unity of the kingdom a matter of policy rather than chance. And yet, ironically, he turned out to be the last Carolingian to rule an undivided Frankish realm. His bold plan for a single succession was foiled by the ambitions of his younger sons who rebelled openly against him and plunged the empire into civil war.

When Louis the Pious's unhappy reign ended in 840, his three surviving sons struggled bitterly for the spoils. The eldest of the three, Lothar, claimed the indivisible imperial title and hegemony over the entire realm. The other two sons, Louis the German and Charles the Bald, struggled to win independent royal authority in East and West Frankland, respectively. In the end, Lothar was obliged to yield to the combined might of his younger brothers. The controversy was settled by the momentous Treaty of Verdun in 843 which permanently divided the empire and foreshadowed the political structure of modern Europe. Lothar was permitted to keep the imperial title but was denied any sort of superior jurisdiction over the realms of Louis the German and Charles the Bald. Louis ruled East Frankland, which became the nucleus of the modern German state. In a very real sense, he was Germany's first king. Charles the Bald became king of West

Frankland, which evolved into modern France. The Emperor Lothar retained a long, narrow, heterogeneous strip of territory which stretched for some thousand miles northward from Italy through Burgundy, Alsace, Lorraine, and the Netherlands, embracing considerable portions of what is now western Germany and eastern France. This Middle Kingdom included the two "imperial capitals," Rome and Aachen, but its long, exposed frontiers were virtually impossible to defend, and it was utterly lacking in unity. It was subdivided at Lothar's death in 855 among his three sons, one of whom inherited Carolingian Italy and the increasingly insignificant imperial title. From the ninth century to the twentieth the fragments of Lothar's middle kingdom have been the source of endless bitter territorial disputes between Germany and France.

The struggles among Charlemagne's grandsons occurred against a background of Viking, Hungarian, and Saracen invasions which accelerated and vastly increased the tendency toward political fragmentation brought about by internal weaknesses. But even without the invasions, and without the Frankish tradition of divided succession, it was unlikely that Charlemagne's huge, unwieldy empire could have long remained intact once his iron hand had been removed from control. As it turned out, even the more modest political units arising from the Treaty of Verdun were too large—too far removed from the desperate realities of the countryside—to cope successfully with the lightning raids of Viking shipmen or Hungarian horsemen. During the ninth and tenth centuries Carolingian leadership was visibly failing, and the incapacity of the later Carolingians is nowhere better illustrated than in their names: Charles the Fat, Charles the Simple, Louis the Child, Louis the Blind.

THE SARACEN AND HUNGARIAN INVASIONS

The Saracens, Hungarians, and Vikings, who plundered the declining Carolingian state, were in part drawn by the growing political vacuum, in part impelled by forces operating in their own homelands. Europe suffered grievously from their marauding; yet it was strong enough in the end to survive the invasions and absorb the invaders. As it happened, the ninth- and tenth-century invasions were the last that Western Christendom was destined to endure. From about 1000 to the present, the West has had the unique opportunity of developing on its own, sheltered from the alien attacks that have so disrupted other civilizations over the past millennium. As the historian Marc Bloch has said, "It is surely not unreasonable to think that this extraordinary immunity, of which we have shared the privilege with scarcely any people but the Japanese, was one of the fundamental factors of European civilization. . . ."*

Yet in the ninth and tenth centuries Europe's hard-pressed peoples had no way of knowing that the invasions would one day end. A Frankish historian of the mid-ninth century writes in a tone of anguish:

> The number of ships grows larger and larger; the great host of Northmen continually increases; on every hand Christians are the victims of massacres, looting, and incendiarism—clear proof of which will remain as long as the world itself endures. The Northmen capture every city they pass through, and none can withstand them.

In southern Gaul people prayed for divine protection against the Saracens: "Eternal Trinity . . . deliver thy Christian people from the oppression of the pagans". To the north they prayed, "From the savage nation of the Northmen, which lays waste our realms, deliver us, O God". And in northern Italy: "Against the arrows of the Hungarians be thou our protector."

The Saracens of the ninth and tenth centuries, unlike their predecessors in the seventh and early eighth, came as brigands rather than conquerors and settlers. From their pirate nests in Africa, Spain, and the Mediterranean islands they preyed on shipping, plundered coastal cities, and sailed up rivers to carry their devastation far inland. Saracen bandit lairs were established on the southern coast of Gaul, from which the marauders conducted raids far and wide through the countryside and kidnapped pilgrims crossing the Alpine passes. Charlemagne had never possessed much of a navy, and his successors found themselves helpless to defend their coasts. In 846 Saracen brigands raided Rome itself,

* Marc Bloch, *Feudal Society*, tr. L. A. Manyon (Chicago, 1961), p. 56.

profaning its churches and stealing its treasures. As late as 982 a German king was severely defeated by Saracen bandits in southern Italy, but by then the raids were tapering off. Southern Europe, now bristling with fortifications, had learned to defend itself and was even beginning to challenge Saracen domination of the western Mediterranean.

The Hungarians or Magyars, fierce nomadic horsemen from the Asiatic steppes, settled in the land now known as Hungary. From the late 800s to 955 they terrorized Germany, northern Italy, and eastern Gaul. Hungarian raiding parties ranged far and wide seeking defenseless settlements to plunder, avoiding fortified towns, outriding and outmaneuvering the armies sent against them. In time, however, they became more sedentary, gave more attention to their farms, and lost much of their nomadic savagery. In 955 King Otto the Great of Germany crushed a large Hungarian army at the battle of Lechfeld and brought the raids to an end at last. Within another half century, the Hungarians had adopted Christianity and were becoming integrated into the community of Christian Europe.

THE VIKINGS

The Vikings, or Norsemen, were the most fearsome invaders of all. These redoubtable warrior-seafarers came from Scandinavia, the very land that had, centuries before, disgorged many of the Germanic barbarians into Europe. Thus the ninth century Vikings and the Germanic invaders of Roman times had similar ethnic backgrounds. But to the ninth century European—the product of countless Germanic-Celtic-Roman intermarriages, tamed by the Church and by centuries of settled life—the Vikings seemed an utterly alien people.

Then, as now, the Scandinavians were divided roughly into three groups: Danes, Swedes, and Norwegians. During the great age of Viking expansion in the ninth and tenth centuries, the Danes, who were brought cheek to jowl with the Carolingian Empire by Charlemagne's conquest of Saxony, focused their attention on Frankland and England. The Norwegians raided and settled in Scotland, Ireland, and the North Atlantic. The Swedes concentrated on the East—the Baltic shores, Russia, and the Byzantine Empire. Yet the three Norse peoples had much in common, and the distinctions between them were by no means sharp. It is therefore proper to regard their raids, their astonishing explorations, and their far-flung commercial enterprises, as a single great international movement.

The breakdown of Carolingian leadership doubtless acted as a magnet to Viking marauders, but their raids on the West began as early as Charlemagne's age. The basic causes for their great outward thrust must be sought in Scandinavia itself. Pre-tenth-century Scandinavia is almost a closed book to historians, and their explanations for the Viking outburst are little more than educated guesses. It is likely, however, that the Scandinavian population, sharply reduced by the outward migrations of Roman times, had increased by the later 700s to a level which the primitive Norse agriculture was scarcely able to support. The pressure of over-population was probably aggravated by the fact that centralized royal power was slowly developing at this time, cramping the more restless spirits and driving them to seek adventures and opportunities abroad. A third factor was the development of improved Viking ships, eminently seaworthy, propelled by both sail and oars, and capable of carrying crews of 40 to 100 warriors at speeds up to 10 knots.

In these long ships the tall, muscular, reddish-haired Viking warriors struck the ports of northern Europe. They sailed up rivers far into the interior, plundering the towns and monasteries of Frankland and England, sometimes stealing horses and riding across the countryside to spread their devastation still further.

THE VIKINGS IN WESTERN CHRISTENDOM

England suffered the first of the Viking attacks. In c. 787 three long ships touched the Channel coast in Dorset, and the Vikings poured out of them to loot and sack a nearby town. Thenceforth the Anglo-Saxon kingdoms were tormented by incessant Viking raids. In 794 Norse brigands annihilated the Northumbrian monastery of Jarrow, where Bede had lived and died, and the other great monastic cultural centers of Northumbria suffered a like fate.

In 842 the Danes plundered London, and a few years thereafter they began to establish permanent winter bases in England which freed them from the necessity of returning to Scandinavia after the raiding season. By the later 800s they had turned from simple piracy to large-scale occupation and permanent settlement. They overran one Anglo-Saxon kingdom after another until at length, in the 870s, only the southern kingdom of Wessex remained free of Danish control—and even Wessex came within a hair of falling before the Danish onslaught.

To mariners such as the Vikings the English Channel was a boulevard rather than a barrier, and the same raiding parties attacked the English and Frankish shores indiscriminately. They established permanent bases at the mouths of great rivers and sailed up them to plunder defenseless monasteries and sack towns. Antwerp was ravaged in 837, Rouen in 841, Hamburg and Paris in 845, Charlemagne's old capital at Aachen in 881. Europe was truly under siege.

But if some Europeans were driven to helpless resignation, others fought doggedly to protect their lands and their heritage. King Alfred the Great of Wessex saved his kingdom from Danish conquest in the late 870s and began the arduous task of rolling back the Danish armies in England. King Arnulf of East Frankland won a decisive victory over the Norsemen in 891 at the battle of the Dyle and thereby vastly decreased the Viking pressure on Germany, although it was at this very moment that the Hungarian raids began. West Frankland continued to suffer for a time, but in about 911 King Charles the Simple created a friendly Viking buffer state in northern France by concluding an epoch-making treaty with a Norse chieftan named Rollo. The Vikings in Rollo's band had been conducting raids from their settlement at the mouth of the Seine River. Charles, less simple than his name would imply, determined that if he could make Rollo his ally the Seine settlement might well prove an effective barrier against further raids. Rollo became a Christian, married Charles the Simple's daughter, and recognized—at least in some sense—the superiority of the West Frankish monarchy. Thus Rollo's state acquired legitimacy in the eyes of Western Christendom. Expanding gradually under Rollo and his successors it became known as the land of the Northmen or "Normandy." Over the next century and a half the Normans became as good Christians as the Franks.

ATLANTIC

OCEAN

NORWAY

SWEDEN

DENMARK

Drieper

Rhine R.

Rouen   Aachen   Kiev   R.

Paris   Seine

Loire R.

Tours

LOMBARDY   Hungarians

Danube   R.   BLACK SEA

PROVENCE

Marseilles   PAPAL STATES

CORSICA

BALEARICS   SARDINIA   Rome   Monte Cassino

Naples

SICILY

KEY   MEDITERRANEAN   SEA

→ Vikings

- - ▶ Moslems

- - - ▶ Hungarians

SCALE OF MILES

0   200   400   600

Map VIII.   The Viking, Hungarian, and Moslem invasions.

They adopted French culture and the French language, yet retained much of their old energy. In the eleventh century Normandy was producing some of Europe's most vigorous warriors, Crusaders, administrators, and monks.

THE VIKINGS IN THE NORTH ATLANTIC
AND EASTERN EUROPE

France, England, and Germany formed only a part of the vast Viking world of the ninth and tenth centuries. By the mid-800s Norwegians and Danes had conquered the greater part of Ireland,

and between 875 and 930 they settled remote Iceland. There a distinctive Norse culture arose which for several centuries remained only slightly affected by the main currents of Western Civilization. In Iceland the magnificent oral tradition of the Norse saga flourished and was eventually committed to writing. The Icelandic Norsemen were perhaps the greatest sailors of all. They settled on the coast of Greenland in the late 900s and established temporary settlements on the northern coasts of North America itself in the eleventh century, thereby anticipating Columbus by half a millennium.

To the east, Swedish Vikings overran Finland and penetrated far southward across European Russia to trade with Constantinople and Baghdad. The Byzantine emperors took inordinate pride in the tall Norse mercenaries who served in their imperial guard. In Russia itself, a Swedish dynasty established itself at Novgorod in the later ninth century, ruling over the indigenous Slavic population. In the tenth century a Norse ruler at Novgorod captured the strategic Russian city of Kiev, which became the nucleus of a powerful, well-organized Russian state. Deeply influenced by the culture of its subjects, the dynasty at Kiev became far more Slavic than Scandinavian. It adopted Byzantine Christianity around the turn of the millennium and looked to Constantinople rather than the West for its religious and cultural inspiration. Nevertheless, in Russia, as in Iceland and elsewhere, the Norsemen had shown that they could build kingdoms as well as destroy them.

THE TWILIGHT OF THE VIKING AGE

The development of centralized monarchies in Denmark, Norway, and Sweden, which may have been a factor in driving the restless Viking raiders outward from Scandinavia, ultimately resulted in taming the Viking spirit. As Scandinavia became increasingly civilized, its kings discouraged the activities of roaming independent warrior bands, and its social environment gave rise to a somewhat more humdrum, sedentary life. Far into the eleventh century England continued to face the attacks of Norsemen, but the eleventh century invaders were no longer pirate bands; rather, they were royal armies led by Scandinavian kings. The nature of the Scandinavian threat had changed profoundly, and by the late eleventh century the threat had ceased altogether. Around the year 1000 Christianity was winning converts all across the Scandinavian world. In Iceland, in Russia, even in the kingdoms of Scandinavia itself, the ferocious Northmen were adopting the religion of the monks who had once so feared them. Thereafter Scandinavia ceased to be a reservoir of barbarian invaders and became a creative part of Western European culture.

Even at the height of the invasions the Norsemen were by no means pure barbarians. They excelled at commerce as well as piracy. They were the greatest seafarers of the age. They introduced Europe to the art of ocean navigation and immeasurably enlarged the horizons of Western Christendom. In a word, they injected a spirit of enterprise and cosmopolitanism into the conservative, parochial outlook of Carolingian civilization.

10

Europe Survives the Siege

The invasions of the ninth and tenth centuries wrought significant changes in the political and social organization of Western Europe. Generally speaking, political authority tended to crumble into small local units, as cumbersome royal armies proved themselves incapable of coping with the lightning raids. This was the case in France, but it was less true of Germany where the monarchy, after a period of relative weakness, underwent a spectacular recovery in the tenth century. In England, paradoxically, the hammer blows of the Danes had the ultimate result of unifying the several Anglo-Saxon states into a single kingdom.

In the later eighth century, on the eve of the Viking invasions, England was politically fragmented, just as it had been ever since the Anglo-Saxon conquests. But over the centuries the several smaller kingdoms had gradually been passing under the control of three larger ones—Northumbria in the north, Mercia in the midlands, and Wessex in the south. The Danish attacks of the ninth century, by destroying the power of Wessex's rivals, cleared the field for the Wessex monarchy and thereby hastened the trend toward consolidation that was already under way. But if the Danes were doing the Wessex monarchy a favor, neither side was aware of the fact during the dark days of the later ninth century. England suffered grievous devastation, and for a time it looked as though the Danes might conquer Wessex itself. At the moment of crisis, however, a leader rose to the Wessex throne who was perhaps the most remarkable king England has known, Alfred the Great (871–899). Alfred did everything in his power to save his kingdom from the Vikings. He fought ferocious battles against them. He even resorted to bribing them. In the winter of 878 the Danes invaded Wessex by surprise and forced Alfred to take refuge, with a handful of companions, on the isle of Athelney in a remote swamp. Athelney was England's Valley Forge. In the following spring, 878, Alfred rallied his forces and smashed a Danish army at the battle of Edington. This crucial victory turned the tide of the war, for the Danish leader agreed to take up Christianity, to withdraw from Wessex, and to accept a "permanent" peace. Wessex was never again seriously threatened.

But other Danes under other leaders refused to honor the peace, and Alfred, in his later campaigns, conquered Kent and most of Mercia and captured London—even then England's greatest city. In the 880s a new peace treaty gave Wessex most of southern and southwestern England. The remainder of England—the "Danelaw"—remained hostile, but all non-Danish England was now united under King Alfred.

Like all successful leaders of the age, Alfred was an exceedingly able warrior. But he was far more than that. He was a brilliant, imaginative organizer who systematized military recruitment and founded the English navy, seeing clearly that Christian Europe could not hope to drive back the Vikings without challenging them on the seas. He filled his land with fortresses which served both as defensive strongholds and as places of sanctuary for the agrarian population in time of war. And gradually, as the Danes were rolled back, new fortresses were built to secure the territories recently reconquered. Alfred clarified and rationalized the laws of his people, enforced them strictly, and ruled with an authority such as no Anglo-Saxon king had exercised before his time.

This remarkable monarch was not only a great warrior-statesman; he was also a scholar and a patron of learning. His intellectual environment was even less promising than Charlemagne's. The great days of Bede, Boniface, and Alcuin were far in the past, and by Alfred's time, Latin—the key to Classical-Christian culture—was almost unknown in England. Like Charlemagne, Alfred gathered scholars from far and wide—from England,

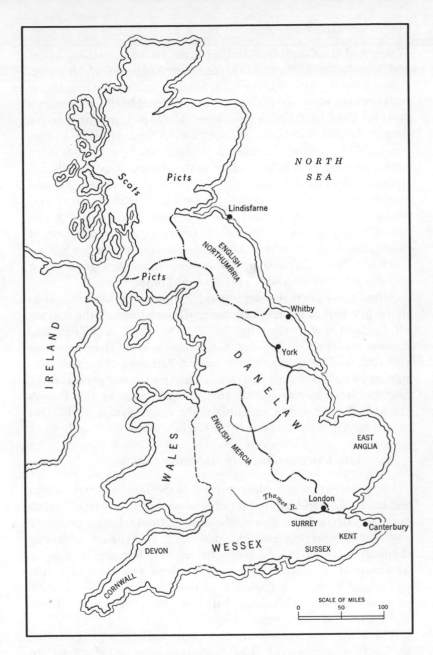

Map IX.   England about 885.

Wales, and the Continent—and set them to work teaching Latin and translating Latin classics into the Anglo-Saxon language. Alfred himself participated in this work of translation, rendering such works as Boethius' *Consolation of Philosophy*, Pope Gregory's *Pastoral Care*, and Bede's *Ecclesiastical History* into the native tongue. In his translation of Boethius, Alfred added a wistful comment of his own: "In those days one never heard tell of ships armed for war," and in his preface to the *Pastoral Care* he alluded with nostalgia to the days "before everything was ravaged and burned, when England's churches overflowed with treasures and books." Alfred's intellectual revival, even more than Charlemagne's, was a salvage operation rather than an outburst of originality, and Alfred was both modest and accurate when he described himself as one who wandered through a great forest collecting timber with which others could build.

Alfred's task of reconquest was carried on by his able successors in the first half of the tenth century. Midway through the century all England was in their hands, and the kings of Wessex had become the kings of England. Great numbers of Danish settlers still remained in northern and eastern England—the amalgamation of Danish and English customs required many generations— but the creative response of the Wessex kings to the Danish threat had transformed and united the Anglo-Saxon world. Out of the agony of the invasions the English monarchy was born.

THE RENEWAL OF THE DANISH ATTACK

For a generation after the conquest of the Danelaw, from about 955 to 980, England enjoyed relative peace and prosperity. English flotillas patrolled the shores, the old fortresses began to evolve into commercial centers, and dedicated churchmen addressed themselves to the task of monastic reform. But the Danish inhabitants of northern and eastern England remained only half committed to the new English monarchy, and with the accession of an incompetent child-king, Ethelred the Unready (978–1016), the Danish invasions began anew.

The new invasions evolved into a campaign of conquest directed by the Danish monarchy. The English defense was characterized by incompetence, treason, and panic. In 991 Ethelred began paying a tribute to the Danes, known thereafter as *danegeld*. In later years the danegeld evolved into a land tax which was exceedingly profitable to the English monarchy, but for the time being it was a symbol of a profound humiliation. In 1016 Ethelred fled the country altogether, and in the following year King Canute of Denmark became the monarch of England (1017–1035).

Canute has been described as very nearly a dwarf and very nearly a genius. He conquered Norway as well as England, and joining these two lands to his kingdom of Denmark, he became the master of a vast, heterogeneous empire centering on the North Sea. No bloodthirsty Viking, he was a product of the new civilizing forces at work in eleventh-century Scandinavia: he issued law codes, practiced Christianity, and kept the peace. Devoting much of his time to England, he cast himself as an English king in the old Wessex tradition. He respected and upheld the ancient customs of the land and gave generously to the monasteries. Despite his Danish background he was a far better English monarch than Ethelred, and his reign was, in a very real sense, a continuation of the past, adding luster to the crown which Alfred's dynasty had forged. English religion and culture prospered as before: "Merry sang the monks of Ely as Canute the king rowed by."

Canute's immense Danish-Norwegian-English empire was hopelessly disunited and failed to survive his death in 1035. When the last of his sons died in 1042, the English realm fell peacefully to Edward the Confessor, a member of the old Wessex dynasty who had grown up in exile in Normandy.

Edward the Confessor was a poor general and a mediocre administrator, but he was a man of genuine piety who won the love of his people despite his political ineptitude. His pious insistence on his own virginity ensured a disputed succession on his death in 1066 and set the stage for the Norman Conquest. When William the Conqueror, duke of Normandy, invaded England and won its crown in 1066 he inherited a prosperous kingdom with strong and well-established political and legal traditions—a kingdom still divided by differences in custom, but with a deep-seated respect for royal authority. Ethelred the Unready notwithstanding, the Wessex dynasty had done its work well. With the timber that Alfred collected, his successors had built an ample and sturdy edifice.

RESPONSES TO THE INVASIONS: FRENCH FEUDALISM

In England the invasions stimulated the trend toward royal unification; in France they encouraged a shattering of political authority into small local units. This paradox can be explained in part by the fact that France, unlike England, was far too large for the Vikings to conquer. Although many settled in Normandy, the chief Norse threat to France came in the form of plundering expeditions rather than large conquering armies. Distances were too great, communities too primitive, and the national territorial army too unwieldy for the king to take the lead in defending his realm. Military responsibility descended to local lords who alone could hope to protect the countryside from the swift and terrible Viking assaults. The French Carolingians became increasingly powerless until at length, in 987, the crown passed to a new dynasty—the Capetians. During the twelfth and thirteenth centuries, the Capetian family produced some of France's most illustrious kings, but for the time being the new dynasty was as powerless as the old one. After 987, as before, the nobles overshadowed the king. About all one can say for the French monarchy in these dark years is that it survived.

The Viking Age witnessed the birth of feudalism in France. In a very real sense feudalism was a product of France's response to the invasions; yet in another sense the Franks had long been drifting in a feudal direction. The roots of feudalism ran deep; one root was the honorable bond of fidelity and service of a warrior to his lord—which characterizes the lord-vassal relationship of late-Merovingian and early-Carolingian times, and the still-earlier comitatus of the Germanic barbarians. Another root was the late-Roman and early-medieval concept of land holding in return for some services to the person who granted the land. An estate granted to a tenant in return for service was known as a *benefice*.

Charles Martel took an important step toward feudalism by joining the institutions of benefice and vassalage. He undertook heavy confiscations of Church property and granted the appropriated estates to his military vassals. There were several reasons for this step. For one thing, money was in very short supply throughout the Early Middle Ages, and it was almost impossible for a ruler to support his soldiers with wages. Often the vassals of an important Frankish lord were fed and sheltered in his household. Indeed, the "household knight" persisted throughout the feudal age. But these warrior-vassals, as their military importance grew, exhibited an ever-increasing hunger for land, and their lords were therefore under considerable pressure to grant them estates—benefices—in return for their loyalty and service.

This tendency was associated with a profound revolution in Frankish military tactics which occurred around the 730s. Previously the Franks had been foot soldiers for the most part. Thereafter, cavalry became increasingly important; within a century and a half it had become all important. The Frankish warrior *par excellence* was now the armored, mounted knight, far more effective than the infantryman but also far more expensive to support or maintain. The knight needed a fine mount, heavy armor and weapons, several attendants, and many years of training. Hence the tendency for a lord to support his knightly vassals by granting them estates in return for their service. The knight did not, of course, labor on his own fields; rather he administered them and collected dues, chiefly in kind, from his peasants.

The Carolingian military vassal was typically a knight. As knightly tactics came more and more to dominate warfare, the custom of vassalage spread widely. The great Frankish magnates of Charlemagne's time pledged their allegiance to their emperor and thereby recognized that they were his vassals and he, their lord. Moreover, these royal vassals had vassals of their own who owed primary allegiance to their immediate lords rather than to the emperor. Charlemagne himself approved of this situation and encouraged the freemen of his realm to become vassals of his magnates. In time of war these vassals' vassals or sub-vassals were expected to join their lords' contingents in the royal army. The centrifugal tendencies implicit in such an arrangement should be obvious. Yet Charlemagne, lacking a coherent civil service or adequate funds to hire a professional army of his own, was obliged to depend on this potentially unstable hierarchy of authority and allegiance.

With the removal of Charlemagne's commanding personality, and under the pressure of the invasions, the rickety hierarchy began to crumble into its component parts. Charlemagne's old territorial officials, the dukes, counts, and margraves, backed by their own vassals, tended increasingly to usurp royal rights, revenues, and prerogatives. They administered justice and collected taxes without regard for the royal will. In time they built castles and assumed all responsibility for the defense of their districts. These feudal magnates remained nominally the vassals of the kings of France, but they were soon much too powerful to be coerced by the crown. Their authority was limited chiefly by the independence of their own vassals, who began to create sub-vassals or sub-sub-vassals of their own. At the height of the feudal age, the lord-vassal relationship might run down through some ten or twenty levels, and there was scarcely a vassal to be found who was not the lord of some still lower vassal.

The ultimate consequences of these developments have been described as "feudal anarchy." In a sense the term is well chosen, but it should not mislead us into thinking of feudalism simply as a "bad thing." Given the instability of the Carolingian Empire, given the desperate plight of France in the Viking era, feudalism emerges as a realistic accommodation to the hard facts of the age. It must never be forgotten that whereas Roman Europe succumbed to barbarian invasions, feudal Europe survived its invaders and ultimately absorbed them.

French feudalism reached its height in the tenth and eleventh centuries. Its key institution was the military benefice, the estate granted by a lord to his vassal in return for allegiance and service— primarily knightly military service. This military benefice was commonly known as a *fief* (rhyming with beef). It was a logical response to the desperate requirements of local defense, the perpetuation of at least some degree of political authority, and the scarcity of money, which necessitated the paying for service in land rather than wages. A great lord would grant an estate—a fief—to his vassal. The vassal might then grant a part of the estate—another fief—to a vassal of his own. And so, on and on, down and down, the process of enfeoffment went. The result was a hierarchically organized landed knightly aristocracy, each knight giving homage and fealty—that is, pledging his personal allegiance —to his immediate lord, each living off the labor and dues of a dependent peasantry which tilled the fields that his fief embraced, each administering a court and dispensing justice to those below him.

Such were the essential ingredients of feudalism. The term has been frequently abused and misunderstood. Indeed, it is extremely difficult to define, and if we wish to sum up the whole institution we can do no better than repeat the definition of medieval feudalism's greatest modern scholar, the French historian Marc Bloch:

> A subject peasantry; widespread use of the service tenement (i.e., the fief) instead of a salary, which was out of the question; the supremacy of a class of specialized warriors; ties of obedience and protection which bind man to man and, within the warrior class, assume the distinctive form called vassalage; fragmentation of authority—leading inevitably to disorder; and in the midst of all this, the survival of other forms of association, family and state . . .—such then seem to be the fundamental features of European feudalism.*

With this definition in mind, it may be helpful to emphasize some of the things that feudalism was not. It was not, for one thing, a universal and symmetrical system. Born in northern France in the Viking age, it took on many different forms as it spread across Europe. In northern France itself it varied widely from one region to another. It by no means encompassed all the land, for even at its height many landowners owed no feudal obligations and had no feudal ties. The feudal hierarchy or feudal "pyramid" was riddled with ambiguities: a single vassal might hold several fiefs from several lords; a lord might receive a fief from his own vassal, thereby putting himself in the extraordinary position of being his vassal's vassal. The degree of confusion possible in feudalism can best be appreciated by examining a typical document of the age:

> I, John of Toul, affirm that I am the vassal of the Lady Beatrice, countess of Troyes, and of her son Theobald, count of Champagne, against every creature living or dead, excepting my allegiance to Lord Enjourand of Coucy, Lord John of Arcis, and the count of Grandpre. If it should happen that the count of Grandpre should be at war with the countess and count of Champagne in his own quarrel, I will aid the

---

* Bloch, *Feudal Society*, p. 446.

count of Grandpre in my own person, and will aid the count
and countess of Champagne by sending them the knights
whose service I owe them from the fief which I hold of them.

So much for feudal order!

Feudalism was not, in its heyday, associated with the romantic
knight errant, the many-turreted castle, or the lady fair. The
knight of the ninth, tenth, and eleventh centuries was a rough-
hewn warrior; his armor was simple, his horse was tough, his
castle was a crude wooden tower atop an earthen mound, and his
lady fair was any available wench. Chivalry developed after a
time, to be sure, but not until the foundations of the old feudal
order were being eroded by the revival of commerce and a money
economy and the rise of strong monarchies. Only then did feudalism soften and become chivalric. Only then did the knight
seek to disguise his declining social usefulness by turning to
elaborate shining armor, lace and ruffles, courtly phrases, and
wedding-cake castles.

Feudalism was not entirely military. The vassal owed his lord
not only military service but a variety of additional obligations
as well. Among these were the duty to join his lord's retinue on
tours of the countryside; to serve, when summoned, in his lord's
court of justice; to feed, house, and entertain his lord and his
lord's retinue on their all-too-frequent visits; to give money to
his lord on a variety of specified occasions; to contribute to his
lord's ranson should he be captured in battle. Early in its history
the fief became hereditary, but the lord retained the right to
confiscate it should his vassal die without heirs, to supervise and
exploit it during a minority, and to exercise a power of veto over
the marriage of a female fief-holder. In return for such rights as
these, the lord was obliged to protect and uphold the interests
of his vassals. The very essence of feudalism was the notion of
reciprocal rights and obligations, and consequently the feudal
outlook played a key role in steering medieval Europe away from
autocracy or absolutism.

Feudalism was not, strictly speaking, a system that embraced
the whole of society from serf to king. Although it rested on the
labor of peasants, the feudal structure itself encompassed only
the warrior class of lords and vassals. There was, in short, a world

of difference between a vassal and a serf. Beneath the level of the feudal warrior class, 80 or 90 per cent of the population continued to labor on the land. In a book of this sort it is customary to discuss at great length the organization of peasant life on the "typical medieval manor." But, in fact, agrarian organization was infinitely diverse, and to discuss the typical medieval manor would be as fruitless as to discuss the typical American business. Medieval agriculture exhibited infinite variations. It ranged from small farms to large manors divided between the peasants' fields and the lord's demesne fields. The peasants themselves varied from slaves to freemen, although the majority of them, between the ninth and eleventh centuries, occupied an intermediate status and were known as villains or serfs. Like the Roman *coloni* they were bound to their land. They owed various dues, chiefly in kind, to their manorial lord, who was ordinarily the knightly vassal to whose fief the manor belonged, and were normally expected to labor for a certain number of days per week on their lord's fields. But they were by no means chattel slaves. Legally they could not be sold, nor could their own hereditary fields be taken from them. After paying manorial dues, the produce of their own fields was theirs to keep. Hardly enviable, their situation could have been worse.

The feudal chaos of the ninth and tenth centuries, with its extreme fragmentation of sovereign power and its incessant private wars, gradually gave way to a somewhat more orderly regime as great territorial magnates, such as the count of Anjou or the duke of Normandy, extended their frontiers at the expense of weaker neighbors and tightened their control over their own vassals and sub-vassals. But it was not until the twelfth century that the French monarchs began to rise above the level of their great feudal magnates and assert real authority over the realm. The age of feudalism was a period of virtual eclipse for the French crown.

RESPONSES TO THE INVASIONS: GERMANY

England's response to the invasion was royal unification; France's response was feudal particularism. Germany's response differed from those of both England and France, owing to the special character of the invasions which Germany faced and the unique conditions prevailing in Germany itself. The East Frankish kingdom—which evolved directly into the medieval German state —was subject to Viking attacks, but the real threat came from the Hungarian horsemen of the East. The late Carolingian kings of Germany—the successors of Louis the German, who was granted East Frankland at the Treaty of Verdun—proved incapable of coping with the Hungarian raids. As in France, real authority descended to the great magnates of the realm. But these magnates were not the dukes and counts of Carolingian officialdom. Most of Germany had remained outside Frankish control until the Carolingian conquests of the eighth century; consequently the Frankish system of local administration was only imperfectly established there. The ancient tribal consciousness of Saxons, Bavarians, and Swabians was still strong. In the critical decades of the late ninth and early tenth centuries ambitious aristocrats exploited this tribal patriotism by grasping leadership over the old tribal districts. These men of the hour assumed the title of duke, and the regions that they ruled came to be known as tribal duchies. The "tribal" dukes sought to dominate the local ecclesiastical organizations, to seize the royal Carolingian estates in their duchies, and to usurp royal power. It was they who assumed the responsibility of meeting the Hungarian threat.

In the early tenth century there were five important tribal duchies—Saxony, Bavaria, Swabia, Franconia, and Lorraine. Saxony, Swabia, and Bavaria had been incorporated only superficially into the Carolingian state, whereas the western duchies of Franconia and Lorraine were much more strongly Frankish in outlook and organization.

The five tribal dukes might well have become the masters of Germany. Their ambitions were frustrated by two closely related factors, (1) their failure to curb the Hungarians and (2) the reinvigoration of the German monarchy under an able new dynasty. The Carolingian line came to an end in Germany in 911 with the death of King Louis the Child. He was succeeded first by the duke of Franconia and then, in 919, by the duke of Saxony—the first of a remarkable and illustrious line of kings who based their royal power on their domination of the powerful Saxon duchy.

The Saxon kings struggled vigorously to assert their authority over the tribal duchies. The duchy of Saxony was now under the authority of the monarchy, and the Saxon kings quickly grasped direct control over Franconia as well. But the semi-independent dukes of the two southern duchies, Swabia and Bavaria, continued to be a problem. The real victory of the Saxon monarchy occurred in the reign of the second and greatest of the Saxon kings, Otto I (936–973).

Otto I, or Otto the Great as he is often called, devoted his considerable talents to achieving three goals: (1) defending Germany against the Hungarian invasions, (2) establishing royal power over the remaining tribal duchies, and (3) extending German royal control to the crumbling, unstable Middle Kingdom which the Treaty of Verdun had assigned to Emperor Lothar back in 843. We have already seen how this heterogeneous Middle Kingdom began to fall to pieces after Lothar's death. By the mid-tenth century it had become a confused political shambles. Parts of it had been seized by Germany, other parts by France, but its southern districts—Burgundy and Italy—retained a chaotic independence. The dukes of Swabia and Bavaria both had notions of seizing these territories, and Otto the Great, in order to forestall the development of an unmanageable rival power to his south, led his armies into Italy in 951 and assumed the title "King of Italy."

From 951 onward, events developed rapidly. Otto the Great was obliged to leave Italy in haste to put down a major uprising in Germany. His victory over the rebels enabled him to establish his power over Germany more strongly than ever. And in 955 he won the crucial battle of the age, crushing a large Hungarian army at Lechfeld. At a blow he terminated once and for all the Hungarian menace. Lechfeld served as a vivid demonstration of royal power—a vindication of the monarch's claim that he, not the tribal dukes, was the true defender of Germany. The Hungarians were defeated, and Germany's eastern frontier now lay open to the gradual eastward penetration of German-Christian culture. The day of the tribal duchies was over and the monarchy reigned supreme. Otto the Great now towered over his contemporaries as the greatest monarch of the West and the most powerful ruler since Charlemagne. The invasions of Germany, which had begun by uplifting the tribal duchies, ended by contributing to the revival of royal authority.

THE GERMAN EMPIRE

After Lechfeld there remained for Otto I one important piece of unfinished business. Since his departure from Italy a usurper had seized the Italian throne and was harassing the pope. In response to a papal appeal—which harmonized beautifully with the pursuit of his own interests—Otto returned to Italy in force, conquered the usurper, and recovered the Italian crown. In 962 the pope hailed Otto as Roman Emperor and placed the imperial crown on his head. It is this momentous event, rather than the coronation of Charlemagne in 800, that marks the true genesis of the medieval institution known as the Holy Roman Empire. The events of 962 are reminiscent of those of 800, but Otto's empire was vastly different from Charlemagne's. Above all, Otto and his imperial successors made no pretensions of universal jurisdiction over France or the remainder of Western Christendom. The medieval Holy Roman Empire had its roots deep in the soil of Germany, and most of the emperors subordinated imperial interests to those of the Germany monarchy. From its advent in 962 to its long-delayed demise in the early nineteenth century, the Holy Roman Empire remained fundamentally a German phenomenon.

The German orientation of Otto's empire is illustrated dramatically by the fact that neither he nor the majority of his successors over the next two centuries made any real effort to establish tight control over Italy. Only when they marched south of the Alps could they count on the obedience of the Italians; when they returned to Germany they left behind them no real administrative structure but depended almost solely on the fickle allegiance of certain Italian magnates. The medieval German emperors were never really successful in straddling the Alps.

In Germany conditions were quite different. There the coming of feudalism was delayed for more than a century after Otto's imperial coronation. The great magnates, to be sure, became vassals of the king, but they normally had no vassals of their own. The chief tool which Otto and his successors employed in governing their state was the Church. In an era of a weak papacy, the German kings dominated the Church within their realm and kept a close control over important ecclesiastical appointments.

KEY

The Five Stem Duchies

SCALE OF MILES
0   100   200

SAXONY

Slavs

Elbe R.

LORRAINE

FRANCONIA

BOHEMIA

Rhine R.

Danube R.

SWABIA   Lechfeld
BAVARIA

KINGDOM OF BURGUNDY

Rhone R.

Hungarians

Rome

APULIA

BALEARICS

SARDINIA

CALABRIA

MEDITERRANEAN SEA

SICILY

Map X.   The Holy Roman Empire in 962.

Otto had successfully wrested control of the Church in the various tribal duchies from the defunct dukes, and in a very real sense the great bishops and abbots of Germany were the king's men. These churchmen made ideal royal lieutenants. They could not make their estates hereditary; when a bishop or abbot died his successor could be hand picked by the king. Thus the loyalty and political capacity of the churchly royal administrators were assured. After 962 the German monarchy was even moderately successful in appointing popes. There would come a time when churchmen would rebel at such high-handed treatment, but in Otto's reign the time was still far off.

Otto's lofty position as proprietor of the imperial Church was supported by both tradition and theory. Otto was regarded as far more than a mere secular monarch. He was *rex et sacerdos*, king and priest, sanctified by the holy anointing ceremony which accompanied his coronation. He was the vicar of God—the living symbol of Christ the King—the "natural" leader of the Church in his empire. In the closing years of his reign his actual political power over Church and state came close to matching his lofty pretensions.

Otto's remarkable reign provided the impulse for an impressive intellectual revival which reached its culmination under his two successors, Otto II (973–83) and Otto III (983–1002). This "Ottonian Renaissance" produced a series of able administrators and scholars, the greatest of whom was the brilliant churchman Gerbert of Aurillac—later Pope Sylvester II (d. 1003). Gerbert visited Spain and returned with a comprehensive knowledge of Islamic science. The intellectual legacy of Arab civilization was beginning to filter into Western Christendom at last. Gerbert had an encyclopedic though unoriginal mind. A master of classical literature, logic, mathematics, and science, he astonished his contemporaries by teaching the Greco-Arab doctrine that the earth was spherical. There were widespread rumors that he was some kind of wizard in league with the Devil—rumors which were somewhat dampened by his elevation to the papacy. Gerbert was no wizard; rather he was an advance agent of the momentous intellectual awakening that Europe was about to undergo—a harbinger of the High Middle Ages.

The successors of Otto the Great were no longer troubled by the tribal duchies or the Hungarians, but they were obliged, as all men are, to cope with new problems and devise new solutions. In 1024 the Saxon dynasty died out and was replaced by a Franconian family known as the Salian dynasty (1024–1125). The tribal dukes gave way to a new, particularistic aristocracy whose impulse toward independence taxed the ingenuity of the emperors. Still, the Salian dynasty was generally successful in maintaining its power. Working hand in glove with the German Church, the Salians improved and elaborated the royal administrative system and ultimately came to exercise even greater authority than Otto I had known. In the mid-eleventh century the mightiest of the Salian emperors, Henry III (1039–1056), ruled unrivaled over Germany and appointed popes as effortlessly as he selected his own bishops. In 1050, at a time when France was still a medley of feudal principalities and England, under Edward the Confessor, was relatively small and relatively isolated, the German Emperor Henry III dominated central Europe and held the papacy in his palm.

EUROPE ON THE EVE OF THE HIGH MIDDLE AGES

By 1050 both England and Germany were comparatively stable, well-organized kingdoms. The French monarchy was still weak, but within another century it would be on its way toward dominating France. Meanwhile feudal principalities such as Normandy, Flanders, and Anjou were well advanced toward political coherence. Warfare was still endemic, but it was beginning to lessen as Europe moved toward political stability. Above all, the invasions were over—the siege had ended. Hungary and the Scandinavian world were being absorbed into Western Christendom, and Islam was by now on the defensive. The return of prosperity, the increase in food production, the rise in population, the quickening of commerce, the intensification of intellectual activity, all betokened the coming of a new era. Western Civilization was on the threshold of an immense creative upsurge which was destined, ultimately, to transform the world.

CHRONOLOGY OF THE AGE OF SIEGE AND ITS AFTERMATH

England	France	Germany
c.787: First Danish raid	814–840: Louis the Pious	814–840: Louis the Pious
	840–877: Charles the Bald	840–876: Louis the German
871–899: Reign of Alfred	843: Treaty of Verdun	843: Treaty of Verdun
878: Battle of Edington	911: Normandy recognized	891: Vikings defeated by Arnulf
c.954: Reconquest of Danelaw completed		936–973: Reign of Otto the Great
		955: Otto defeats Hungarians at Lechfeld
		962: Otto crowned Roman Emperor
978–1016: Reign of Ethelred	987: Capetians replace Carolingians	973–983: Reign of Otto II
1017–1035: Reign of Canute		983–1002: Reign of Otto III
1042–1066: Reign of Edward the Confessor		1003: Gerbert of Aurillac dies
1066: Norman Conquest of England		1039–1056: Reign of Henry III

Suggested Readings

The asterisk indicates a paperback edition.

GENERAL HISTORIES OF THE EARLY MIDDLE AGES

Margaret Deanesly, *A History of Early Medieval Europe, 476–911* (2nd ed., Methuen). An excellent, accurate, and highly detailed text.

H. St. L. B. Moss, *The Birth of the Middle Ages* (*Oxford). A brief, thoughtful survey running from the Principate through Charlemagne.

J. M. Wallace-Hadrill, *The Barbarian West* (*Harper). Still more condensed; the discussion of the Carolingian Renaissance is especially illuminating.

William C. Bark, *Origins of the Medieval World* (*Anchor). A provocative interpretive study.

Robert Latouche, *The Birth of Western Economy* (Methuen). A splendid, up-to-date account of early medieval economic trends.

M. L. W. Laistner, *Thought and Letters in Western Europe, A.D. 500 to 900* (rev. ed., Methuen). The best intellectual history of the period.

Christopher Dawson, *The Making of Europe* (*Meridian). A brilliant analysis of early medieval culture by a distinguished Catholic scholar.

BYZANTIUM

N. H. Baynes and H. St. L. B. Moss (Eds.), *Byzantium, An Introduction to East Roman Civilization* (*Oxford). An anthology of essays by scholarly specialists, organized topically.

Two short general accounts of Byzantine history and civilization, available in paperback, are highly recommended:

J. M. Hussey, *The Byzantine World* (*Harper).

Steven Runciman, *Byzantine Civilization* (*Meridian).

G. Ostrogorsky, *History of the Byzantine State* (Blackwell). Longer and more detailed than the above works, this is the best single-volume history of Byzantium.

THE WEST BEFORE THE CAROLINGIANS

J. M. Wallace-Hadrill, *The Long-Haired Kings* (Barnes and Noble). A collection of illuminating essays on the Merovingian period.

A. F. Havinghurst (Ed.), *The Pirenne Thesis—Analysis, Criticism, and Revision* (*Heath). An excellent approach to one of the central problems in early medieval history through excerpts from the writing of contending historians. For a fuller account of Pirenne's thesis see:

Henri Pirenne, *Mohammed and Charlemagne* (*Meridian).

ISLAM

G. E. von Grunebaum, *Medieval Islam* (2nd ed., University of Chicago Press). A learned and original work, the best on the subject.

P. K. Hitti, *History of the Arabs* (St. Martin's Press). Broad yet full; a monumental work. For a good introduction to Hitti's work, see:

P. K. Hitti, *The Arabs: A Short History* (*Gateway).

Two other useful surveys in paperback are

H. A. R. Gibb, *Mohammedanism: An Historical Survey* (*Mentor).

Bernard Lewis, *The Arabs in History* (*Arrow Books).

CAROLINGIAN AND POST-CAROLINGIAN EUROPE

H. Fichtenau, *The Carolingian Empire* (*Harper). The best English-language work on the subject.

P. H. Sawyer, *The Age of the Vikings* (St. Martin's Press). A rather technical, highly significant reappraisal of the Viking age.

Marc Bloch, *Feudal Society* (U. of Chicago Press). A masterly work, challengingly written and boldly original in its conclusions.

Lynn White, Jr., *Medieval Technology and Social Change* (*Oxford). An important and provocative pioneering work which defies categorization. Beautifully written and opulently annotated.

Geoffrey Barraclough, *The Origins of Modern Germany* (*Capricorn). Incorporates recent scholarship in medieval German constitutional history.

Sidney Painter, *French Chivalry* (*Cornell). Short, witty, and perceptive.

F. M. Stenton, *Anglo-Saxon England* (2nd ed., Oxford). A massive masterpiece.

H. R. Loyn, *Anglo-Saxon England and the Norman Conquest* (St. Martin's Press). An authoritative recent work emphasizing economic and social history.

Carl Stephenson, *Mediaeval Feudalism* (*Cornell). A brief, lucid, well-organized account.

SOURCES

Norman F. Cantor (Ed.), *The Medieval World* (*Macmillan). A good recent collection of medieval sources.

Einhard, *Life of Charlemagne*, tr. S. E. Turner (*Ann Arbor Paperbacks). A short, reasonably trustworthy biography by Charlemagne's secretary.

Bede, *A History of the English Church and People*, tr. Leo Sherley-Price (*Penguin).

Part 3

THE High Middle Ages:
The First Flowering of European Culture

11

Economic Revolution
and New Frontiers

THE HIGH MIDDLE AGES: 1050-1300

History, it has often been said, is a seamless web. But the human mind can only cope with the flow of historical reality by dividing it into arbitrary chronological units—forcing it into compartments of the historian's own making. In this sense every historical "period" is a kind of falsehood—an affront to the continuity of human development. Yet unless we concoct historical epochs, unless we invent ages, unless we force the past into some relatively tidy chronological framework, we cannot make history intelligible to the human mind. Thus the historian speaks of "Classical Antiquity," "The Early Middle Ages," "The High Middle Ages," "The Renaissance," etc. These are all historical lies, to be sure, but they are necessary lies—white lies—without which the past would have little meaning. We cannot get along without "eras," but we should never forget that they are inventions of our own. We should never lose sight of their limitations.

The term *High Middle Ages* has been applied to the great cultural upsurge of the later eleventh, twelfth, and thirteenth centuries. Yet no spectacular event occurred in 1050 to signal the advent of the new era; no cataclysm occurred in 1300 to mark its end. The transition from Early Middle Ages to High Middle Ages was gradual and uneven. It might even be argued that the High

Middle Ages came to Germany as early as the tenth century, under the Ottos, or that it was delayed in France until the twelfth century when the Capetian monarchy rose from its torpor. Ever since the waning of the Viking, Hungarian, and Saracen invasions—many decades prior to 1050—Europe had been pulsing with new creative energy. Broadly speaking, however, the scope and intensity of the revival did not become evident until the later eleventh century. By the century's end, Europe's lively commerce and bustling towns, her intellectual vigor and political inventiveness, her military expansion and her heightened religious enthusiasm left no doubt that vast new forces were at work—that Western Christendom had at last become a great creative civilization. As the historian would say, a new age had dawned.

The causes of an immense cultural awakening such as occurred in the High Middle Ages are far too complex to be identified precisely or listed in order of importance. One essential element was the ending of the invasions and the increasing political stability that followed. We know that in the eleventh century Europe's population was beginning to increase significantly and that her food production was rising. Whether increased productivity led to increased population or vice-versa is difficult to say. But productivity could not have risen as it did without the revolutionary developments in agricultural technology; the three-field system which spread across much of northern Europe, the windmill, the water mill (by 1086 there were over 5000 water mills in England alone) the heavy, wheeled plow, the horseshoe and improved horse collar which transformed horses into efficient draught animals, and the tandem harness which made it possible to employ horses and oxen in large teams to draw plows or to pull heavy wagons. These and numerous related inventions came to the West gradually over the centuries, but they had a powerful cumulative influence on the great economic boom of the High Middle Ages.

TOWNS AND COMMERCE

The rise in productivity and population was accompanied by a great commercial revival and a general reawakening of urban life. In turn, the new towns became the foci of a brilliant, reinvigorated culture. The intimate human contacts arising from town life stimulated European thought and art. The cathedral and the university, perhaps the two greatest monuments of high medieval culture, were both urban phenomena; the Franciscan order, possibly the loftiest and most dynamic religious institution that the new age produced, devoted itself primarily to evangelical work among the new urban population. Yet the towns were also, and above all, centers of commercial and industrial enterprise. The European economy in the High Middle Ages remained fundamentally agrarian, but the towns were the great economic and cultural catalysts of the era. In them, God and mammon stood face to face and often worked hand in hand.

There had been towns in Europe ever since antiquity. The administrative-military town of the Roman Empire gave way in time to the far humbler cathedral town of the Early Middle Ages. But both had one crucial thing in common: both were economic parasites, living off the blood, labor, and taxes of the countryside; both consumed more than they produced. The towns of the High Middle Ages, on the other hand, represented something radically new. With few exceptions they were true commercial entities that earned their own way, living off the fruits of their merchant and industrial activities. Small, foul, disease-ridden, and often torn by internal conflict, they were nevertheless Western Europe's first cities in the modern sense of the word.

These commercial towns arose in rhythm with the upsurge of commerce. Often they began as suburbs of older cathedral towns or as humble settlements outside the walls of some of the many fortresses that had arisen in ninth- and tenth-century Europe. These fortresses were generally known by some form of the Germanic word *burgh*, and in time the term came to apply to the town itself rather than the fortress that spawned it. By the twelfth century a *burgh* or *borough* was an urban commercial center, inhabited by *burghers* or *burgesses*, who constituted a new class known later as the bourgeoisie.

At the end of the eleventh century, towns were developing rapidly all over Europe. They were thickest in Flanders and northern Italy, where the immense opportunities of international commerce were first exploited. The greatest Italian city of the age was Venice, long a Byzantine colony but now an independent republic, whose merchants carried on a lucrative trade with Constantinople and

the East. Other Italian coastal towns—Genoa, Pisa, and Amalfi—
soon followed Venice into the profitable markets of the eastern
Mediterranean, and the ramifications of their far-flung trade
brought vigorous new life to the towns of interior Italy, such as
Milan and Florence. During the High Middle Ages the Moslems
were virtually driven from the seas and Italian merchants dominated the Mediterranean.

Meanwhile, the towns of Flanders were growing wealthy from
the commerce of the North—from trade with northern France and
the British Isles, the Rhineland and the shores of the Baltic Sea.
Flanders itself was a great sheep-growing district; her towns became centers of woolen textile production. In time the towns were
processing more wool than Flemish sheep could supply so that
from the twelfth century onward Flemish merchants began to
import wool on a huge scale from England. By then Flanders was
the great industrial center of northern Europe, with the textile
industry the supreme manufacturing enterprise of the age.

The rise of towns and commerce injected a vigorous new urban
class into a society that had theretofore been almost exclusively
agrarian. The merchant class was drawn from vagabonds, runaway
serfs, avaricious minor noblemen, and, in general, the surplus of a
mushrooming population. At an early date these ambitious traders
began to form themselves into merchant guilds in order to protect
themselves against confiscatory tolls and other exactions levied
by a hostile landed aristocracy. A town was almost always situated
on the territories of some lord—sometimes a duke or even a king—
and the merchants found that only by collective action could they
win the privileges essential to their calling: personal freedom from
serflike status, freedom of movement, freedom from inordinate
tolls at every bridge or feudal boundary, the rights to own property
in the town, to be judged by a town court, to execute commercial
contracts, and to buy and sell freely. By the twelfth century, a
number of lords, recognizing the economic advantages of having
flourishing commercial centers on their lands, were issuing town
charters which guaranteed many of these rights. Indeed, some
farsighted lords began founding and chartering new towns on
their own initiative.

At first the urban charters differed greatly from one another,
but in time it became customary to pattern them after certain

well-known models. The charter granted by the king of England to Newcastle-on-Tyne, and that of the French King to the town of Lorris, were copied repeatedly throughout England and France. In effect, these charters transformed the commercial communities into semiautonomous political and legal entities, each with its own local government, its own court, its own tax-collecting agencies, and its own customs. These urban communes paid well for their charters and continued to pay regular taxes to their lord. But—and this is all important—they did so as political units. Individual merchants were not normally subject to the harassments of their lords' agents. These townsmen enforced their own law in their own courts, collected their own taxes, and paid their dues to their lord in a lump sum. In short, they had won the invaluable privilege of handling their own affairs.

One should not conclude, however, that the medieval towns were even remotely democratic. It was the prosperous merchants and master craftsmen who profited chiefly from the charters, and it was they who normally came to control the town governments, ruling as narrow oligarchies over the towns' less exalted and less fortunate inhabitants. Some towns witnessed the beginnings of a significant split between large-scale producers and wage-earning workers along the lines of modern capitalism. It can be said, in fact, that the medieval town was the birthplace of European capitalism. For as time passed, towns tended to become centers of industry as well as commerce. Manufacturing followed in the footsteps of trade. And although most industrial production took place in small shops rather than large factories, some enterprising businessmen employed considerable numbers of workers to produce goods—usually textiles—on a large scale. Normally these workers did not labor in a factory but rather in their own shops or homes. Since the entrepreneur sent his raw materials out to his workers, instead of bringing the workers to the materials, this mode of production has been called the "putting-out system." As a direct antecedent of the factory system, it was a crucial phase in the early history of capitalism.

The more typical medieval manufacturer worked for himself in his own shop, producing his own goods and selling them directly to the public. As early as the eleventh century these craftsmen were organizing themselves into craft guilds—as distinct from merchant guilds. In an effort to limit competition and protect their market, the craft guilds established strict admission requirements and stringent rules on prices, wages, standards of quality, and operating procedures. A young craftsman would learn his trade as an apprentice in the shop of a master craftsman. After a specified period, sometimes as long as seven years, he ended his apprenticeship. With good luck and rich parents he might then become a master himself. Normally, however, he had to work for some years as a day laborer—a journeyman—improving his skills and saving his money, until he was able to demonstrate sufficient craftsmanship to win guild membership and accumulate enough money to establish a shop of his own. Toward the end of the High Middle Ages, as prosperity began to wane and urban society became more crystalized, it became increasingly common for journeymen to spend their whole lives as wage earners, never becoming masters at all. Accordingly, the town became the scene of bitter class feelings which erupted from time to time into open conflict.

There were many who made their fortunes in commerce and manufacturing. Europe was astir with new life; for a clever, enterprising man the possibilities were vast. In the twelfth and thirteenth century, merchants were moving continuously along the roads and rivers of Europe. Italians crossed the Alps bringing spices and luxury goods from the Near East and the Orient to the aristocracy of France and Germany. French, Flemish, and German merchants carried goods far and wide across the Continent, "buying cheap and selling dear." A series of annual fairs along the overland trade routes provided the long-distance merchants with excellent opportunities to sell their goods. As large-scale commerce grew, credit and banking grew with it, and by the thirteenth century several banking families had amassed immense fortunes. It may seem paradoxical that the period which is often regarded as the supreme age of faith witnessed the rise of large-scale commerce and a money economy. Yet it was money that built the Gothic cathedrals and supported the Crusades, that financed the pious charities of St. Louis and gave zest to the magnificent religious culture of the thirteenth century—money, and, of course, an ardent faith. In time faith itself would fall victim to the acquisitive spirit which was evolving in the towns, but during the High

Middle Ages the townsmen, by and large, exhibited a piety that was far more vibrant and intense than that of the peasantry and the aristocracy. Indeed, the powerful upsurge of lay piety among the European townsmen became a crucial factor in the evolution of medieval Christianity.

THE DECLINE OF FEUDALISM

Feudalism, based as it was on hereditary land tenure in return for service, was a characteristic product of a money-poor society which could not afford to pay wages to its warriors. With the rise of a money economy in Europe, the basic feudal relationship began to dissolve. The deep impact of feudal custom on the European mind is demonstrated by the various ingenious ways in which the aristocracy sought to adopt feudalism to the new economic realities. Indeed, during the eleventh and twelfth centuries the feudal system spread from France into England, Germany, and the Crusader States of the Holy Land. At the same time, however, kings and dukes were resorting increasingly to the hiring of mercenaries for warfare and professional judges and civil servants for the administration of their realms. As the twelfth century progressed, the feudal vassal was, oftener than not, asked to pay a tax in lieu of his personal service in the feudal army. With the income from this tax—which was sometimes called *scutage*—a monarch could hire professional warriors who were better trained, better disciplined, and more obedient than the landed knights. The feudal aristocracy retained its lands and much of its power for centuries to come, and even continued to produce warriors. But the knights of the new age expected to be paid. They no longer served at their own expense in return for their fiefs. Once the paying of taxes had replaced personal service as the vassal's primary obligation—and this was the case almost everywhere by the thirteenth century—feudalism had lost its soul.

THE EVOLUTION OF AGRARIAN LIFE

The new social and economic conditions of the High Middle Ages wrought a profound transformation in the European countryside. Doubtless the most spectacular change was the immense expansion of arable land. The great primeval forest of northern Europe was reduced to isolated patches, swamps and marshes were drained, and vast new territories were opened to cultivation. This prodigious clearing operation was stimulated by the soaring population and the rising money economy. Agricultural surpluses could now be sold to townsmen and thereby converted into cash. Consequently, the peasant was strongly motivated to produce as far in excess of the consumption level as he possibly could. Every new field that could be put into operation was likely to bring a profit.

A second change, no less significant than the first, was the elevation of the peasant. Slavery, which was rare in Carolingian times, had virtually disappeared from Europe by the eleventh century. The tillers of the land were chiefly freemen and serfs. Often the freeman owned his own small farm, but the serf was generally to be found on a manor. Normally the manor included the peasants' fields and the lord's fields—his *demesne*—the produce of which went directly and entirely to the lord. Among the obligations which the serf normally owed his lord were a rent in kind from the serf's own fields and labor service for a stipulated number of days on the lord's demesne. In Carolingian times, manorial lords had augmented the part-time serf labor on their demesne fields by using slaves. As slavery gradually died out, the lords were faced with a severe labor shortage on their demesne.

As a result of this problem, and in keeping with the trend toward transforming service obligations into money payments, the lords tended to abandon demesne farming altogether. They leased out their demesne fields to peasants and, in return for a fixed money payment, released their serfs from the traditional obligation of working part-time on the demesne. At about the same time they translated the serf's rent-in-kind from his own fields into a money rent. By freeing the serf of his labor obligation they transformed him, in effect, into a tenant farmer, thereby improving his status immensely. The obligations of the serf, like those of the feudal vassal, were gradually being placed on a fiscal basis.

The abandonment of demesne farming was a slow and uneven trend which progressed much more rapidly in some areas than in others. In thirteenth-century England, a countertrend developed whereby many lords successfully reclaimed and enlarged their demesnes. But on the Continent the demesne gradually disappeared and, in quite a literal sense, the peasant inherited the earth.

When the lords transformed the dues and services of their serfs into fixed money rents they failed to reckon with inflation. The booming economy of the High Middle Ages was accompanied by an upward spiral of prices and a concomitant decline in the purchasing power of money. Hence the real value of the peasants' rents steadily diminished, and many lords of the later Middle Ages came to regret the bargains their ancestors had made. Inflation ruined more than one lord, but it was a godsend to the medieval peasantry. The lords could do little to recoup their losses; they were often obligated to improve the condition of their peasants still more in order to keep them from fleeing to the towns or to the newly cleared lands. The peasant was in great demand, and the enterprising land developers who were engaged in turning woods and marshes into fields competed for his services. As a consequence, the High Middle Ages witnessed the elevation of innumerable peasants from servile status to freedom. Rural communes emerged—peasant villages whose lords had granted them charters closely paralleling those of townsmen. One should be careful not to idealize the lot of the thirteenth-century peasant —it was still impoverished and brutish by present standards—yet it was distinctly superior to peasant life in the Roman Empire or the Early Middle Ages. The terrifying peasants' rebellions of early Modern Europe were products of a later and different era when the expansion and prosperity of the High Middle Ages had given way to an epoch of recession and closed frontiers.

THE NEW FRONTIERS

The open, expanding frontier is one of the most characteristic aspects of the High Middle Ages. The clearing of forests and draining of swamps represent the conquest of a great internal frontier. They were paralleled by an external expansion all along the periphery of Western Christendom, which brought vast areas of the Arab, Byzantine, and Slavic worlds within the ballooning boundaries of European civilization and added wealth to the flourishing economy.

Western Europe had been expanding ever since Charles Martel repelled the Arabs in 733. Charlemagne had introduced Frankish government and Christianity into much of Germany and had established a Spanish bridgehead around Barcelona. The stabilization and conversion of Hungary and Scandinavia around the turn of the millennium pushed the limits of Western Civilization far northward and eastward from the original Carolingian core. Now, in the eleventh, twelfth, and thirteenth centuries, the population boom produced multitudes of landless aristocratic younger sons who sought land and military glory on Christendom's frontiers. And the ever-proliferating European peasantry provided a potential labor force for the newly conquered lands. While the Christian warrior of the frontier was carving out new estates for himself, he was also storing up treasures in heaven, for as a result of his aggressive militancy Christendom was everywhere expanding at the expense of the heathen Slavs of eastern Europe and the infidel Moslems of Spain, Sicily, and Syria. Land, gold, and eternal salvation—these were the alluring rewards of the medieval frontier.

SPAIN

So it was that knightly adventurers from all over Christendom— and particularly from feudal France—flocked southwestward into Spain during the eleventh century to aid in the reconquest of the Iberian Peninsula from Islam. The powerful Moslem caliphate of Cordova had broken up after 1002 into a kaleidoscope of small, warring Moorish states, thereby providing the Christians with a superb opportunity. Unfortunately, the Christians were themselves divided into several kingdoms which consumed more energy fighting one another than fighting the Moors. Taking the lead in the reconquest, the Christian kingdom of Castile captured the great Moslem city of Toledo in 1085. In later years Toledo became a crucial point of contact between Islamic and Christian culture. Here numerous Arab scientific and philosophical works were translated into Latin and then disseminated throughout Europe to challenge and invigorate the Western mind.

Early in the twelfth century the Spanish Christian kingdom of Aragon contested the supremacy of Castile and undertook an offensive of its own against the Moors. In 1140 Aragon was greatly strengthened by its unification with Catalonia—the wealthy state whose center was Barcelona—the Spanish March of Charlemagne's time. During the greater part of the twelfth century Aragon, Castile, and the smaller Christian kingdoms exhausted themselves in fighting one another and the reconquest momentarily stalled. But in 1212 the powerful Pope Innocent III proclaimed a crusade against the Spanish Moslems, and the king of Castile advanced from Toledo with a powerful pan-Iberian army, winning a decisive victory over the Moors at the battle of Las Navas de Tolosa. Thereafter Moorish power was permanently crippled. Cordova fell to Castile in 1236, and by the later thirteenth century the Moors were confined to the small southern kingdom of Granada where they remained until 1492. Castile now dominated central Spain, and the work of re-Christianization proceeded apace as Christian peasants were imported en masse into the reconquered lands. Aragon, in the meantime, was conquering the islands of the western Mediterranean from the Moslems and establishing a powerful maritime empire.

Thus the High Middle Ages witnessed the Christianization of nearly all the Iberian Peninsula and its organization into two powerful Christian kingdoms and several weaker ones. The long crusade against the Moslems was the chief factor in the molding of Spanish life in the Middle Ages, and its ultimate result was to produce the intense blend of piety and patriotism which inspired the saints, soldiers, and *conquistadores* of Spain's sixteenth-century Golden Age.

SOUTHERN ITALY AND SICILY

Probably the most vigorous and militant force in Europe's eleventh-century awakening was the warrior-aristocracy of Normandy—largely Viking in ancestry but now thoroughly adapted to French culture. These Norman knights, French in tongue, Christian in faith, feudal in social organization, plied their arms across the length and breadth of Europe: in the reconquest of Spain, on the Crusades to the Holy Land, on the battlefields of England and France, and in southern Italy and Sicily. Normandy itself was growing in prosperity and political centralization, and

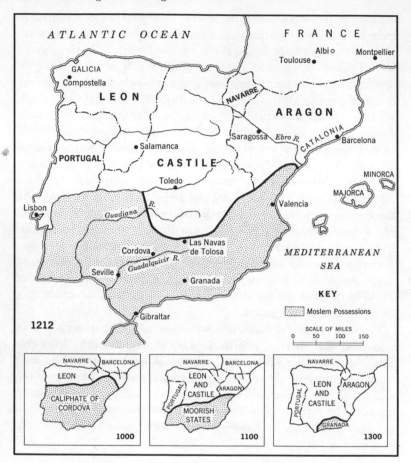

Map XI.   The Christian reconquest of Spain.

an ever-increasing population pressure drove the greedy and ad-
venturous Norman warriors far and wide on distant enterprises.
    Early in the eleventh century the Normans began to try their
luck in the chaotic politics of southern Italy. Here Byzantine
coastal cities—a legacy of Justinian's conquests—struggled with
old Lombard principalities and rising seaport republics such as
Naples and Amalfi. The great offshore island of Sicily was controlled by the Moslems or, rather, it was divided among several

mutually hostile Moslem princes. In short, the area was a tremendous, chaotic melting pot of Islamic, Byzantine, and Western Christian culture, politically unstable, and, from the standpoint of the Normans, enormously promising.

At first hiring themselves out as mercenaries to one side or another, the Norman adventurers quickly began to found states of their own. In the later eleventh century all of southern Italy fell under the control of a ruthless, cunning Norman duke named Robert Guiscard (d. 1085) who organized the district into a hierarchical feudal state of the Norman pattern. A younger brother of Robert Guiscard's conquered Sicily after a long campaign (1060–1091) and established himself as its master. Now the whole area of Sicily and southern Italy was in Norman hands, and in 1130 Robert Guiscard's nephew, Roger the Great (d. 1154), fused it into a single kingdom and became its first king.

Although Roger the Great's new realm embraced both Sicily and southern Italy it was called simply the kingdom of Sicily; it would later be called the kingdom of the Two Sicilies. Roger and his successors ruled strongly but tolerantly over the manifold peoples of the realm with their variety of faiths, customs, and languages. Byzantine, Islamic, Lombard, and Northern French cultural traditions were synthesized, and a highly effective administrative structure was created. The Sicilian capital of Palermo, with its superb harbor and magnificent palace, its impressive public buildings and luxurious villas, was known as the city of the three-fold tongue. Here Islamic, Byzantine, and Western scholars worked under royal patronage, producing invaluable translations of Arabic and Greek texts into Latin and doing important original work of their own. East and West met in Roger the Great's glittering, sun-drenched realm and worked creatively side by side to make the kingdom of Sicily the most sophisticated European state of its day.

THE CRUSADES

The Crusades to the Holy Land were the most spectacular and self-conscious acts of Western Christian expansionism in the High Middle Ages, although by no means the most lasting. They arose in response to a major political crisis in the Near East. A new warlike tribe from Central Asia, the Seljuk Turks, had recently swept into Persia, taken up the Islamic faith, and turned the Abbasid caliphs of Baghdad into their pawns. In 1071 the Seljuk Turks inflicted a nearly fatal blow on the Byzantine Empire, smashing a Byzantine army at the battle of Manzikert and seizing Asia Minor, the essential reservoir of Byzantine manpower. Stories began filtering into the West of Turkish atrocities against Christian pilgrims to Jerusalem, and when the desperate Byzantine emperor swallowed his pride and appealed to the West for help, Europe, under the leadership of a reinvigorated papacy, was only too happy to respond.

The Crusades represented a happy fusion of three characteristic impulses of medieval man—sanctity, pugnacity, and greed. All three were essential. Without Christian idealism the Crusades would be inconceivable; yet the pious dream of liberating Jerusalem and the Holy Land from the infidel was reinforced mightily by the lure of new lands and unimaginable wealth. The Crusades provided a magnificent opportunity to the Christian warrior aristocracy to perform their knightly skills in the service of the Lord—and to make their fortunes in the bargain.

Accordingly, when Pope Urban II summoned the European nobility in 1095 to take up the Cross and reconquer the Holy Land, the response was overwhelming. By 1096 the First Crusade was under way. A great international army—with a large nucleus of feudal knights from France, Normandy, and Norman Sicily—hurled itself into Syria and Palestine. In 1099 Jerusalem itself fell to the Crusaders. The great mission had been accomplished after only three years of vigorous campaigning. A long strip of territory along the eastern Mediterranean shore had been wrested from Islam and was now divided, according to feudal principles, among the Christian knights. The Crusaders consolidated their conquests by erecting elaborate castles whose ruins still excite the admiration of travelers.

The conquered lands were organized into four Crusader States, the most important of which was the kingdom of Jerusalem. The king of Jerusalem was the theoretical overlord of the four states, but he had difficulty enforcing his authority outside his own kingdom. Indeed, the feudal knights who settled in the Holy Land

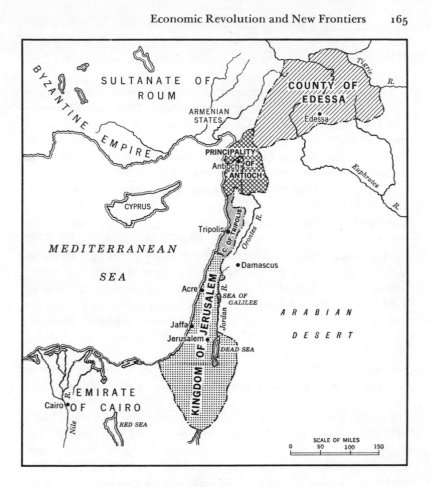

Map XII.   The Crusader states.

were far too proud and warlike for their own good, and the
Crusader States were characterized from the beginning by dangerous rivalries and dissensions.

Gradually, over the years, the Moslems began to reconquer their
lost lands. Jerusalem fell to them in 1187, less than a century
after its capture by the Christians. Europe sent new Crusading
armies eastward, but to no avail. In later years some of Europe's
most illustrious monarch took up the Cross—Richard the Lion-
Hearted of England, Emperor Frederick Barbarossa of Germany,

St. Louis of France—but always in vain. In 1291 the last Christian bridgehead on the Syrian coast fell to the Moslems, and the Crusader States came to an end.

Yet the Crusades were more than simply a splendid failure. For the greater part of the High Middle Ages Christian Crusaders ruled portions of the Holy Land. Their activities caught the imagination of Europe and held it for two centuries. During the Crusading age European merchants established permanent bases in Syria and vastly enlarged their role in inter· ational commerce. As a surprising side-effect of the Crusading movement a considerable portion of the Byzantine empire passed for a time into Western Christian hands. This came about as a consequence of the Fourth Crusade (1201–1204), which, by a curious series of circumstances, was diverted from the Holy Land to Constantinople. The Crusaders took the city by siege in 1204, succeeding where so many before them had failed, and actually established a dynasty of Western emperors in Constantinople which ruled the city for half a century until a Greek dynasty displaced them. In the Latin Empire of Constantinople as well as in the Holy Land, Christian knights broadened their horizons by contacts with other civilizations. The effect of such contacts in dissolving the provincial narrowmindedness of the Western European nobility is incalculable.

Finally, the Crusades gave rise to several semimonastic orders of Christian warriors—for example, the Knights Templars, the Knights Hospitallers, and the Teutonic Knights—which represented the ultimate synthesis of the military and the Christian life. In the thirteenth century the Teutonic Knights transferred their activities from the Holy Land to northern Germany and devoted themselves to the eastward thrust of German-Christian civilization against the heathen Slavs.

THE GERMAN EASTWARD EXPANSION

Eastern Germany was still another of Europe's expanding frontiers. The German expansion eastward was not a product of active royal policy but rather a movement led by enterprising local aristocrats. They succeeded, over a long period running from c. 1125 to c. 1350, in moving the eastern boundary of Germany from the Elbe

River past the Oder to the Vistula at Slavic expense. They consolidated their gains by building innumerable agrarian villages and encouraging a massive eastward migration of German peasants. Consequently, the new areas were not only conquered; they were in large part Christianized and permanently Germanized. As a by-product of the movement, the Slavic kingdom of Poland was converted to Catholic Christianity and incorporated into the fabric of Western Christendom.

The later phases of the German push were spearheaded by the Teutonic Knights who penetrated temporarily far northward into Lithuania, Latvia and Estonia and even made an unsuccessful bid to conquer Byzantine Russia. During the fourteenth and fifteenth centuries the Teutonic Knights were forced to forfeit many of their conquests, but much of the great German expansion proved to be permanent. The epoch between 1125 and 1350 witnessed the conquest and Germanization of what ultimately became the eastern two-fifths of modern Germany.*

In the later thirteenth and early fourteenth centuries the great European expansion was clearly coming to an end. The internal frontiers of forest and swamp had by then been won, and the external frontiers were everywhere hardening, sometimes even receding as in the Holy Land. The closing of the frontiers was accompanied by diminishing prosperity and a drying up of high medieval culture. For the brilliant cultural achievements of the High Middle Ages were products of a buoyant, expanding, frontier society, fired by a powerful faith, driven by immense ambitions, and beguiled by a world in which, so it seemed, anything was possible.

* Prior to World War II.

CHRONOLOGY OF THE EUROPEAN FRONTIER MOVEMENT

Spain	Sicily	Holy Land
1002: Breakup of Caliphate of Cordova	1016: Norman infiltration begins	
	1060–1091: Sicily conquered	
1085: Capture of Toledo	1085: Death of Robert Guiscard	1095: Calling of First Crusade
1140: Aragon unites with Catalonia	1130: Coronation of Roger the Great	1099: Crusaders take Jerusalem
	1154: Death of Roger the Great	
		1187: Crusaders lose Jerusalem
1212: Great Christian victory at Las Navas de Tolosa		1204: Crusaders take Constantinople
1236: Castile takes Cordova		1291: Crusaders driven from Holy Land

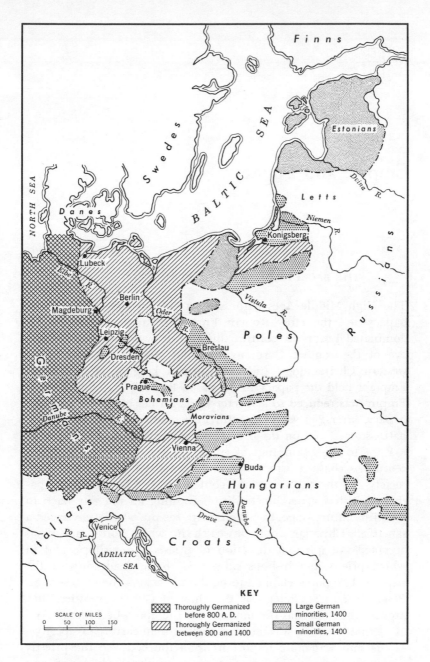

Map XIII.   The German eastward penetration.

12

Empire and Papacy

THE BACKGROUND OF THE STRUGGLE

The High Middle Ages witnessed an epic struggle between the papacy and the Holy Roman Empire—a tragic conflict which dominated European political history for two centuries. On the eve of the conflict Germany had the mightiest monarchy in western Christendom, and the German king or Holy Roman Emperor held the papacy in his palm. By 1300 the Holy Roman Empire was reduced to a specter of its former greatness, and the papacy, after 250 years of political prominence, was exhausted, battle-scarred and on the brink of a prolonged decline.

Prior to the beginnings of papal reform in the mid-eleventh century, a chasm existed between the papal theory of Christian society and the realities of the contemporary Church. The papal theory, with a venerable tradition running all the way back to the fifth-century pope, Leo the Great (see pp. 50–51), envisaged a sanctified Christian commonwealth in which lords and kings accepted the spiritual direction of priests and bishops, and in which priests and bishops submitted to the leadership of the papacy. The popes claimed to be the successors—the *vicars*—of St. Peter. Just as St. Peter was the chief of Christ's apostles, they argued, the pope was the monarch of the apostolic Church. And as eternal salvation was more important than earthly prosperity— as the soul was more important than the body—so the priestly power was greater than the power of secular lords, kings, and emperors. The properly ordered society—the truly Christian society—was a society dominated by the Church, which, in turn, was dominated by the pope. In the intellectual climate of the High Middle Ages this view had great pertinence and caught the imagination of many thoughtful men. It provided the papacy with a dynamic, convincing, almost irresistible intellectual position.

The reality of mid-eleventh-century society was far different. Almost everywhere the Church was under the control of aristocratic lay proprietors. Petty lords appointed their priests; dukes and kings selected their bishops and abbots. As we have seen, the Holy Roman Emperors used churchmen extensively in the administration of Germany. In France, the Church provided warriors from its estates for the feudal armies, clerks for the feudal chanceries, and shrewd political advisers for the feudal princes. The Church played a vital role in the operation of tenth- and early-eleventh-century society but it was always subordinate to the lay ruling class. Its spiritual and sacramental role was compromised by its secular administrative responsibilities. As was bound to happen under such conditions, the Church tended to neglect its sacred mission. From the lay standpoint it was an effective administrative tool, but from the spiritual standpoint it was inadequate and often corrupt. Monasteries all too frequently ignored the strict Benedictine rule. Some priests had concubines, and a great many had wives, despite the canonical requirement of priestly celibacy. Lay lords often sold important ecclesiastical offices to the highest bidder, and the new prelate customarily recouped the expense of buying his office by ruthlessly exploiting his tenants and subordinates. This flourishing commerce in ecclesiastical appointments was known as *simony*. It was regarded by some contemporary reformers as the arch sin of the age.

Ecclesiastical corruption was nowhere more evident than in Rome itself. The papacy of the earlier eleventh century had fallen into the soiled hands of the Roman nobility and had become a prize disputed among the several leading aristocratic families. In 1032 the prize fell to a callow, sensuous young man, Pope Benedict IX, whose outrageous pontificate was scandalous even by contemporary Roman standards. Pope Benedict sold the papacy, then changed his mind and reclaimed it. By 1046 his claim to the papal throne was challenged by two other men, both of whom claimed to be pope. The papacy had disintegrated into a three-way schism.

THE REFORM MOVEMENT

Such were the conditions of the European Church as the mid-eleventh century approached. A Church dominated by lay proprietors had long existed in Europe and had long been accepted. But with the dawning of the High Middle Ages, Western Christendom underwent a momentous upsurge in lay piety which marked the culmination of the long, heroic struggle during the Early Middle Ages for the Christianization of Europe. In an age of deep and widespread spiritual awakening, the comfortable Church-state relationship of the previous epoch seemed profoundly wrong to many sensitive spirits. Some took up a saintly hermit life; others flocked into new, austere monastic orders. And still others set about on the onerous task of reforming the Church and the world. A powerful reform movement began to make itself felt across the length and breadth of Christendom.

In general, the reformers fell into two groups: (1) a conservative group which sought to eliminate simony, enforce clerical celibacy, and improve the moral calibre of churchmen, but without challenging the Church's traditional subordination to the lay aristocracy—a subordination which had been sweetened by countless generous gifts of lands and powers to submissive prelates; (2) a radical group which sought to demolish the tradition of lay control and to rebuild society on the pattern of the papal monarchy theory. The radical reformers dreamed of an ideal Christian commonwealth in which laymen no longer appointed churchmen—in which kings deferred to bishops and a reformed papacy ruled the Church. The conservative reformers endeavored to heal society; the radicals wished to overturn it.

One of the chief centers of conservative reform in the eleventh century was the Burgundian abbey of Cluny, a great Benedictine monastery which had been an island of spiritual rectitude ever since its foundation in 910. Departing from the earlier Benedictine tradition of individual autonomy, Cluny became the nucleus of a great congregation of monasteries extending throughout Christendom—a mother house with hundreds of daughter houses, all of them obedient to the abbot of Cluny. The Cluniac spiritual life was pure but not puritanical. Without going to ascetic extremes Cluny set a high standard of Christian morality for its day, inspiring other monasteries to join its congregation, and attracting rich bequests from the lay aristocracy. In the mid-eleventh century the congregation of Cluny was both powerful and wealthy. Its high ideals were tempered by a sense of dignity—and perhaps also by a comfortable feeling of spiritual success and social acceptance. Cluny energized the European movement toward reform but accepted the lay-dominated social order.

Conservative reform was also espoused by several of the more enlightened rulers of the age, among them, Emperor Henry III, the powerful Salian monarch of Germany. Shocked by the scandalous antics of Pope Benedict IX and the three-way tug-of-war for the papal throne, Henry intervened in Italy in 1046, arranged the deposition of Benedict and his two rivals, and drastically improved the quality of papal leadership by appointing a series of able reform popes. These energetic imperial appointees carried on a vigorous campaign against simony and clerical marriage, traveling far and wide across Europe, holding synods, and deposing guilty churchmen. Empire and papacy worked hand in hand to raise the moral level of the European Church.

But however successful this reform movement might have been, there were those who felt that it was not going far enough. The real evil, they believed, was lay supremacy over the Church, and Henry III's domination of the papacy, however well intentioned, was the supreme illustration of a profound social sin. These radical reformers had their opportunity when Henry III died prematurely in 1056, leaving behind him an infant son and a weak queen-regent. By then many of the cardinals—the chief administrators of the Roman Church—had become captivated by the radical reform ideology and, above all, by the notion of a papacy free of both imperial and Roman aristocratic control. At the death of Henry III's last papal appointee in 1057, the cardinals began electing reform popes on their own. In 1059 they issued a daring and momentous declaration of independence known as the *Papal Election Decree,* which stated that thenceforth emperors and Roman laymen would merely give formal approval to the candidate whom the cardinals elected. In the years that followed, this revolutionary

Model after drawings by Professor K. J. Conant; Photograph courtesy of J. Combier.

Plate VI. Model of the Abbey Church at Cluny showing the form of the apse which is basic to the Romanesque style.

proclamation was challenged by both the empire and the Roman aristocracy, but in the end the cardinals won out. The papacy had been wrested free of lay control. The first step toward papal monarchy had been taken.

THE INVESTITURE CONTROVERSY

The next step was infinitely more difficult. It involved nothing less than the annihilation of lay control over the entire Church. At a time when the Church possessed untold wealth, including perhaps a third of the land in Europe, the total realization of such a goal would cripple secular power and revolutionize European society. Yet only by its realization, so the radical reformers believed, could a true Christian commonwealth be achieved.

The immense struggle over lay appointments broke out in earnest in 1075 when Gregory VII (1073–1085), the greatest of the reform popes, issued a proclamation banning lay investiture. Traditionally, a newly chosen bishop or abbot was invested by a lay lord with a ring and a pastoral staff, symbolic of his marriage to the Church and his duty toward his Christian flock. Pope Gregory VII attacked this custom of lay investiture as the crucial symbol of lay authority over churchmen. Its prohibition was a grave threat to every ruler in Christendom but especially to the Holy Roman Emperor, whose administrative system depended on his control of the German Church. By Gregory VII's time, Henry III's infant son, Henry IV, had grown to vigorous manhood and was showing promise of being as strong a ruler as his father. Refusing to accept the decree against lay investiture, Henry IV sent a flaming letter of defiance to Gregory VII. The pope responded with a startling and unprecedented exercise of spiritual authority: he excommunicated and deposed Henry IV. In so doing, he was repudiating the traditional concept of sacred, divinely commissioned kingship. The king, in Gregory's view, was in no sense God's earthly vicar; he was a purely secular figure, charged with keeping order in the Christian society. It was for the pope, the supreme spiritual monarch of Christendom, to judge whether or not the king was fit to rule. Gregory's actions were nothing less than revolutionary, for in banning lay investiture and deposing the king of Germany he was putting into practice the papal theory in its most radical form and striking at the very bedrock of the established order.

Gregory's deposition of Henry IV shook Germany to its foundations and unleashed a powerful aristocratic reaction that had long been building up against the centralizing policies of the Salian dynasty. Many Germans, churchmen and laymen alike, refused to serve an excommunicated sovereign. The great aristocrats took the revolutionary step of threatening to elect a new king in Henry's place, thereby challenging the ingrained German tradition of hereditary kingship with the fateful counter-doctrine of elective monarchy.

Desperate to keep his throne, Henry IV crossed into Italy to seek the pope's forgiveness. In January, 1077, at the castle of Canossa in Tuscany, the two men met in what was perhaps medieval history's most dramatic encounter—Henry IV barefoot and humble, clothed in rough, penitential garments, Gregory VII torn between his conviction that Henry's change of heart was insincere and opportunistic, and his priestly duty to forgive a repentant sinner. Finally, Pope Gregory lifted Henry's excommunication, and the monarch, promising to amend his ways, returned to Germany to rebuild his authority.

Down through the centuries Canossa has symbolized the ultimate royal degradation before the power of the Church. Perhaps it was. But in the immediate political context it was a victory—and a much-needed one—for Henry IV. It did not prevent a group of German nobles from electing a rival king; it did not restore the powerful centralized monarchy of Henry III; but it did save Henry IV's throne. Restored to communion, he was able to rally support, to check for a time the forces of princely particularism, and to defeat the rival king. As his power waxed, however, he ignored his promises at Canossa and continued to support lay investiture. In 1080 Gregory VII excommunicated the defiant king a second time, only to find that this potent spiritual weapon was losing its strength through overuse. In the early 1080s Henry IV returned to Italy, this time with an army at his back. In the confusion that followed, Gregory VII was forced to flee Rome and seek refuge among the Normans in southern Italy. In 1085 Gregory died, consumed by bitterness and a conviction of failure. His last words were these: "I have loved justice and hated iniquity; therefore I die in exile."

Although Gregory VII failed to transform Europe into what he conceived to be a proper Christian society, his theory of papal monarchy retained its potency. The reform papacy soon fell into the able hands of Urban II (1088–99), a former prior of Cluny, who seized the moral leadership of Europe by calling the First Crusade. Urban II and his successors made life miserable for the unlucky Henry IV, stirring up rebellions in Germany and eroding the power of the imperial government. In 1106 Henry IV died as unhappily as had Gregory VII. In the end, Henry's own son and heir, Henry V, led an army of hostile aristocrats against his father. As Henry IV died, the German Empire seemed to be collapsing in ruins around him.

Henry V (1106–1125) enjoyed a happier reign than his father's, but only because he forsook his father's struggle to recover the fullness of imperial power as it had existed in the mid-eleventh century. The independence-minded aristocracy consolidated the gains it had made during the preceding era of chaos, and Henry V could do nothing about it.

Toward the end of his reign, Henry V worked out a compromise settlement with the Church which brought the Investiture Controversy to an end at last. Already the Controversy had been settled by compromise in England and France, where the Church-state struggle had been considerably less bitter than in Germany. As time progressed both papacy and Empire tended to withdraw somewhat from the extreme positions they had taken during Gregory VII's pontificate. At length they reconciled their differences in the Concordat of Worms of 1122. Henry V agreed that the investiture ceremony would no longer be performed by laymen, but the pope conceded to the emperor the important privilege of bestowing on the new prelate the symbols of his *territorial* and *administrative* jurisdiction. Bishops and abbots were thenceforth to be elected according to the principles of canon law, by the monks of a monastery or the canons of a cathedral, but the emperor had the right to be present at such elections and to make the final decision in the event of a dispute. These reservations enabled the emperor to retain a considerable degree of *de facto* control over the appointment of important German churchmen. The reconciliation of royal control and canonical election is illustrated in a delightful twelfth-century charter of King Henry II of England to the monks at Winchester: "I order you to hold a free election, but nevertheless I forbid you to elect anyone except Richard, my clerk, the archdeacon of Poitiers."

There was no real victor in the Investiture Controversy. The Church had won its point—lay investiture was banned—but monarchs still exercised very real control over their churches. The theory of papal monarchy over a reconstituted Christian society remained unrealized.

Still, the papal-imperial balance of power had changed radically since the mid-eleventh century. The papacy was now a mighty force in Europe, and the power of the emperor had declined sharply. During the chaotic half-century between the onset of the Investiture Controversy in 1075 and Henry V's death in 1125, feudalism came to Germany. In these decades of civil strife a powerful new aristocracy emerged. Ambitious landowners rose to great power, built castles, extended their estates, and usurped royal rights. They forced minor neighboring noblemen to become their vassals and, in some instances, forced free peasants to become their serfs. The monarchy was helpless to curb this ominous process of fragmentation.

In northern Italy the emperors had traditionally exercised their power through the pro-imperial Lombard bishops, who possessed wide jurisdictional rights over their cities and the surrounding countryside. In the anarchy wrought by the papal-imperial struggle, the pious and fiercely independent inhabitants of the rising commercial cities on the Lombard Plain took up the cause of papal reform, rebelled against episcopal and imperial control, and established quasi-independent communes or city states. By 1125 they had broken the power of the Lombard bishops and had reduced imperial control to little more than a formality. Lombardy had become a region of free urban communes.

In Germany and Italy alike, imperial power was receding before the whirlwind of local particularism, invigorated by the soaring popular piety of the age. Long before the Concordat of Worms, the downfall of the medieval empire had begun.

THE AGE OF FREDERICK BARBAROSSA (1152–1190)

The Salian dynasty died out with the passing of Henry V in 1125. During the next quarter century Germany reaped the bitter harvest of princely particularism. The great nobles ignored the principle of hereditary royal succession and reverted to the elective principle which they had asserted at the time of Canossa. Their choice always fell to a man of royal blood but never to the most direct heir. In the turbulent decades between 1125 and 1152 a great rivalry developed between two powerful families which had risen to power in the anarchic era of the Investiture Controversy: the Welfs of Saxony and the Hohenstaufens of Swabia. In 1152 the princes elected as king a powerful and talented Hohenstaufen, Frederick Barbarossa (the Red-Bearded), duke of Swabia, who took as his mission the revival and reconstruction of the German monarchy.

Emperor Frederick Barbarossa recognized fully that the mighty imperial structure of Henry III was beyond recovery. His goal was to harness the new feudal forces of his age to the royal advantage. He actually encouraged the great princes of the realm to expand their power and privileges at the expense of the lesser lords, but at the same time he forced them to recognize his own feudal lordship over all the kingdom. In other words, he succeeded in establishing the leading feudal magnates as his vassals—his tenants-in-chief. He was the supreme overlord at the apex of the feudal pyramid.

But as the sorry state of the early French monarchy well illustrates, feudal overlordship was an ephemeral thing if the royal overlord lacked the power and resources to support his position. Frederick Barbarossa, therefore, set about to increase his revenues and extend the territories under his direct authority. A strong feudal monarchy required a substantial territorial core under exclusive royal control—an extensive royal demesne to act as a counterweight to the great fiefs of the chief vassals of the realm. Frederick enlarged his demesne territories, most of which were concentrated in Swabia, by bringing many of the new monasteries and rising towns under imperial jurisdiction. The crux of his imaginative policy was the establishment of imperial authority over the wealthy cities of Lombardy. With Lombardy under his control and its revenues pouring into the imperial treasury, no German lord could challenge him.

Barbarossa's Lombard policy earned him the hostility of the papacy, which had always feared the consolidation of imperial power in Italy. Indeed, at one point the papacy evoked the ghost of Gregory VII by excommunicating and deposing the emperor. And the papacy had dedicated allies in the intensely independent Lombard cities which were determined to give up as little of their wealth and autonomy as they possibly could. Goaded by Barbarossa's pressure and encouraged by the papacy, these cities formed an association called the Lombard League and organized a powerful interurban army to oppose the Holy Roman Empire. A long, bitter struggle involving Barbarossa, the papacy, and the Lombard League ended in the total victory of the Lombard army at the battle of Legnano in 1176. Barbarossa submitted as graciously as he could, granting *de facto* independence to the Lombard cities in return for their admission of a vague imperial overlordship. Pope and emperor tearfully embraced, and Barbarossa promised thereafter to be a dutiful son of the Roman See.

Barbarossa had lost a battle, but he had by no means lost the war. Leaving Lombardy severely alone, he shifted his operations southward to Tuscany, establishing administrative control over this rich province immediately to the north of the Papal States. At the same time he arranged a fateful marriage between his son and the future heiress of the Norman kingdom of southern Italy and Sicily—a marriage which ultimately brought that opulent kingdom within the imperial fold. The papacy had been outwitted and was in grave danger of being encircled and stifled by the empire. In 1180 Barbarossa consolidated his power in Germany by crushing the greatest and most hostile of his vassals, the Welf duke of Saxony. The farsighted emperor was at the height of his power in 1190 when he died while leading his army toward the Holy Land to participate in the Third Crusade.

Barbarossa had taken pains to circumvent the princely policy of elective monarchy by forcing the princes, prior to his death, to elect his son, Henry VI. In 1190 Henry VI succeeded to the German throne without difficulty, and in 1194 he made good his claim to the Kingdom of Sicily. The Papal States were now an island completely surrounded by the Holy Roman Empire, and the papacy was powerless to alter the situation. The bounteous revenues of southern Italy and Sicily fattened the imperial purse. The territories under imperial rule had never been so extensive.

But for an age in which the emperor had to remain ever vigilant against the centrifugal forces of local particularism and, above all,

Map XIV.   The Holy Roman Empire in 1190.

against the boundless ambitions of the great German vassals, the imperial frontiers had become dangerously overextended. It remained ominously uncertain whether a single man could rule Italy and Germany concurrently. Whether Henry VI could have accomplished this task we shall never know, for he died prematurely in 1197 leaving as his heir his infant son, Frederick II. The problems the empire faced in 1197 would have taxed the ablest of leaders, yet at this crucial moment imperial leadership failed. The papacy had its opportunity at last.

THE HIGH NOON OF THE MEDIEVAL PAPACY

During the twelfth century, the papacy lost much of its former zealous reform spirit as it evolved into a huge, complex administrative institution. Revenues flowed into its treasury from all the states of Western Christendom; bishops traveled vast distances to make their spiritual submission to the Roman pontiff; the papal curia served as a court of last appeal for an immense network of ecclesiastical courts. Papal authority over the European Church had increased immeasurably since the mid-eleventh century. As the dream of a papal monarchy came ever-nearer to realization, the traditional theory of papal supremacy over Christian society was magnified and elaborated by a new class of canon lawyers, products of the momentous upsurge of scholarship and rationalism. These subtle ecclesiastical scholars pored over ancient canons and customs to find new arguments in support of the papal cause. Whereas many of the eleventh-century reform popes had been monks, the greatest popes of the later twelfth and thirteenth centuries were canon lawyers.

The greatest of these lawyer-popes, Innocent III (1198–1216), came to power in the year following Emperor Henry VI's death. It was he who seized the opportunity offered by the succession of an infant to the throne of the overextended empire. Innocent III was history's most powerful pope—a brilliant, astute diplomat, an imperious, self-confidant aristocrat, genuinely pious yet distinctly aloof from the surging religious emotionalism of the humbler folk of his age. Animated by the theory of papal monarchy in its most uncompromising form, he forced his will on the great monarchs of

Christendom, playing off one king against another with consummate skill. A long struggle with King John of England over the appointment of an archbishop of Canterbury ended with John's complete submission and recognition of papal lordship over England. Innocent suspended all church services in France and excommunicated the French king in order to make him repudiate an uncanonical second marriage. He summoned a new Crusade against the Holy Land and also called Crusades against the Spanish Moors and against a powerful group of heretics in Southern France known as the Albigensians (see p. 221). In short, he exercised a moral sway over Christendom that no pope before or since has ever approached.

Germany, during Innocent III's pontificate, was torn by a bitter struggle for the throne between the Welf and the Hohenstaufen families. Innocent III supported first one rival, then the other, and at length settled on the child Hohenstaufen heir, Frederick II. Innocent wrung many promises from Frederick, making him swear to sever the kingdom of Sicily from the empire, to go on a Crusade, to follow the spiritual direction of the papacy. Yet no sooner had Innocent died than Frederick II, now a grown man, made it clear that he would ignore papal advice and would rule as he pleased. In choosing Frederick II, Innocent III had made a fearful miscalculation.

FREDERICK II (1211–1250)

Frederick II, whose Sicilian childhood exposed him to several faiths, grew up to be a brilliant, anticlerical skeptic, more concerned with his harem and his exotic menagerie than with the salvation of his soul. He dazzled his contemporaries and earned the name *Stupor Mundi*, the "Wonder of the World." His dream of unifying all Italy and making it the nucleus of the empire won him the undying hatred of the papacy. Indeed, some churchmen regarded Frederick quite literally as the incarnate Antichrist.

Frederick II was a talented, many-sided man—perhaps the most flamboyant product of an intensely creative age. He was a writer of considerable skill and an amateur scientist, curious about the world around him, but in some matters deeply superstitious. After much delay he kept his promise to lead a Crusade (1228), but instead of fighting the Moslems he negotiated with them, and did so with such success that Jerusalem itself came into his hands for a time. The amicable spirit of Frederick's Crusade against the infidel struck many churchmen as unholy, and its success infuriated them. That this irreverent skeptic should win the crown of Jerusalem was almost more than they could stand.

Frederick II ruled his kingdom of Sicily in the autocratic but enlightened manner of a Renaissance despot, establishing a uniform legal code, tightening and broadening the centralized system of his Norman-Sicilian predecessors, encouraging agriculture, industry and commerce, abolishing interior tariffs and tolls, and founding a great university at Naples. He had promised Innocent III that he would cut Sicily off from his empire, but he made no effort to keep the promise. He had always preferred his urbane, sunny Sicilian homeland to the cold forests and gloomy castles of Germany. Although he tried to follow Frederick Barbarossa's policy of strengthening the royal demesne and enforcing the feudal obligations of his great German vassals, he did so half-heartedly. To him, Germany was important chiefly as a source of money and military strength with which to carry out his policy of bringing all Italy under his rule.

As it happened, this policy proved disastrous. Frederick's aggressions in Italy evoked the opposition of a revived Lombard League and the implacable hostility of the papacy. He gave up lands and royal rights in Germany with an almost careless abandon in order to keep the peace with the German princes and win their support for his persistent but inconclusive Italian campaigns. In the end, he was even obliged to tax his beloved Sicily to the point of impoverishment in order to support his endless wars. In 1245 the pope presided over a universal council of the Church at Lyons which condemned and excommunicated Frederick II. The emperor was deposed, a rival emperor was elected in his place, and a Crusade was called to rid the empire of its ungodly tyrant. Revolts now broke out against Frederick throughout his empire. The royal estates in Germany slipped more and more from his grasp, and his Italian holdings were ridden with rebellion. Against this unhappy background Frederick II died in 1250.

THE FAILURE OF THE MEDIEVAL EMPIRE

In a very real sense, the hopes of the medieval empire died with Frederick II. His son succeeded him in Germany but died after a brief and unsuccessful reign. For the next nineteen years Germany endured a crippling Interregnum (1254–1273) during which no recognized emperor held the throne. In 1273 a vastly weakened Holy Roman Empire re-emerged with papal blessing under Rudolph of Hapsburg, the first emperor of a family that was destined to play a crucial role in modern European history. Rudolph attempted to rebuild the shattered royal demesne and shore up the foundations of imperial rule, but it was much too late. The monarchy's one hope had been to strengthen and extend the crown lands, gradually transforming them into the nucleus of a modern state. This was the policy on which the medieval French monarchy had risen to a position of dominance in France; it was a policy that Frederick Barbarossa had pursued so promisingly in Germany. But it was a policy that aroused the unremitting opposition of the great princes, who had no desire to see their own rights and territories eaten away by royal expansion. On the contrary, they longed to extend their own principalities at the expense of the crown.

The civil strife during Innocent III's pontificate, the Italian involvements of Frederick II, and the Interregnum of 1254–1273 gave the princes their opportunity, and by 1273 the crown lands were hopelessly shrunken and disorganized. Germany was now drifting irreversibly toward the loose confederation of principalities and the anemic elective monarchy which characterized its constitutional structure from the fourteenth to the later nineteenth century. The tragic failure of the medieval empire doomed Germany to six-hundred years of agonizing disunity—a bitter heritage which may well have contributed to her catastrophic career in the twentieth century.

Italy, too, emerged from the struggles of the High Middle Ages hopelessly divided. During the Interregnum the papacy succeeded in permanently severing the kingdom of Sicily from the empire. In later years southern Italy and Sicily became a battleground for the conflicting claims of French and Spanish dynasties. Once the most prosperous and enlightened region of Italy, Sicily became backward, pauperized and divided. .Northern Italy was now a chaos of totally independent warring city states—Florence, Siena, Venice, Milan, and many others—whose rivalries would form the backdrop for the Italian Renaissance.

THE PAPACY AFTER INNOCENT III

To judge by the disintegration of the Holy Roman Empire in the thirteenth century, one would conclude that the papacy had won an overwhelming victory. But the victory was an empty one. For ultimately the strength of the medieval papacy depended on its prestige as a spiritual force; as popes like Innocent III became increasingly involved in power politics their spiritual role was more and more obscured. In the thirteenth century the papacy's international religious mission was being steadily subordinated to its local political interests. It was winning its battles but slowly, almost imperceptibly, losing its hold on the heart of Europe. Papal excommunication, after several centuries of overuse—often for political purposes—was no longer the terrifying weapon it once had been. To call a Crusade against Frederick II was doubtless an effective means of harassing that troublesome emperor, but the crusading ideal was debased in the process. The time would come when a pope would call a Crusade and nobody would answer.

As the papacy became a great political power and a big business, it found itself in need of ever-increasing revenues. By the end of the thirteenth century the papal tax system was admirably efficient, with the result that the papacy acquired an unsavory reputation for boundless greed. As one contemporary observer complained, the supreme pastor of Christendom was supposed to lead Christ's flock but not to fleece it. Ironically, the fiscal and political cast of the later medieval papacy came as a direct consequence of its earlier dream of becoming the spiritual dynamo of a reformed Christendom. Rising to prominence in the eleventh century on the floodtide of the new popular piety, the papacy became in the twelfth and thirteenth centuries increasingly insensitive to the deep spiritual aspirations of European Christians as it became more and more absorbed in the complex problems of political power.

The papacy humbled the empire only to be humbled itself by
the rising power of the new centralized monarchies of northern
Europe. By the end of the thirteenth century a new concept of
royal sovereignty was in the air. The kings of England and France
were finding it increasingly difficult to tolerate the existence of a
semi-independent, highly privileged, internationally controlled
Church within their realms. By endeavoring to bring these ecclesiastical "states within states" under royal control, the two monarchies encountered vigorous papal opposition. The issue of papal
versus royal control of the Church was an old one, but the ancient
controversy now took on a new form. The growing monarchies of
the late thirteenth century found themselves increasingly in need
of money. This was particularly true after 1294 when England and
France became locked in a series of costly wars. Both monarchies
adopted the novel policy of systematically taxing the clergy of
their realms, and Pope Boniface VIII (1294–1303) retaliated in
1296 with a papal bull that expressly forbade this practice. Once
again, Church and state were at an impasse.

Boniface VIII was another lawyer-pope—a man of ability but
not of genius—proud and intransigent, with a vision of absolute
papal power that transcended even the notions of Innocent III but
a fatal blindness to the momentous implications of the new centralized monarchies of late-thirteenth-century Europe. His great
weakness was his inability to bend his stupendous concepts of
papal authority to the hard realities of contemporary European
politics.

In King Philip the Fair* of France (1285–1314), Boniface had a
powerful and ruthless antagonist. Philip ignored the papal bull
prohibiting clerical taxation; he set his agents to work spreading
scandalous rumors about the pope's morals, and exerted serious
financial pressure on Rome by cutting off all papal taxes from his
French realm. Boniface VIII was obliged to submit for the moment, and Philip taxed his clergy unopposed. But a vast influx of
pilgrims into Rome in the Jubilee year of 1300 restored the pope's
confidence. He withdrew his concession to Philip the Fair on clerical taxation and in 1302 issued the famous bull *Unam Sanctam*
which asserted the doctrine of papal monarchy in uncompromis-

* Fair in the sense of "handsome." See pp. 209 ff.

ing terms: " . . . we declare, announce, affirm, and define that for
every human creature, to be subject to the Roman pontiff is absolutely necessary for salvation." Philip the Fair now summoned an
assembly of the realm and accused Pope Boniface of every imaginable crime from murder to black magic. A small French military
expedition crossed into Italy in 1303 and took Pope Boniface
prisoner at his palace at Anagni with the intention of bringing
him to France for trial. Anagni, the antithesis of Canossa, symbolized the humiliation of the medieval papacy. The French plan
failed—Boniface was freed by local townsmen a few days after his
capture—but the proud old pope died shortly thereafter, outraged
and chagrined that armed Frenchmen should have dared to lay
hands on his person.

The great age of the medieval papacy was now at an end. In
1305 the cardinals elected the Frenchman Clement V (1305–1314),
who pursued a policy of timid subservience to the French throne.
Clement V submitted on the question of clerical taxation, repudiated *Unam Sanctam,* and took the disastrous step of abandoning
faction-ridden Rome for a new papal capital at Avignon on the
Rhone. Here the popes remained for the better part of the fourteenth century, under the shadow of the French monarchy, their
independence dangerously compromised and their spiritual prestige plunging.

It is easy to criticize the inflexibility of a Boniface VIII or the
limpness of a Clement V, but the momentous papal collapse at
the close of the High Middle Ages did not result primarily from
their personal shortcomings. Rather it stemmed from an ever-
widening gulf between papal government and the spiritual hunger
of ordinary Christians, combined with the hostility to Catholic
internationalism on the part of increasingly powerful centralized
states. It would be grossly unfair to describe the high medieval
papacy as "corrupt." Between 1050 and 1300 men of good intentions and high purposes sat on the papal throne. Not satisfied
merely to chide the society of their day by innocuous moralizing
from the sidelines, they plunged bodily into the world and struggled vigorously to transform and sanctify it. Tragically, perhaps
inevitably, they soiled their hands.

CHRONOLOGY OF THE PAPAL-IMPERIAL CONFLICT

1039–1056: Reign of Henry III
1046:   Henry III deposes 3 rival popes, inaugurates papal reform movement
1056–1106: Reign of Henry IV
1059:   Papal Election Decree
1073–1085: Pontificate of Gregory VII
1075:   Gregory VII bans lay investiture
1076:   Gregory VII excommunicates and deposes Henry IV
1077:   Henry IV humbles himself at Canossa
1080:   Second excommunication of Henry IV
1088–1099: Pontificate of Urban II
1106–1125: Reign of Henry V
1122:   Concordat of Worms
1152–1190: Reign of Frederick Barbarossa
1176:   Lombards defeat Frederick at Legnano
1180:   Frederick defeats duke of Saxony
1190–1197: Reign of Henry VI
1194:   Henry VI becomes king of Sicily
1198–1216: Pontificate of Innocent III
1211–1250: Reign of Frederick II
1245:   Council of Lyons
1254–1273: Interregnum
1273–1291: Reign of Rudolf of Hapsburg
1294–1303: Pontificate of Boniface VIII
1285–1314: Reign of Philip the Fair of France
1302:   Boniface VIII issues *Unam Sanctam*
1303:   Boniface VIII humiliated at Anagni
1305–1314: Pontificate of Clement V. Papacy moves to Avignon

13

England and France

THE ANGLO-NORMAN MONARCHY

While empire and papacy were engaged in their struggle, France and England were evolving into centralized states. Strong monarchy came earlier to England than to France; yet it was the English who were most successful in imposing constitutional limitations on the crown. French royal absolutism and English parliamentary monarchy are both rooted in the High Middle Ages.

The Anglo-Saxon period of English history came to an end when Duke William of Normandy won the English crown with his victory at Hastings in 1066. In the centuries that followed, England was more closely tied to the Continent than before; her rulers were at once kings of England and great feudal vassals of the kings of France. England's involvement in France continued from 1066 until the mid-sixteenth century. It was a source of cultural enrichment to the English, but it also led to centuries of hostilities between the two monarchies.

William the Conqueror brought a number of fundamental changes to his new kingdom. He divided much of the conquered land among the leading warriors of his victorious army, thereby introducing into England a new, knightly, French-speaking aristocracy. He established a feudal regime in England more-or-less on the Norman pattern by transforming most English estates, both lay and ecclesiastical, into fiefs, held by crown vassals in return for a specified number of mounted knights and various other feudal services. The crown vassals or tenants-in-chief, in order to raise the numerous knights required by the monarchy, subdivided portions of their fiefs into smaller fiefs and granted them to knightly subvassals. In other words, the process of subinfeudation proceeded in much the way that it had centuries earlier on the Continent. As a natural by-product of the establishment of feudalism in England, scores of castles were hastily erected across the land.

But feudalism in England was not accompanied by political disintegration as it had been in Carolingian Frankland. The Norman kings of England were careful to reserve vast stretches of land for their own demesne and to keep their vassals under tight rein. Indeed, under William the Conqueror and his energetic successors, royal centralization—which had progressed far under the Anglo-Saxon kings—was significantly accelerated. William had come to England not as a mere aggressor but as a legitimate claimant to the throne, related (distantly) to the Anglo-Saxon royal family and designated—so he claimed—by King Edward the Confessor, who had died childless early in 1066.

Taking up the role of Edward the Confessor's rightful successor, William promised to preserve the laws and customs of Edward's day. Indeed, it was only natural that he should do so, for many of these customs were highly beneficial to the monarchy. The danegeld, for example, had evolved into a unique and highly lucrative royal land tax. Good Anglo-Saxon that he was, King William faithfully preserved it, although he did not hesitate to augment it with various new feudal dues imposed on his tenants-in-chief. The Anglo-Saxon custom of general allegiance to the crown was even more valuable to the Norman kings than the danegeld. It enabled them to demand oaths of loyalty from every vassal and subvassal in the English feudal hierarchy. A knight's allegiance to his lord was now secondary to his direct allegiance to the crown. Private war between vassals was prohibited, and private castles could be built only by royal license. In brief, the new institution of feudalism was molded by the powerful Anglo-Saxon tradition of royal supremacy into something far more centralized—far less centrifugal—than the feudalism of the Continent.

On the Conqueror's death, his kingdom passed in turn to his two sons, William II (1087–1100) and Henry I (1100–1135). Both were strong, ruthless men, but Henry I was the abler of the two. A skillful general and brilliant legal and administrative innovator, Henry I rid England of rebellion and exploited the growing prosperity of his day by a policy of severe taxation. He was not a kindly man, but his was an age in which firmness and military skill were the chief requisites to successful rule and excessive geniality was a grave weakness. His great service to his English subjects was his pitiless enforcement of the peace.

The reigns of William the Conqueror and his sons witnessed a significant growth in royal administrative institutions. The unique survey of land holdings known as Domesday Book—the product of a comprehensive census of the realm undertaken by royal order in 1086—testifies eloquently to the administrative vigor of William the Conqueror. Between 1066 and 1135 royal administration became steadily more elaborate and efficient. By Henry I's reign, royal justices were traveling around England, hearing cases in the various counties, and thereby extending the king's jurisdiction far and wide across the land. The baronial courts and the ancient folk courts of the counties and local districts continued to function. But the extension of royal jurisdiction under Henry I was the initial step in a long and profoundly significant process whereby folk justice and baronial justice were overshadowed and finally superseded by the king's justice.

Administrative efficiency and royal centralization were the keynotes of Henry I's reign. Royal dues were collected systematically by local noblemen in the king's service—the sheriffs—who passed the money on to a remarkably effective accounting agency known as the Exchequer. A powerful royal bureaucracy was gradually coming into being. The growing efficiency of the Exchequer and the expansion of royal justice were both motivated chiefly by the king's desire for larger revenues. For the more cases the royal justices handled, the more fines went into the royal coffers; the more closely the sheriffs were supervised, the less likely it was that royal taxes would stick to their fingers. The Norman kings discovered that strong government was good business.

HENRY II (1154-1189)

Henry I's death in 1135 was followed by a period of unrest and a disputed royal succession. He was survived by a daughter, Matilda, who was wed to Geoffrey Plantagenet, count of Anjou. Henry I had arranged the marriage with the hope of healing the bitter rivalry between the two great powers of northern France: Normandy and Anjou. Shortly before Henry I's death, his daughter Matilda bore him a grandson, Henry Plantagenet, who was destined ultimately to inherit a vast territory including Anjou, Normandy, and England. But when the old king died, his grandson was still an infant, and the English crown was seized by Henry I's nephew, Stephen of Blois (King of England 1135-1154). For two turbulent decades Stephen and Matilda struggled for control of England while the English barons, often playing one side against the other, threw up unlicensed castles and usurped royal rights. English churchmen and commoners, tormented by the endemic warfare of the period, looked back longingly toward the peaceful days of Henry I.

During Stephen's troubled reign Henry Plantagenet grew to vigorous manhood and established control over Anjou and Normandy. A marriage with Eleanor of Aquitaine, the heiress of that large, heterogeneous southern duchy, extended still further the territories under his jurisdiction. And at King Stephen's death in 1154 Henry peacefully acquired the English throne and became King Henry II of England. He now held sway over an immense constellation of territories north and south of the English Channel which has been called the Angevin Empire. It was not an integrated realm but rather a medley of individual states held together only by their subordination to a single man. On the map, the Angevin Empire dwarfs the modest territory controlled by the King of France. But Henry II and his sons who succeeded him had difficulty in keeping order throughout their vast, diverse territories. The Angevin Empire was doubtless a source of power and prestige to the English monarchy, but it was also a grave burden.

Henry II was an energetic, brilliant man—short, burly, and red-headed. Named after his grandfather, he ruled in Henry I's imperious tradition and consciously imitated him. In many re-

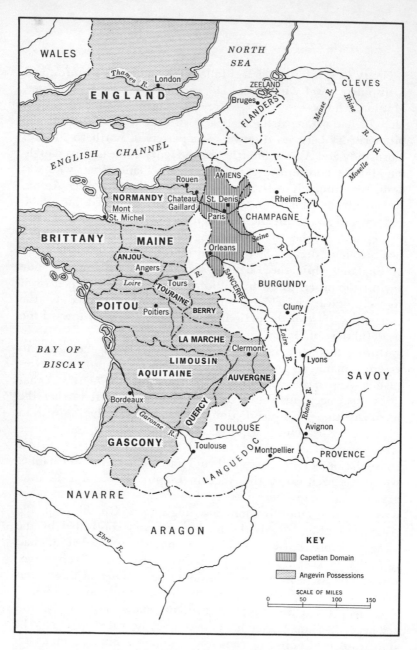

Map XV.   The Angevin Empire in 1154.

spects he was a creature of his age—a product of the great intellectual and cultural outburst of twelfth-century Europe. He was a
literate monarch who consorted with scholars, promoted the growing towns, and presided over an age of economic boom. A chaos of
feverish activity pervaded his court, which was constantly on the
move and, in the opinion of one contemporary observer, "a perfect
portrait of Hell."

Henry II's goals were the preservation of the Angevin Empire,
the strengthening of royal power, and the increasing of his revenues. During his thirty-five year reign the royal administration
grew steadily in complexity and effectiveness. The illegal baronial
castles of Stephen's reign were destroyed, and traditional royal
privileges were recovered and expanded. More and more, the older
feudal relationship of service in return for land gave way, under
the pressure of royal ambition and a growing money economy, to
wage service. The Exchequer grew, the sheriffs were kept under
strict royal control, separate administrative departments evolved,
and public records became fuller and more extensive. Many Englishmen were delighted at the return of peace and order; others
were uneasy over the steady rise of "Big Government."

Henry II has been called the father of English common law.
Like his predecessors, he favored the extension of royal jurisdiction chiefly for its financial rewards to the crown, and in his quest
for ever-greater judicial revenues he was able to push the powers
of the royal courts far beyond their former limits. His Assize of
Clarendon of 1166 provided that local inquest juries should meet
periodically under royal auspices to identify and denounce notorious neighborhood criminals. The inquest jury had been used
before but never in such a systematic fashion. He also extended
royal jurisdiction over the vast and turbulent field of land disputes, employing local juries to determine the rightful possessors
of disputed estates. Previous kings had intervened in territorial
quarrels but never in a consistent, systematic way. Now, itinerant
royal justices made periodic circuits of the countryside, bringing
the king's law to vast numbers of Englishmen who had previously
been untouched by it. Henry II's subjects learned to turn to his
courts for quick, modern, rational justice. Feudal law, with its
archaic and time-consuming procedures, had little chance in the
competition. Gradually the patchwork of local laws and customs

which had so long divided England gave way to a uniform royal law—a *common* law by which all Englishmen were governed. The *political* unification of the tenth century was consummated by the *legal* unification under the Angevin kings.

Predictably, Henry II also sought to expand royal justice at the expense of the ecclesiastical courts. In this matter he was opposed by his implacable archbishop of Canterbury, Thomas Becket. King and archbishop became locked in a furious quarrel which centered on the issue of whether churchmen accused of crimes should be subject to royal jurisdiction or tried by Church courts alone. The issue was brought to a violent climax in 1170 when four overenthusiastic knightly supporters of Henry II, acting without royal order, murdered Becket in Canterbury Cathedral. This dramatic crime made a profound impact on the age. Becket became a martyr; miracles were alleged to have occurred at his tomb, and he was quickly canonized. Acutely embarrassed by the episode, Henry II was obliged to do penance by walking barefoot through the streets of Canterbury and submitting to a flogging by the Canterbury monks. But his campaign against the ecclesiastical courts was delayed only momentarily. By the end of his reign, royal justice had made significant inroads on the authority of the Church courts, and the crown had succeeded in bringing the English Church under tight rein. Here, as elsewhere, Henry II was remarkably successful in steering England toward administrative and legal centralization.

RICHARD AND JOHN

Henry II was succeeded by his eldest surviving son, Richard the Lion-Hearted (1189–1199), a cruel, skillful warrior who devoted himself chiefly to two great projects: defending the Angevin Empire against the French crown and crusading against the Moslems. He was a superb general but a second-rate administrator who spent less than six months of his ten-year reign in England. During his protracted absences, the administrative system of Henry II proved its worth; it governed England more-or-less satisfactorily for ten years without a king. Meanwhile Richard was engaging in romantic but fruitless adventures in the Holy Land and was successfully defending the Angevin Empire against the remorseless pressure of King Philip Augustus of France.

The fortunes of the Angevin Empire veered sharply with the accession of King John (1199–1216), Richard the Lion-Hearted's younger brother. John is an enigmatic figure—brilliant in certain respects, a master of administrative detail, but a suspicious and unscrupulous leader. He trusted nobody, and nobody trusted him. Consequently, his subjects never supported him more than half-heartedly in moments of crisis.

In Philip Augustus of France (1180–1223) John had a shrewd and unremitting antagonist. Philip took full advantage of his position of feudal overlord over John's continental possessions. In 1202 John was summoned to the French royal court to answer charges brought against him by one of his own Aquitainian vassals. When John refused to come, Philip Augustus declared his French lands forfeited and proceeded to invade Normandy. The duchy quickly fell into Philip's hands (1203–4) as John's demoralized vassals defected, one after another, and John himself fled ignominiously to England. In the chaos that followed Philip Augustus was able to wrest Anjou and most of the remaining continental possessions of the Angevin Empire from John's control. Only portions of distant Aquitaine retained their connection with the English monarchy. King John had sustained a monstrous political and military disaster.

For the next ten years John nursed his wounds and wove a dextrous web of alliances against King Philip in hopes of regaining his lost possessions, but his careful plans were shattered by Philip's decisive victory over John's Flemish and German allies at the battle of Bouvines in 1214 (see p. 205). With Bouvines went John's last hope of reviving the Angevin Empire.

These catastrophies destroyed what remained of John's royal prestige and paved the way for the epoch-making English baronial uprising that culminated in the signing of Magna Carta in 1215. John's barons had good reason to oppose him. He had pushed the centralizing tendencies of his Norman and Angevin predecessors to new limits and was taxing his subjects as they had never been taxed before. The baronial reaction of 1215 may be regarded both as a protest against John and as an effort to reverse the trend toward royal authoritarianism of the past 150 years. Magna Carta has been interpreted in contradictory ways: as the fountainhead of English constitutional monarchy, and as a reactionary, backward-looking document designed to favor the particularistic feudal aristocracy at the expense of the enlightened Angevin monarchy.

In reality, Magna Carta was both feudal and constitutional—both backward-looking and forward-looking. Its more important clauses were designed to keep the king within the bounds of popular tradition and feudal custom. Extraordinary taxes, for example, were to be levied only by the common council of the kingdom. But implicit in the traditional feudal doctrine that the lord had to respect the rights of his vassals—and in the age-old Germanic notion that the monarch had to adhere to the customs of his people—was the profound constitutional principle of government under the law. In striving to make King John a good feudal lord, the barons in 1215 were moving uncertainly, perhaps unconsciously, toward constitutional monarchy. For this was the crucial moment when the English nobles were just beginning to represent a national point of view. In the past, baronial opposition to royal autocracy had taken the form of a selfish insistence on local aristocratic autonomy. But one finds in Magna Carta the notion that the king is bound by traditional legal limitations in his relations with all classes of free Englishmen. It would be misleading to lay too much stress on the underlying principles of this intensely practical document, which was concerned primarily with correcting specific abuses of royal power, but it would be equally misleading to ignore the momentous implication in Magna Carta of an overarching body of law which limited and circumscribed royal authority.

The chief constitutional problem in the years following Magna Carta was the question of how an unwilling king might be forced to stay within the bounds of law. A series of royal promises was obviously insufficient to control an ambitious monarch who held all the machinery of the central government in his grasp. Magna Carta itself relied on a committee of twenty-five barons who were empowered, should the king violate the Charter, to call on the English people "to distrain and distress him in every way possible." Thus the monarch was to be restrained by the crude sancton of baronial and popular rebellion—a desperate and unwieldly weapon against an unscrupulous king.

John himself seems to have had no intention of carrying out his promises. He repudiated Magna Carta at the first opportunity and died in 1216 in the midst of a full-scale revolt. With John's death the revolt ended and the crown passed to his nine-year-old son, Henry III (1216–1272), who was supervised during his minority by a baronial council. In the decades that followed, Magna Carta was reissued many times, but the great task of the new age was to create political institutions capable of limiting royal autocracy by some means short of rebellion. The ultimate solution to this problem was found in Parliament.

HENRY III AND EDWARD I

Henry III was a petulant, erratic monarch—pious without being holy, bookish without being wise. Surrounding himself with foreign favorites and intoxicated by grandiose, impractical foreign projects, he ignored the advice of his barons and gradually lost their confidence.

Ever since its beginning the English monarchy had customarily arrived at important decisions of policy with the advice of a royal council of nobles and officials. The composition of this royal council or *curia regis* had always been vague, and it had never possessed anything resembling a veto power over royal decisions, but many Englishmen, particularly noblemen, put much importance in the fact that royal policies were framed in consultation with the barons.

Traditionally English royal councils were of two types. Ordinary royal business was conducted in a small council consisting of the king's household officials and whatever barons happened to be at court at the time. But in moments of crisis, or when some important decision was pending, the kings supplemented their normal coterie of advisers by summoning all the important noblemen of the realm to meet as a great council. It was this great baronial council that eventually evolved into Parliament.

A key factor in the evolution from great council to Parliament was the trend in the thirteenth century toward including representatives of the country gentry and the townsmen alongside the great barons. This notable development resulted from the royal policy, particularly evident after Magna Carta, of summoning the great council for the purpose of obtaining approval for some un-customary tax. As wealth gradually seeped downward into the sub-baronial classes, the king found it expedient to obtain the consent of these lesser orders to new royal taxes by summoning their representatives to the great council.

The vigorous baronial opposition to Henry III arose from the fact that he summoned the great council not for the purpose of consulting his magnates on policy matters but chiefly for the pur-pose of obtaining their consent to new taxes. The barons resented being asked to finance chimerical foreign schemes in which they had not been consulted and of which they disapproved. They might well have chosen as their motto, "no taxation without con-sultation." They responded to Henry III's fiscal demands with increasing reluctance, and for a time they were able to use their financial leverage to force the king to accept their advice. But in the end the conflict between king and baronage proved irrecon-cilable and a major rebellion broke out. In 1264 the baronial leader, Simon de Montfort, defeated Henry III, and for the next fifteen months he ruled England through a nine-man baronial committee augmented periodically by a great council of all the barons.

In 1265 the monarchy rallied and crushed Simon de Montfort's rebellion. But the effect of the uprising proved to be lasting. Eng-land had undergone an interesting experience in baronial gov-ernment and, far more important, a significant step had been taken in the development of Parliament. For earlier in 1265 Simon de Montfort had summoned a great council—a Parliament—which included for the first time all three of the classes that were to characterize the Parliaments of the later Middle Ages. Simon de Montfort's Parliament included, in addition to the barons, two knights from every shire, and two burghers from every town. Simon's chief motive in summoning this Parliament was probably to broaden the base of his rebellion, but in later years Parliaments were summoned for many purposes: to sit as a high court of law, to advise the king on important matters of policy, to declare their support in moments of crisis, and, most important of all, to give their consent to the ever-increasing royal taxes.

The English Parliament was built on a sturdy foundation of local government, and all three of the major parliamentary orders—barons, burghers, and shire knights—brought with them a wealth of local political experience. The burghers in Parliament were usually veterans of town government. The shire knights had long been involved in the administration of the counties and the county courts. Intermediate between the baronial nobility and the peasantry, these men constituted a separate class—a country gentry—rooted to their shires and their ancestral estates, experienced in local government, and ideally suited to represent their counties in Parliament.

In 1272 Henry III was succeeded by his able son, Edward I (1272–1307), a far wiser man than his father. Edward I was a monarch of strong will and independence, but he had the sagacity to take the barons into his confidence and he was successful in winning their support. Although he, like his father, regarded Parliaments chiefly as means of winning approval for new taxes, he used them for many other purposes as well. He summoned Parliaments frequently and experimented endlessly in their composition. In the later years of his reign the inclusion of shire knights and townsmen became customary. It was not until the fourteenth century, however, that the knights and burghers began meeting separately from the barons, thereby giving birth to the great parliamentary division into Lords and Commons.

As the thirteenth century closed, the actual powers of Parliament remained exceedingly vague and its composition was still fluid. At best, it might bargain discreetly with the king for concessions in return for financial aid. Still, a beginning had been made. The deep-rooted medieval concept of limited monarchy had given rise to an institution that would develop over the centuries into a keystone of representative government. Ultimately Parliament became the crucial institutional bridge between medieval feudalism and modern democracy.

The reign of Edward I witnessed the culmination of many trends that had been developing throughout the High Middle Ages. Through his creative legislation Edward completed the great work of his predecessors in creating an effective and complex royal administrative system and building an enlightened, comprehensive body of common law. He was a skillful general who added Wales to the English realm, came close to conquering Scotland, and fought vigorously but inconclusively with King Philip the Fair over the remaining English territories in southern France. But his most significant contribution, in the long run, was his policy of developing Parliament into an integral organ of government. It is ironic, therefore, that King Edward regarded Parliament primarily as a useful instrument for raising the necessary revenues to support his far-flung projects. He would have been appalled to learn that his royal descendants would one day be figurehead kings and that Parliament was destined to rule England.

THE EARLY CAPETIANS

When William of Normandy conquered England in 1066, the French monarchy exerted a feeble control over a small territory around Paris and Orleans known as the Île de France and was virtually powerless in the lands beyond. To be sure, the French kings had as their vassals great feudal magnates such as the dukes of Normandy and Aquitaine and the counts of Anjou, Flanders, and Champagne, but vassalage was a slender bond indeed when the king lacked the power to enforce his lordship. In theory the anointed king of the French, with his priestly charisma, with the sovereign power traditionally associated with royalty, and with the supreme feudal overlordship, was a mighty figure indeed. But in grim reality he was impotent to control his great vassals and unable to keep order even in the Île de France itself.

Since 987 the French crown had been held by the Capetian dynasty. The achievement of the Capetians in the first century or so of their rule was modest enough. Their one triumph was their success in keeping the crown within their own family. The Capetians had gained the throne originally by virtue of being elected by the magnates of the realm, but from the first they sought to purge the monarchy of its elective character and to make it hereditary. This they accomplished by managing to produce male heirs at the right moment and by arranging for the new heir to be crowned before the old king died. They may have been aided by the fact that the crown was not a sufficiently alluring prize to attract powerful usurpers.

In the early twelfth century the Capetians remained weaker than several of their own vassals. While vassal states such as Normandy and Anjou were becoming increasingly centralized, the

Capetian Île de France was still ridden with fiercely insubordinate robber barons. If the Capetians were to realize the immense potential of their royal title, they had three great tasks before them: (1) to master and pacify the Île de France, (2) to expand their political and economic base by bringing additional territories under direct royal authority, and (3) to make their lordship over the great vassals real rather than merely theoretical.

During the twelfth and thirteenth centuries a series of remarkable Capetian kings pursued and achieved these goals. Their success was so complete that by the opening of the fourteenth century the Capetians controlled all France, either directly or indirectly, and had developed an efficient and sophisticated royal bureaucracy. They followed no hard and fast formula. Rather their success depended on a combination of luck and ingenuity—on their clever exploitation of the powers which, potentially, they had always possessed as kings and feudal overlords. They were surprisingly successful in avoiding the family squabbles that had at times paralyzed Germany and England. Unlike the German monarchs, they maintained comparatively good relations with the papacy. They had the enormous good fortune of an unbroken sequence of direct male heirs from 987 to 1328. Above all, they seldom overreached themselves: they avoided grandiose schemes and spectacular strokes of policy, preferring instead to pursue modest, realistic goals. They extended their power gradually and cautiously by favorable marriages, by confiscating the fiefs of vassals who died without heirs, and by dispossessing vassals who violated their feudal obligations toward the monarchy. Yet the majority of the Capetians had no desire to absorb all the territories of their vassals. Rather they sought to build a kingdom with a substantial core of royal domain lands surrounded by the fiefs of loyal, obedient magnates.

LOUIS VI AND LOUIS VII

The first Capetian to work seriously toward the consolidation of royal control in the Île de France was King Philip I (1060–1108), a bloated, repugnant man who grasped the essential fact that the Capetian monarchy had to make its home base secure before turning to loftier goals. Philip's realistic policy was pursued far more vigorously by his son, Louis VI, "the Fat" (1108–1137). Year after year Louis the Fat battled the petty brigand-lords of the Île de France, besieged their castles one after another, and at last reduced them to obedience. At his death in 1137 the Île de France was relatively orderly and prosperous, and the French monarchy was beginning to pull abreast of its greater vassals.

Louis the Fat received invaluable assistance in the later part of his reign from Abbot Suger of the great royal abbey of Saint Denis. This talented and dedicated statesman served as chief royal adviser from 1130 to 1151 and labored hard and effectively to extend the king's sway, to systematize the royal administration, and, incidentally, to augment the wealth and prestige of Saint Denis. Suger provided an invaluable element of continuity between the reigns of Louis the Fat and his son, Louis VII (1137–1180), who pursued his father's goals with less than his father's skill. Pious and gentle, Louis VII was, in the words of a contemporary observer, "a very Christian king, if somewhat simple-minded."

When Abbot Suger died in 1151, Louis VII was left to face unaided a new and formidable threat to the French monarchy. The Angevin Empire was just then in the process of formation, and in 1154 the ominous configuration was completed when Henry Plantagenet, Count of Anjou and Duke of Normandy and Aquitaine, acceded to the English throne as King Henry II. Louis VII sought to embarrass his mighty vassal by encouraging Henry's sons to rebel, but his efforts were too half-hearted to be successful. Still, Louis VII's reign witnessed a significant extension of royal power. Indeed, as one historian has aptly said, it was under Louis VII that "the prestige of the French monarchy was decisively established." * The great vassals of the crown, fearful of their powerful Angevin colleague and respectful of Louis VII's piety and impartiality, began for the first time to bring cases to the court of their royal overlord and to submit their disputes to his judgment. Churchmen and townsmen alike sought his support in struggles with the nobility. These developments resulted not so much from royal initiative as from the fundamental trends of the age toward peace, order, and increased commercial activity. Frenchmen in

* R. Fawtier, *The Capetian Kings of France* (London, 1962), p. 23.

increasing numbers were turning to their genial, unassuming monarch for succor and justice, and, little by little, Louis VII began to assume his rightful place as feudal suzerain and supreme sovereign of the realm.

PHILIP AUGUSTUS (1180–1223)

The French monarchy came of age under Louis VII's talented son, Philip II "Augustus" (1180–1223). By remorseless insistence on his feudal rights, and by a policy of dextrous and ruthless opportunism, Philip Augustus enlarged the royal territories enormously and, beyond the districts of direct royal jurisdiction, transformed the chaotic anarchy of the vassal states into an orderly hierarchy subordinate to the king.

Philip Augustus' great achievement was his destruction of the Angevin Empire and his establishment of royal jurisdiction over Normandy, Anjou, and their dependencies. For two decades he plotted with dissatisfied members of the Angevin family against King Henry II and King Richard the Lion-Hearted, but it was not until the reign of King John (1199–1216) that his efforts bore fruit. Against John's notorious faithlessness and greed, Philip was able to play the role of the just lord rightfully punishing a disobedient vassal. And when Philip Augustus moved against Normandy in 1203–4, John's remarkable unpopularity played into his hands. The prize which Philip had sought so long fell with surprising ease, and once Normandy was his, John's remaining fiefs in northern France fell like dominoes. Ten years later, in 1214, Philip extinguished John's last hope of recovering the lost territories by winning a decisive victory over John's German allies at Bouvines. Settling the fate of Normandy and Anjou, Bouvines was also a turning point in the power balance between France and Germany in the High Middle Ages. For thereafter the waxing Capetian monarchy of France replaced the faltering kingdom of Germany as the great continental power in Western Europe.

Under Philip Augustus and his predecessors significant developments were occurring in the royal administrative system. The *curia regis* had assumed its place as the high feudal court of France and was proving an effective instrument for the assertion of royal rights over the dukes and counts. Hereditary noblemen, who had traditionally served as local administrators in the royal territories, were gradually replaced by salaried middle-class officials known as *baillis*. These new officials, whose functions were at once financial, judicial, military, and administrative, owed their positions to the royal favor and were therefore fervently devoted to the interests of the crown. Throughout the thirteenth century the *baillis* worked tirelessly and often unscrupulously to erode the privileges of the feudal aristocracy and extend the royal sway. This intensely loyal and highly mobile bureaucracy, without local roots and without respect for feudal and local traditions, became in time a powerful instrument of royal absolutism. The *baillis* stood in sharp contrast to the local officials of England—the sheriffs and the shire knights—who were customarily drawn from the local gentry and whose loyalties were divided between the monarch whom they served and the region and class from which they sprang.

LOUIS VIII (1223–1226)

The closing years of Philip Augustus' reign were concurrent with the savage Albigensian Crusade in southern France, called by Philip's great contemporary, Pope Innocent III, against the supporters of the Albigensian heresy which was spreading rapidly through Languedoc and northern Italy (see pp. 221 ff). Philip Augustus declined to participate personally in the Crusade, but his son, Prince Louis, took an active part in it, and when the prince succeeded to his father's throne in 1223 as Louis VIII (1223–1226), he threw all the resources of the monarchy behind the southern campaign. The Crusade succeeded in eliminating the Albigensian threat to Western Christendom but only by devastating large portions of southern France and exterminating the brilliant culture which previously had flourished there. Thenceforth southern France tended to be dominated by northern France, and the authority of the French monarchy was extended to the Mediterranean.

It may perhaps be surprising to discover that Louis VIII, who inherited a vastly expanded royal jurisdiction from his father and extended it still further himself, granted about a third of the hard-won royal territories as fiefs to junior members of the Capetian family. These family fiefs, created out of the royal domain, are known as *appanages*. Their emergence should serve as a warning that the growth of the Capetian monarchy cannot be understood simply as a linear process of expanding the royal territories. The Capetians had no objection to vassals as long as they were obedient and subject to royal control. Indeed, given the limited transportation and communication facilities of twelfth- and thirteenth-century France, the kingdom was far too large to be controlled directly by the monarchy. The new vassals, bound to the crown by strong family ties, played an essential role in the governance of the realm and strengthened rather than weakened the effectiveness of Capetian rule.

SAINT LOUIS (1226–1270)

Louis VIII died prematurely in 1226, leaving the land in the capable hands of his stern and pious Spanish widow, Blanche of Castile, who acted as regent for the boy-king Louis IX (1226–1270)—the later St. Louis. Even after St. Louis came of age in 1234 he remained devoted to his mother, and Queen Blanche continued for years to be a dominant influence in the royal government.

St. Louis possessed both his mother's sanctity and his mother's firmness. Unlike many saint-kings, he was a strong monarch, obsessed with the obligation to rule justly and firmly and to promote moral rectitude throughout the kingdom of France. His sanctity although thoroughly genuine was perhaps too orthodox—too conventional. He persecuted heretics and crusaded against the Moslems. He once remarked that the only possible response for a Christian toward Jews who blasphemed was "to plunge his sword into their bellies as far as it would go." Still, in asserting these attitudes he was merely mirroring his age. His reign was far different from that of Philip Augustus, for he oriented his life not toward political ends but toward what he conceived to be religious ends. He believed in war against the infidel, but he believed just as fervently in peace among Christian rulers. Accordingly, he arranged treaties with Henry III of England and with the king of Aragon which settled peacefully all outstanding disputes. He played the role of peacemaker among Christian princes and was even called on to arbitrate between King Henry III and his barons.

St. Louis was content, in general, to maintain the royal rights established by his predecessors. His *baillis* and other officials were

Map XVI.   The expansion of the French royal domain, 1180–1314.

actually far more aggressive than he in extending the royal power; as one modern historian puts it, "In this reign monarchial progress was the complex result of the sanctity of a revered ruler, and the patient and obstinately aggressive policy of the king's servants." Indeed, St. Louis went to the length of establishing a system of itinerant royal inspectors—*enquêteurs*—who reported local grievances and helped keep the ambitious local officials in check.

In France under Louis IX medieval culture reached its climax. Town life flourished under St. Louis' rule, and in the towns magnificent Gothic cathedrals were being erected. This was the great age of the medieval universities, and at the most distinguished university of the age, the University of Paris, some of the keenest intellects of medieval Europe—St. Bonaventure, Albertus Magnus, Thomas Aquinas—were assembled concurrently. The universities produced brilliant and subtle theologians, but they also produced learned and ambitious lawyers—men of a more secular cast, who devoted their talents to the king and swelled the ranks of the royal bureaucracy. The Capetian government became steadily more complex, more efficient and, from the standpoint of the feudal nobility, more oppressive.

PHILIP THE FAIR (1285–1314)

St. Louis died in the midst of his second Crusade. Under his successors the bureaucracy pursued its ruthless centralizing policies without restraint. The saint-king was succeeded by his inept son, Philip III (1270–1285), and his frigid, unscrupulous grandson, Philip IV, "the Fair" or "the Handsome" (1285–1314). Philip the Fair was a mysterious, silent figure, conventionally pious but with a real flair for choosing able, aggressive, and thoroughly unprincipled ministers—chiefly middle-class lawyers from southern France—who devoted themselves with remarkable singlemindedness to the exaltation of the French monarchy.

The reign of Philip the Fair was an age of unceasing royal aggression—against the territories of neighboring states, against the papacy, and against the traditional privileges of the French nobility. Philip waged an indecisive war against King Edward I of England over Edward's remaining fiefs in southern France. He made a serious effort to absorb Flanders, imprisoning the Flemish count and ruling the district directly through a royal agent, but he was foiled by a bloody Flemish revolt in 1302. He pursued a successful policy of nibbling aggression to the east against the Holy Roman Empire. He suppressed unscrupulously the rich Crusading order of Knights Templars, ruined their reputation by an astonishingly modern campaign of vituperative propaganda, and confiscated their wealth. We have seen in the previous chapter how he struggled with Pope Boniface VIII, how his agents held Boniface captive for a brief time, and how he finally engineered the election of the pliable French Pope Clement V who took up residence at Avignon (see pp. 187–8). Against his nobles he pursued a rigorously anti-feudal policy. He short-circuited the feudal hierarchy and demanded direct allegiance and obedience from all Frenchmen. All these activities were manifestations of the prevailing political philosophy of his reign: that the French king was by rights the secular and spiritual master of France and the dominating figure in Western Europe. We encounter this same philosophy in ambitious French statesmen of succeeding centuries—in Cardinal Richelieu, in Louis XIV, and, stripped of its monarchial trappings, in Napoleon and de Gaulle.

Throughout the thirteenth century the French royal bureaucracy had been developing steadily. The royal revenues came to be handled by a special accounting bureau, roughly parallel to the English Exchequer, called the *Chambre des Comtes.* The king's judicial business became the responsibility of a high court known as the *Parlement of Paris,* which was to play a highly significant political role in later centuries. Under Philip the Fair the bureaucracy became an exceedingly refined and supple tool of the royal interest, and its middle-class background and fanatical royalism gave the king a degree of independence from the nobility that was quite unknown in contemporary England.

Still, the king could not rule without a degree of support from his subjects. Philip's victory over the papacy on the issue of royal taxation of the clergy and his rape of the Knights Templars brought additional money into his treasury, but the soaring expenses of government and warfare forced him to seek ever-new sources of revenue and, as in England, to secure his subjects' approval for extraordinary taxation. But instead of summoning a great assembly—a parliament—for this purpose, he usually negotiated individually with various tax-paying groups.

Nevertheless, it was under Philip the Fair that France's first great representative assemblies were summoned. Beginning in 1302, the Estates General was assembled from time to time, primarily for the purpose of giving formal support to the monarchy in moments of crisis—during the height of the struggle with Pope Boniface VIII, for example, or in the midst of the Knights Templars controversy. The assembly included members of the three great social classes or "estates"—the clergy, the nobility, and the townsmen. It continued to meet occasionally during the succeeding centuries, but it never became a real organ of government as did the English Parliament. Its failure resulted in part from a premature and unsuccessful bid for power during the fourteenth century in the midst of the Hundred Years' War. But even under Philip the Fair the Estates General lacked the potential of the contemporary Parliaments of England. It had no real voice in royal taxation and was therefore not in a position to bargain with the king through increasing control of the purse strings. It was not, as in England, an evolutionary outgrowth of the royal council but rather an entirely separate and therefore somewhat exotic body. There was no real opportunity for the bourgeoisie and the gentry to join ranks as in the English House of Commons; lacking the important responsibilities in local government which fell on the English shire knights, the knights in France remained an inarticulate and subordinate part of the aristocratic class. Above all, the French nobility and bourgeoisie lagged far behind the English in developing a national consciousness or a feeling of cohesion. Late-thirteenth-century France was too large, too heterogeneous, and too recently consolidated under royal authority, for its inhabitants to have acquired a meaningful sense of identification as a people; their outlook remained provincial and parochial.

Yet despite the significant differences between the English Parliament and the French Estates General, the two institutions had much in common. Both were products of a European-wide evolution out of feudal monarchy and out of the vague but pervading medieval notion of government by the consent of the realm. Similar representative institutions were emerging concurrently all over Western Christendom: in the Christian kingdoms of Spain, in Italy under Frederick II, in the rising principalities of Germany, and in innumerable counties, duchies, and communes across the length and breadth of Europe. Of these many experiments, only the English Parliament survives today. But Parliament was not merely the outgrowth of an isolated English experience; it was one particular manifestation of a broad and fundamental trend in European civilization during the High Middle Ages.

CHRONOLOGY OF THE ENGLISH AND FRENCH MONARCHIES
IN THE HIGH MIDDLE AGES

	England		*France*
1066:	Norman Conquest of England	987–1328:	Rule of the Capetian Dynasty
1066–1087:	Reign of William the Conqueror	1060–1108:	Reign of Philip I
1087–1100:	Reign of William II		
1100–1135:	Reign of Henry I	1108–1137:	Reign of Louis VI, "the Fat"
1135–1154:	Disputed succession; King Stephen		
1154–1189:	Reign of Henry II	1137–1180:	Reign of Louis VII
1189–1199:	Reign of Richard the Lion-Hearted	1180–1223:	Reign of Philip II, "Augustus"
1199–1216:	Reign of John		
1203–1204:	Loss of Normandy	1214:	Battle of Bouvines
1215:	Magna Carta	1223–1226:	Reign of Louis VIII
1216–1272:	Reign of Henry III	1226–1270:	Reign of St. Louis IX
1264–1265:	Simon de Montfort's rebellion	1270–1285:	Reign of Philip III
1272–1307:	Reign of Edward I	1285–1314:	Reign of Philip IV, "the Fair"

14

New Dimensions

in Medieval Christianity

THE CHURCH IN THE HIGH MIDDLE AGES

Although the Middle Ages witnessed the beginnings of European nationhood, it was not until much later that nationalism began to play an important role in the European mind. In the twelfth and thirteenth centuries the majority of Europeans were still intensely local in their outlook, only vaguely aware of what was going on beyond their immediate surroundings. But alongside their localism was an element of cosmopolitanism—a consciousness of belonging to the great international commonwealth of Western Christendom, fragmented politically, but united culturally and spiritually by the Church. Paradoxically, high medieval Europe was at once more localized and more internationalized than the Europe of modern times.

The Church in the High Middle Ages was a powerful unifying influence. It had made notable progress since the half-heathen pre-Carolingian era. A flourishing parish system had by now spread across the European countryside to bring the sacraments and a modicum of Christian instruction to the peasantry. New bishoprics and archbishoprics were formed, and old ones were becoming steadily more active. The papacy never completely succeeded in breaking the control of kings and secular lords over their local bishops, but in the wake of the Investiture Controversy it exercised a very real control over the European episcopacy, and the growing efficiency of the papal bureaucracy evoked the envy and imitation of the rising royal governments.

The buoyancy of high medieval Europe is nowhere more evident than in the accelerating impact of Christian piety on European society. The sacraments of the Church introduced a significant religious dimension into the life of the typical European layman: His birth was sanctified by the sacrament of *baptism* in which he was cleansed of the taint of original sin and initiated into the Christian fellowship. At puberty he received the sacrament of *confirmation*, which reasserted his membership in the Church and gave him the additional grace to cope with the problems of adulthood. His wedding was dignified by the sacrament of *marriage*. If he chose the calling of the ministry, he was spiritually transformed into a priest by the sacrament of *holy orders*. At his death he received the sacrament of *extreme unction*, which prepared his soul for its journey into the next world. And throughout his life he could receive forgiveness from the damning consequences of mortal sin by repenting his past transgressions and humbly receiving the comforting sacrament of *penance*. Finally, he might partake regularly of the central sacrament of the Church —the *eucharist*—receiving the body of Christ into his own body by consuming the eucharistic bread. Thus the Church, through its seven sacraments, brought God's grace to all Christians, great and humble, at every critical juncture of their lives. The sacramental system, which only assumed final form in the High Middle Ages, was a source of immense comfort and reassurance: it brought hope of salvation not simply to the saintly elite but to the sinful majority; it made communion with God not merely the elusive goal of a few mystics but the periodic experience of all believers. And, of course, it established the Church as the essential intermediary between God and man.

The ever-increasing scope of the Church, together with the rising vigor of the new age, resulted in a deepening of popular piety throughout Europe. The High Middle Ages witnessed a profound shift in religious attitude from the awe and mystery characteristic of earlier Christianity to a new emotionalism and dynamism. This shift is evident in ecclesiastical architecture, as the stolid, earthbound Romanesque style gave way in the later twelfth century to the tense, upward-reaching Gothic (see pp. 232 ff). A parallel change is evident in devotional practices as the divine Christ sitting in judgment gave way to the tragic figure of the human Christ suffering on the Cross for man's sins. And it was in the High Middle Ages that the Virgin Mary came into her own as the compassionate intercessor for hopelessly lost souls. No matter how sinful a person might be, he could be redeemed if only he won the sympathy of Mary, for what son could refuse the petition of his mother? Indeed, a legend of the age told of the devil complaining to God that the soft-hearted Queen of Heaven was cheating Hell of its most promising candidates. The God of Justice became the merciful, suffering God who died in agony to atone for the sins of men and to bring them to everlasting life.

Like all human institutions, the medieval Church fell far short of its ideals. Corrupt churchmen were in evidence throughout the age, and certain historians have delighted in cataloguing instances of larcenous bishops, gluttonous priests, and licentious nuns. But cases such as these were clearly exceptional. The great shortcoming of the medieval Church was not gross corruption but rather a creeping complacency which resulted sometimes in a shallow, even mechanical attitude toward the Christian religious life. The medieval Church had more than its share of saints, but among the rank and file of the clergy the profundity of the Faith was often lost in the day-to-day affairs of the pastoral office and the management of far-flung estates.

THE CRISIS IN BENEDICTINISM

The drift toward complacency has been a recurring problem in Christian monasticism. Again and again, the lofty idealism of a monastic reform movement has been eroded and transformed by time and success until, at length, new reform movements arose in protest against the growing worldliness of the old ones. This cycle has been repeated countless times. Indeed, the sixth-century Benedictine movement was itself a protest against the excesses and inadequacies of earlier monasticism. St. Benedict had regarded his new order as a means of withdrawing from the world and devoting full time to communion with God. But Benedictinism, despite Benedict's ideal, quickly became involved in teaching, evangelism, and ecclesiastical reform, and by the tenth and eleventh centuries the whole Benedictine movement had become deeply involved in worldly affairs. Benedictine monasteries controlled vast estates, supplied contingents of knights in their service to feudal armies, and worked closely with secular princes in affairs of state. Early in the tenth century the Cluniac movement, which was itself Benedictine in spirit and rule, arose as a protest against the worldliness and complacency of contemporary Benedictine monasticism, but by the later eleventh century the Congregation of Cluny had definitely come to terms with the secular establishment and was beginning to display traces of the very complacency against which it had originally rebelled. Prosperous, respected, and secure, Cluny was too content with its majestic abbeys and priories, its elaborate liturgical program, and its bounteous fields to support the radical transformation of Christian society for which Pope Gregory VII was struggling.

The aims of Gregory VII were almost exactly the opposite of St. Benedict's, for whereas Benedict had sought to create monastic sanctuaries in which Christians might retire from the world, Gregory VII endeavored to sanctify society itself. His goal was not *withdrawal* but *conversion*. Rather than making Christians safe from the world, he would make the world safe for Christianity. During the Investiture Controversy and its aftermath, these two contrary tendencies—withdrawal and conversion—both had a profound impact on monastic reform.

In the opening decades of the High Middle Ages the Benedictine movement was showing signs of exhaustion. During the long, troubled centuries of the Early Middle Ages, Benedictine teachers and missionaries, scribes and political advisers, had provided indispensable services to society. Benedictine monasteries had served as the spiritual and cultural foci of Christendom. But in the eleventh and twelfth centuries, the Benedictines saw their pedagogical monopoly broken by the rising cathedral schools and universities of the new towns. These urban schools produced increasing numbers of well-trained scholars who gradually superseded the Benedictine monks as scribes and advisers to princes. In other words, the great urbanizing impulse of the High Middle Ages drastically diminished the traditional Benedictine contribution to the functioning of society.

Still, the Benedictines retained their great landed wealth. The Benedictine monastery was scarcely the sanctuary from worldly concerns that St. Benedict had planned. Nor was it any longer the vital force it had once been in Christianizing the world. Twelfth-century Benedictinism followed neither the path of withdrawal nor the path of conversion, and even in the arena of secular affairs it was losing its grip. The Benedictine life was beginning to appear tarnished and unappealing to sensitive religious spirits caught up in the soaring piety of the new age.

THE NEW MONASTICISM

The monastic revolt against Benedictinism followed the two divergent roads of uncompromising withdrawal from society and ardent participation in the Christianization of society. The impulse toward withdrawal pervaded the Carthusian order which arose in eastern France in the later eleventh century and spread across Christendom in the twelfth. Isolated from the outside world, the Carthusians lived in small groups, worshiping together in communal chapels but otherwise living as hermits in individual cells. This austere order exists to this day and, unlike most monastic movements, its severe spirituality has seldom waned. Yet even in the spiritually charged atmosphere of the twelfth century it was a small movement, offering a way of life for only a minority of heroically holy men. Too ascetic for the average Christian, the Carthusian order was much admired but seldom joined.

The greatest monastic movement of the twelfth century, the Cistercian order, managed for a time to be both austere and popular. The mother house of this order, Citeaux, was established in 1098 on a wild, remote site in eastern France. The Cistercian order grew very slowly at first, then gradually acquired momentum. In 1115 it had four daughter houses; by the end of the century it had five hundred.

The spectacular success of the Cistercians demonstrates the immense appeal of the idea of withdrawal to the Christians of the twelfth century. Like Citeaux, the daughter houses were deliberately built in remote wilderness areas. The abbeys themselves were stark and primitive, in dramatic contrast to the elaborate Cluniac architecture. Cistercian life was stark and primitive, too—less severe than that of the Carthusians but far more so than that of the Cluniacs. The Cistercians sought to resurrect the strict, simple life of primitive Benedictinism, but in fact they were more austere than Benedict himself. The numerous Cistercian houses were bound together tightly, not by the authority of a central abbot as at Cluny but by an annual council of all Cistercian abbots meeting at Citeaux. Without such centralized control it is unlikely that the individual houses could have clung for long to the harsh, ascetic ideals on which the order was founded.

The key figure in twelfth-century Cistercianism was St. Bernard, who joined the community of Citeaux in 1112 and three years later became the founder and abbot of Clairvaux, one of Citeaux's earliest daughter houses. St. Bernard of Clairvaux was the leading Christian of his age—a profound mystic, a brilliant religious orator, and a crucial figure in the meteoric rise of the Cistercian order. His moral influence was so immense that he became Europe's leading arbiter of political and ecclesiastical disputes. He persuaded the king of France and the Holy Roman Emperor to participate in the Second Crusade. He persuaded Christendom to accept his candidate in a hotly disputed papal election in 1130. On one occasion he even succeeded in reconciling the two great warring families of Germany, the Welfs and Hohenstaufens. He rebuked the pope himself: "Remember, first of all, that the Holy Roman Church, over which you hold sway, is the mother of churches, not their sovereign mistress—that you yourself are not the lord of bishops but one among them. . . ." And he took an uncompromising stand against one of the rising movements of his day: the intoxicating dream of reconciling the Catholic Faith with human reason, which was spearheaded by the brilliant twelfth-century philosopher, Peter Abelard. In the long run Bernard failed to halt the reconciliation of faith with reason, but he succeeded in making life miserable for the unfortunate Abelard and in securing the official condemnation of certain of Abelard's teachings (see pp. 245–6).

Bernard's career demonstrates vividly the essential paradox of Cistercianism. For although the Cistercians strove to disassociate themselves from the world, Bernard was drawn inexorably into the vortex of secular affairs. Indeed, as the twelfth century progressed, the entire Cistercian movement became increasingly worldly. Like the later Puritans, the Cistercians discovered that their twin virtues of austere living and hard work resulted in an embarrassing accumulation of wealth and a concomitant corrosion of their spiritual simplicity. Their efforts to clear fields around their remote abbeys placed them in the vanguard of the internal frontier movement. They become pioneers in scientific farming and introduced notable improvements in the breeding of horses, cattle, and sheep. The English Cistercians became the great wool producers of the realm. Altogether the Cistercians exerted a powerful, progressive influence on European husbandry and came to play a prominent role in the European economy. Economic success brought ever-increasing wealth to the order. Cistercian abbey churches became steadily more elaborate and opulent, and the primitive austerity of Cistercian life was progressively relaxed. In later years there appeared new offshoots, such as the Trappists, which returned to the strict observance of original Cistercianism.

The Cistercians had endeavored to withdraw from the world, but despite their goal they became a powerful force in twelfth-century Europe. At roughly the same time, other orders were being established with the deliberate aim of participating actively in society and working toward its regeneration. The Augustinian Canons, for example, submitted to the rigor of a monastic rule, yet carried on normal ecclesiastical duties in the world, serving in parish churches and cathedrals. The fusion of monastic discipline and worldly activity culminated in the twelfth-century Crusading orders—the Knights Templars, the Knights Hospitallers, the Teutonic Knights, and similar groups (see p. 166) whose ideal was a synthesis of the monastic and the military life for the purpose of expanding the political frontiers of Western Christendom. These and other efforts to direct the spiritual vigor of monastic life toward the Christianization of society typify the bold visions and lofty hopes of the new, emotionally charged religiosity that animated twelfth-century Europe.

HERESIES AND THE INQUISITION

The new surge of popular piety also raised serious problems for the Church and society, for it resulted in a flood of criticism against churchmen. It was not that churchmen had grown worse, but rather that laymen had begun to judge them by harsher standards. Popular dissatisfaction toward the work-a-day Church manifested itself in part in the rush toward the austere twelfth-century monastic orders. Yet the majority of Christians could not become monks, and for them, certain new heretical doctrines began to exert a powerful appeal.

The heresies of the High Middle Ages flourished particularly in the rising towns of southern Europe. The eleventh-century urban revolution had caught the Church unprepared; whereas the new towns were the real centers of the burgeoning lay piety, the Church, with its roots in the older agrarian feudal order, seemed unable to minister effectively to the vigorous and widely literate new burgher class. Too often the urban bishops appeared as political oppressors and enemies of burghal independence rather than inspiring spiritual directors. Too often the Church failed to understand the townsmen's problems and aspirations or to anticipate their growing suspicion of ecclesiastical wealth and power. Although the vast majority of medieval townsmen remained loyal to the Church, a troublesome minority, particularly in the south, turned to new, anticlerical sects. In their denunciation of ecclesiastical wealth, these sects were doing nothing more than St. Bernard and the Cistercians had done. But many of the anticlerical sects crossed the boundary between orthodox reformism and heresy by preaching without episcopal or papal approval; far more important, they denied the exclusive right of the priesthood to perform sacraments.

One such sect, the Waldensians, was founded by a merchant of Lyons named Peter Waldo who *c.* 1173 gave all his possessions to the poor and took up a life of apostolic poverty. At first he and his followers worked within the bounds of orthodoxy, but gradually their flamboyant anticlericalism and their denial of special priestly powers earned them the condemnation of the Church. Similar groups, some orthodox, some heretical, arose in the communes of Lombardy and were known as the *Humiliati*. Naturally these groups proved exceedingly troublesome and embarrassing to the local ecclesiastical hierarchies, but generally they escaped downright condemnation unless they themselves took the step of denying the authority of the Church. Many did take that step, however, and by the thirteenth century heretical, anticlerical sects were spreading across northern Italy and southern France, and even into Spain and Germany.

The most popular and dangerous heresy in southern France was sponsored by a group known as the *Cathari* (the pure) or the Albigensians, after the town of Albi, where they were particularly strong. The Albigensians represented a fusion of two traditions, (1) the anticlerical protest against ecclesiastical wealth and power and (2) an exotic theology derived originally from Persian dualism. The Albigensians recognized two gods—the god of good who reigned over the universe of the spirit and the god of evil who ruled the world of matter. The Old-Testament God, as creator of the material universe, was their god of evil; Christ, who was believed to have been a purely spiritual being with a phantom body, was the god of good. Albigensian morality stressed a rigorous rejection of all material things—of physical appetites, wealth, worldly vanities, and sexual intercourse—in the hope of one day escaping from the prison of the body and ascending to the realm of pure spirit. In reality this severe ethic was practiced only by a small elite; the rank and file ate well, begat children, and participated only vicariously in the rejection of the material world— by criticizing the affluence of the Church. Indeed, their opponents accused them of gross licentiousness, and it does seem to be true that certain Provençal noblemen were attracted to the new teaching by the opportunity of appropriating Church property in good conscience.

However this may be, Albigensianism was spreading rapidly as the thirteenth century dawned and was becoming an ominous threat to the unity of Christendom and the authority of the Church. Pope Innocent III, recognizing the gravity of the situation, tried with every means in his power to eradicate Albigensianism. At length, in 1208, he summoned a Crusade against the Albigensians—the first Crusade ever to be called against European Christians. The Albigensian Crusade was a ruthless, savage affair which succeeded in its purpose but only at the cost of ravaging the vibrant civilization of southern France. As we have seen, the French monarchy intervened in the Crusade's final stages and thereby extended its sway to the Mediterranean (see p. 206). The Albigensian Crusade was an important event in the development of French royal power, and it succeeded in reversing the trend toward heresy in southern Europe. It also disclosed the brutality of which the Church was capable when sufficiently threatened.

In the years immediately following the Albigensian Crusade, there emerged an institution that will always stand as a grim symbol of the medieval Church at its worst—the Inquisition. The Christian persecution of heretics dates from the later fourth century, but it was not until the High Middle Ages that heterodox views presented a serious problem to European society. Traditionally, the problem of converting or punishing heretics was handled at the local level, but in 1223 the papacy established a permanent central tribunal for the purpose of standardizing procedures and increasing efficiency in the suppression of heresies. The methods of the Inquisition included the use of torture, secret testimony, conviction on the testimony of only two witnesses, the denial of legal counsel to the accused, and other procedures offensive to the Anglo-American legal tradition but not especially remarkable by standards of the times. Indeed, many of these procedures—including torture—were drawn from the customs of Roman Law. In defense of the Inquisition it might be said that convicted heretics might escape death by renouncing their "errors," and that far from establishing a reign of terror, the Inquisition seems to have enjoyed popular support.

Some historians have adduced other arguments in an attempt to defend an indefensible institution. Let us say here merely that the Christian Faith was far more important to the people of medieval Europe than national allegiance—that the medieval Church, with its elaborate charitable activities, its hospitals and universities, and its other social services, performed many of the functions of the modern state, and that therefore medieval heresy was analogous to modern treason. To the medieval Christian, heresy was a hateful, repugnant thing, an insult to Christ, and a source of contamination to others. Today, when political and economic doctrines are more important to most people than religious creeds, the closest parallel to medieval Waldensianism or Albigensianism is to be found in the Communist and Nazi parties in modern America. In examining popular opposition toward extremist groups such as these, perhaps we can gain an inkling of the state of mind that produced the medieval Inquisition.

MENDICANTISM

The thirteenth century found an answer to the heretical drift in urban piety which was far more compassionate and effective than the Inquisition. In the opening decades of the century two radically new orders emerged—the Dominican and the Franciscan —which were devoted to a life of poverty, preaching, and charitable deeds. Rejecting the life of the cloister, they dedicated themselves to religious work in the world, particularly in the towns. Benedictines and Cistercians had traditionally taken vows of personal poverty, but the monastic orders themselves could and did acquire great corporate wealth. The Dominicans and Franciscans, on the contrary, were pledged to both personal and corporate poverty and were therefore known as mendicants (beggars). Capturing the imagination of thirteenth-century Christendom, they drained urban heterodoxy of much of its former support by demonstrating to the townsmen of Europe that Christian orthodoxy could be both relevant and compelling.

St. Dominic (1170–1221), a Spaniard who had preached in southern France against the Albigensians, conceived the idea of an order of men trained as theologians and preachers, dedicated to poverty and the simple life, and to winning over heretics through argument, oratory, and example. Sanctioned by the papacy in 1216, the Dominicans underwent a notable expansion and, by midcentury, had spread across Christendom. The order produced some of the greatest philosophers and theologians of the age, including St. Thomas Aquinas. Dominicans also participated actively in the Inquisition, but their most effective work was done through persuasion rather than force. In time, the ideal of corporate poverty was dropped, for it was recognized that fulltime scholars and teachers could not beg or do odd jobs or be in doubt as to the source of their next meal. But long after their original mendicant ideals were modified, the Dominicans remained faithful to their mission of championing orthodoxy by word and pen.

Dominic's remarkable achievement was overshadowed by that of his contemporary, St. Francis (c. 1182–1226), a warm and appealing man who is widely regarded as Christianity's greatest saint.

Francis was a true product of the urban revolution. He was the son of a wealthy cloth merchant of Assisi, a northern Italian town with an influential Albigensian minority. After a boisterous but harmless adolescence, he underwent a profound conversion, lived in solitude for a brief time, and then returned to human society with a firm dedication to give up all worldly goods and to devote his life to the service of the poor and diseased. Francis was firm, but he was anything but grim. Indeed, it was his joyousness no less than his deep sanctity that captivated his age. As disciples flocked to his side, he wrote a simple rule for them based on the doctrines of charitable activity in the world, total dedication to the work of God, and the absolute rejection of worldly goods. In 1210 he appealed to Pope Innocent III for approval of his rule and the pope, with some misgivings, authorized the new order. In the years that followed, the Franciscan Order expanded phenomenally. The immensely attractive personality of Francis himself was doubtless a crucial factor in his order's popularity, but it also owed much to the fact that its ideals appealed with remarkable effectiveness to the highest religious aspirations of the age. Urban heresy lost its allure as the cheerful, devoted Franciscians began to pour into Europe's cities, preaching in the crowded streets and setting a living example of Christian sanctity.

Pious men of other times have fled the world; the Albigensians renounced it as the epitome of evil. But Francis embraced it joyfully as the handiwork of God. In his "Song of Brother Sun," he expressed poetically his holy commitment to the physical universe:

Praise to Thee, my Lord, for all Thy creatures,
Above all Brother Sun
Who brings us the day, and lends us his light;
Beautiful is he, radiant with great splendor,
And speaks to us of Thee, O most high.

Praise to Thee, my Lord, for Sister Moon and for the stars;
In heaven Thou hast set them, clear and precious and fair.

Praise to Thee, my Lord, for Brother Wind,
For air and clouds, for calm and all weather
By which Thou supportest life in all Thy creatures.

Praise to Thee, my Lord, for Sister Water
Which is so helpful and humble, precious and pure.

Praise to Thee, my Lord, for Brother Fire,
By whom Thou lightest up the night.
And fair is he, and gay and mighty and strong.

Praise to Thee, my Lord, for our sister, Mother Earth,
Who sustains and directs us,
And brings forth varied fruits, and plants and flowers bright. . . .

Praise and bless my Lord, and give Him thanks,
And serve Him with great humility.

Early Franciscanism was far too good to last. As the order expanded it outgrew its primitive ideals, and even before Francis' death in 1226, the papacy was obliged to authorize a more elaborate and practical rule for his order. In time Franciscan friars began devoting themselves to scholarship and took their places alongside the Dominicans in Europe's universities. Indeed, Franciscan scholars such as Roger Bacon in thirteenth-century England played a central role in the revival of scientific investigation, and the minister general of the Franciscan Order in the later thirteenth century, St. Bonaventure, was one of the most illustrious theologians of the age. The very weight and complexity of the Franciscan organization forced it to compromise its original ideal of corporate poverty. Although it neither acquired nor sought the immense landed wealth of the Benedictines or Cistercians, it soon possessed sufficient means to sustain its members. In time, therefore, the Franciscans followed the course of earlier orders: their primitive simplicity and enthusiasm were exhausted by time and attenuated by popularity and success. A splinter group known as the "Spiritual Franciscans" sought to preserve the apostolic poverty and artless idealism of Francis himself, but the majority of Franciscans were willing to meet reality halfway. They continued to serve society, but by the end of the thirteenth century they had ceased to inspire it.

The pattern of religious reform in the High Middle Ages is one of rhythmic ebb and flow. A reform movement is launched with high enthusiasm and lofty purpose, it galvanizes society for a time, then succumbs gradually to complacency and gives way to a new and different wave of reform. But with the passing of the High Middle Ages one can detect a gradual waning of spiritual vigor. Until the Protestant Reformation, no new religious order attained the immense popularity and social impact of thirteenth-century Franciscanism. Popular piety remained strong, particularly in northern Europe, where succeeding centuries witnessed a significant surge of mysticism. But in the south a more secular attitude was slowly beginning to emerge. Young men no longer flocked into monastic orders; soldiers no longer rushed to Crusades; papal excommunications no longer wrought their former terror. The electrifying appeal of a St. Bernard, a St. Dominic, and a St. Francis was a phenomenon peculiar to their age. By the fourteenth century, their age was passing.

CHRONOLOGY OF HIGH MEDIEVAL
MONASTICISM AND HETERODOXY

910:	Founding of Cluny
1084:	Establishment of Carthusian Order
1098:	Establishment of Citeaux
1112–1153:	Career of St. Bernard of Clairvaux as a Cistercian
1128:	Original rule of Knights Templars
1173:	Beginning of Waldensian sect
1208:	Innocent III calls Albigensian Crusade
1210:	Innocent III authorizes Franciscan Order
1216:	Dominican Rule sanctioned by papacy
1226:	Death of St. Francis
1233:	Inquisition established

15

Thought, Letters, and the Arts

THE DYNAMICS OF HIGH MEDIEVAL CULTURE

Thirteenth-century Paris has been described as the Athens of medieval Europe. It is true, of course, that a vast cultural gulf separates the golden age of Periclean Athens from the golden age of thirteenth-century France, but it is also true that these two golden ages had something in common. Both developed within the framework of traditional beliefs and customs which had long existed but were being challenged and transformed by powerful new forces. The social-religious world of the Early Middle Ages, like the social-religious world of the early Greek polis, was parochial and rather tradition-bound. As the two cultures passed into their golden ages, the values of the past were being challenged by new intellectual currents, and the old economic patterns were breaking down before a sharp intensification of commercial activity. Yet, for a time, these dynamic new forces resulted in a heightened cultural expression of the old values. The Parthenon, dedicated to the venerable civic goddess Athena, and the awesome Gothic cathedral of Notre Dame (Our Lady) are both products of a new creativity harnessed to the service of an older ideology. In the long run, the new creative impulses would prove subversive to the old ideologies, but for a time, both ancient Greece and medieval Europe achieved an elusive equilibrium between old and new. The results, in both cases, were spectacular.

Thus twelfth- and thirteenth-century Europe succeeded, by and large, in keeping its vibrant and audacious culture within the bounds of traditional Catholic Christianity. And the Christian world view gave form and orientation to the new creativity. Despite the intense dynamism of the period, it can still be called, with some semblance of accuracy, an Age of Faith.

Europe in the High Middle Ages underwent a profound artistic and intellectual awakening which affected almost every imaginable form of expression. Significant creative work was done in literature, architecture, sculpture, law, philosophy, political theory, and even science. By the close of the period, the foundations of the Western cultural tradition were firmly established. The pages that follow will provide only a glimpse at a few of the remarkable cultural achievements of this fertile era.

LITERATURE

The literature of the High Middle Ages was abundant and richly varied. Poetry was written both in the traditional Latin—the universal scholarly language of medieval Europe—and in the vernacular languages of ordinary speech that had long been evolving in the various districts of Christendom. Traditional Christian piety found expression in a series of somber and majestic Latin hymns, whose mood is illustrated (through the clouded glass of translation) by these excerpts from "Jerusalem the Golden":

> The world is very evil, the times are waxing late.
> Be sober and keep vigil; the judge is at the gate. . . .
> Brief life is here our portion; brief sorrow, short-lived care.
> The life that knows no ending, the tearless life, is there. . . .
>
> Jerusalem the Golden, with milk and honey blessed,
> Beneath thy contemplation sink heart and voice oppressed.
> I know not, O I know not, what social joys are there,
> What radiancy of glory, what light beyond compare.

At the opposite end of the spectrum of medieval Latin literature one encounters poetry of quite a different sort, composed by young, wandering scholars and aging perpetual-undergraduate types. The deliberate sensuality and blasphemy of their poems are expressions of student rebelliousness against the ascetic ideals of their elders:

For on this my heart is set, when the hour is neigh me,
Let me in the tavern die, with a tankard by me,
While the angels, looking down, joyously sing o'er me . . . etc.

One of these wandering-scholar poems is an elaborate and im-
pudent expansion of the Apostles' Creed. The phrase from the
Creed, "I believe in the Holy Ghost, the Holy [Catholic]
Church . . . " is embroidered as follows:

> *I believe* in wine that's fair to see,
> And in the tavern of my host
> More than *in the Holy Ghost*
> The tavern will my sweetheart be,
> And *the Holy Church* is not for me.*

These sentiments should not be regarded as indicative of a sweeping trend toward agnosticism. Rather, they are distinctively medieval expressions of the irreverent student radicalism that all ages
know.

For all its originality, the Latin poetry of the High Middle Ages
was overshadowed both in quantity and in variety of expression by
vernacular poetry. The drift toward emotionalism, which we have
already noted in medieval piety, was closely paralled by the evolution of vernacular literature from the martial epics of the eleventh
century to the delicate and sensitive romances of the thirteenth.
Influenced by the sophisticated and somewhat feminine romanticism of the southern troubadour tradition, the bellicose spirit of
northern France gradually softened.

In the eleventh and early twelfth centuries, heroic epics known
as *Chansons de Geste* (Songs of Great Deeds) were enormously
popular among the feudal nobility of northern France. Many of
these *Chansons* were exaggerated accounts of events surrounding
the reign of Charlemagne. The most famous of all the *Chansons de
Geste,* the *Song of Roland,* told of a heroic and bloody battle between a hoard of Moslems and the detached rearguard of Charlemagne's army as it was withdrawing from Spain. Like old-fash-
ioned Westerns, the *Chansons de Geste* were packed with action,
and their heroes tended to steer clear of sentimental entanglements
with ladies. Warlike prowess, courage, and loyalty to one's lord

* My italics.

and fellows-in-arms were the virtues stressed in these heroic epics. The battle descriptions were characterized by gory realism:

> He sees his bowels gush forth out of his side
> And on his brow the brain laid bare to sight.

In short, the *Chansons de Geste* were mirrors of the rough, masculine spirit of eleventh-century feudal knighthood.

During the middle and later twelfth century the martial spirit of northern French literature was gradually transformed by the influx of the romantic troubadour tradition of southern France. In Provençe, Toulouse, and Aquitaine, a rich and colorful culture had been developing in the eleventh and twelfth centuries, and out of this vivacious society came a lyric poetry of remarkable sensitivity and enduring value. The lyric poets of the south were known as *troubadours*. Most were court minstrels, but some, including a duke of Aquitaine himself, were members of the upper nobility. Their poems were far more intimate and personal than the *Chansons de Geste* and placed much greater emphasis on romantic love. The delicacy and romanticism of the troubadour lyrics betoken a more genteel and sophisticated nobility than that of the feudal north—a nobility that preferred songs of love to songs of war. Indeed, medieval southern France was the source of the entire romantic-love tradition of Western Civilization, with its idealization of women, its emphasis on male gallantry and courtesy, and its insistence on embroidering the sex drive with an elaborate ritual of palpitating hearts, moonlight, and sentimental lies.

Midway through the twelfth century this courtly love tradition was brought northward to the court of Champagne and began to spread rapidly. As its influence grew, knights discovered that more was expected of them than a life of masculine loyalty and carefree slaughter. They were now expected to be gentlemen as well—to be courtly in manner and urbane in speech, and to idolize some noble lady. Such were the ideals of courtly love. Their impact on knightly behavior was distinctly limited, but their effect on the literature of northern Europe was revolutionary. Out of the convergence of vernacular epic and vernacular lyric there emerged a new poetic form known as the *romance*.

Like the *Chansons de Geste,* the romance was a long narrative poem, but like the southern lyrics, it was exceedingly sentimental and imaginative. It was usually based on some theme from the remote past—the Trojan War, Alexander the Great, and, above all, King Arthur, the half-legendary sixth-century British king. Arthur was transformed into an idealized twelfth-century monarch surrounded by charming ladies and chivalrous knights. His court at Camelot, as described by the great French poet Chrétien de Troyes, was a center of romantic love and refined religious sensitivity, where knights worshiped their ladies fair or went on quests for the Holy Grail.

The romance flourished in twelfth- and thirteenth-century France and among the French-speaking nobility of England. It was also a crucial element in the evolution of German vernacular literature. The German poets—known as *minnesingers*—were influenced by the French lyric and romance but developed these literary forms along highly original lines. The *minnesingers* produced their own deeply sensitive and mystical versions of the Arthurian stories, which, in their exalted symbolism and profundity of emotion, surpass even the works of Chrétian de Troyes and his French contemporaries.

Vernacular poetry came late to Italy, but in the works of Dante (d. 1321) it achieved its loftiest expression. Dante's *Divine Comedy*, written in the Tuscan vernacular, is a magnificent synthesis of medieval literature and medieval thought. Rich in allegory and symbolism, it tells of Dante's own journey through hell, purgatory, and paradise to the very presence of God himself. This device allows Dante to make devastating comments on past and contemporary history by placing all those of whom he disapproved—from local politicians to popes—in various levels of hell. Virgil, the archetype of ancient rationalism, is Dante's guide through hell and purgatory; the lady Beatrice, a symbol of purified love, guides him through the celestial spheres of paradise; and St. Bernard, the epitome of medieval sanctity, leads him to the threshold of Almighty God. In his *Divine Comedy* Dante encompassed the entire universe of medieval man in a single work of art which brought medieval literature to a resplendent climax.

ARCHITECTURE: FROM ROMANESQUE TO GOTHIC

The High Middle Ages are one of the great epochs in the history of Western architecture. Stone churches, large and small, were built in prodigious numbers: In France alone, more stone was quarried during the High Middle Ages than by the pyramid and temple builders of ancient Egypt throughout its three-thousand-year history. Yet the real achievement of the medieval architects lay not in the immense scope of their activities but in the splendid originality of their aesthetic vision. Two great architectural styles dominated the age—the Romanesque style evolved in the eleventh century, rose to maturity in the early twelfth, and during the latter half of the twelfth century gave way gradually to the Gothic style. From about 1150 to 1300 the greatest of the medieval Gothic cathedrals were built. Thereafter, the Gothic style lost some of its inspiration as it became overly elaborate and increasingly showy, but during the High Middle Ages it constituted one of humanity's most audacious and successful architectural experiments.

High medieval architecture was deeply affected by two of the basic cultural trends of the period. First of all, the great cathedrals were products of the urban revolution and the rise of intense urban piety. Second, the evolution from Romanesque to Gothic closely parallels the shift which we have already observed in literature and piety toward emotional sensitivity and romanticism. Romanesque architecture, although characterized by an exceeding diversity of expression, tended in general toward the solemnity of earlier Christian piety and the uncompromising masculinity of the *Chansons de Geste*. Gothic architecture, on the other hand, is dramatic, upward-reaching, and even somewhat feminine. (A vast number of Gothic cathedrals were dedicated to Notre Dame.)

The development from Romanesque to Gothic can also be understood as an evolution in the principles of structural engineering. The key architectural ingredient in the Romanesque churches was the round arch. Romanesque roof design was based on the various elaborations of the round arch, such as the barrel vault and the cross vault (see Figures (a) and (b)). These heavy stone roofs required thick supporting walls with windows that were necessarily few and small. A church in the fully developed Romanesque style conveys a powerful feeling of unity and earthbound solidity. Its massive arches, vaults, and walls, and its somber, shadowy interior give the illusion of mystery and otherworldliness, yet suggest at the same time the steadfast might of the universal Church.

(a)   *Historical Pictures Service — Chicago*   (b)   *Taurgo Slides*

Plate VII.   (a) Engraving of The Cathedral of Worms, illustrating a typical Romanesque exterior.   (b) Photograph of St. Sernin in Toulouse, illustrating a typical Romanesque interior.

Midway through the twelfth century, Abbot Suger, the chief adviser of the French crown, became a pioneer of the new Gothic style by introducing significant novel elements into the construction of his abbey church at St. Denis. The key features of the Gothic style, which now spread rapidly outward from the Île de France, were the pointed arch and the flying buttress. These and related structural devices resulted in a totally new aesthetic experience. The pointed arch, as the accompanying illustration makes clear, permitted the cathedral roof to soar upward. Churches now lost their earth-bound quality and began to reach toward the sky. In the simplest terms, the Romanesque round arch resulted in a structure whose lines were chiefly horizontal, whereas the Gothic pointed arch emphasized the vertical. From the aesthetic standpoint, this shift in orientation made an immense difference.

The flying buttresses were devices to relieve the church walls of the outward and downward thrust of the roof. By so doing, they rendered the walls structurally superfluous and permitted the architects to design huge windows, usually filled with brilliant stained glass, which flooded the interior of the Gothic church with light and color. The Gothic exterior was richly ornamented with sculptural representations of plants and animals, saints and statesmen. Gothic sculpture often sought to tell a story—to reproduce scenes and episodes from the Bible or from the lives of the saints. Sometimes this was done in a straightforward way, sometimes through religious symbolism. And sometimes the Gothic sculptors had no further wish than to portray the variety of the natural world in stone. In many instances they succeeded in reproducing plants, animals, and humans with a remarkable degree of realism.

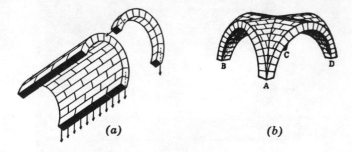

(a) Barrel Vault.   *(b)* Cross Vault.

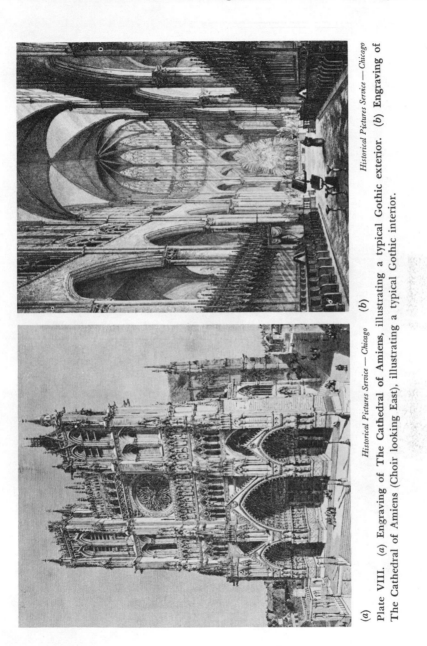

Historical Pictures Service — Chicago   (b)

Historical Pictures Service — Chicago

(a)

Plate VIII. (a) Engraving of The Cathedral of Amiens, illustrating a typical Gothic exterior. (b) Engraving of The Cathedral of Amiens (Choir looking East), illustrating a typical Gothic interior.

Taurgo Slides

Plate IX.   The Flying Buttresses of Notre Dame in Paris.

Taurgo Slides

Plate X.   *Annunciation* and *Visitation*, Gothic sculptures that stand at the west portals of Rheims Cathedral.

The Gothic cathedral was a functional and closely unified work of art. Its soaring silhouette dominated the town in which it stood, and its lofty, richly illuminated interior created a dramatic effect that must have overwhelmed the medieval worshipers whose piety it so superbly reflected. After the physical and spiritual ravages of seven centuries its spell still holds.

THE RISE OF UNIVERSITIES

Like the Gothic cathedral, the university was a product of the medieval town. The urban revolution of the eleventh and twelfth centuries brought about the decline of the old monastic schools which had done so much to preserve culture over the previous centuries. They were superseded north of the Alps by cathedral schools located in the rising towns, and in Italy by semi-secular municipal schools. Both the cathedral schools and the municipal schools had long existed, but it was only in the eleventh century that they arose to great prominence. Many of these schools now became centers of higher learning of a sort that Europe had not known for centuries. Their enrollments increased steadily and their faculties grew until, in the twelfth century, some of them evolved into universities.

In the Middle Ages, *university* was an exceedingly vague term. A university was simply a group of persons associated for any purpose. The word was commonly applied to the merchant guilds and craft guilds of the rising towns. A guild or university of students and scholars engaged in the pursuit of higher learning was given the more specific name, *studium generale*. When we speak of the medieval university, therefore, we are referring to an institution that would have been called a *studium generale* by a man of the thirteenth century. It differed from lesser schools in three significant respects. (1) The *studium generale* was open to students from many lands, not simply those from the surrounding district; (2) the *studium generale* was a large school with a number of teachers rather than merely one omnicompetent master; (3) the *studium generale* offered both elementary and advanced curricula. It offered a basic program of instruction in the traditional "seven liberal arts"—astronomy, geometry, arithmetic, music, grammar, rhetoric, and dialectic—and also instruction in one or more of the "higher" disciplines—theology, law, and medicine. Upon the successful completion of his liberal arts curriculum, the student could apply for a license to teach, but he might also wish to continue his studies by specializing in medicine, theology, or—most popular of all—civil or canon law. Legal training offered as its reward the promise of a lucrative administrative career in royal government or the Church.

Fundamentally, the medieval university was neither a campus nor a complex of buildings but a *guild*—a privileged corporation of teachers, or sometimes of students. With its classes normally held in rented rooms, it was a highly mobile institution, and on more than one occasion when a university was dissatisfied with local conditions it won important concessions from the townsmen simply by threatening to move elsewhere.

In the thirteenth century, flourishing universities were to be found at Paris, Bologna, Naples, Montpelier, Oxford, Cambridge, and elsewhere. Paris, Oxford, and a number of others were dominated by guilds of instructors in the liberal arts. Bologna, on the other hand, was governed by a guild of students who managed to reduce the exorbitant local prices of food and lodgings by threatening to move collectively to another town, and who established strict rules of conduct for the instructors. Professors had to begin and end their classes on time and to cover the prescribed curriculum; they could not leave town without special permission. This, surely, was student government run rampant. It is important to point out, however, that Bologna specialized in legal studies and that its pupils were older professional students for the most part —men who had completed their liberal arts curriculum and were determined to secure sufficient training for successful careers in law.

The students of the medieval universities were, on the whole, rowdier and more exuberant than students of American universities today, more imaginative in their pranks, and more hostile toward the surrounding towns. Thus the history of the medieval universities is punctuated by frequent town-gown riots. New students were hazed unmercifully; unpopular professors were hissed, shouted down, and even pelted with stones. Most of the students were of relatively humble origin—from the towns or the ranks of the lesser nobility—but they were willing to spend their student days in abject poverty if necessary in order to acquire the new knowledge and prepare themselves for the rich social and economic rewards that awaited many graduates.

Despite the enormous difference between medieval and modern university life, it should be clear that the modern university is a direct outgrowth of the institution that came into being in high medieval Europe. We owe to the medieval university the concept of a formal teaching license, the custom—unknown to antiquity—of group instruction, the idea of academic degrees, the notion of a liberal arts curriculum, the tradition of professors and students dressing in clerical garb (caps and gowns) on commencement day, and numerous other customs of university life. Even the letters written by medieval students to their parents or guardians have a curiously modern ring:

> This is to inform you that I am studying at Oxford with the greatest diligence, but the matter of money stands greatly in the way of my promotion, as it is now two months since I have spent the last of what you sent me. The city is expensive and makes demands; I have to rent lodgings, buy necessities, and provide for many other things which I cannot now specify. [A fuller elaboration here would have been illuminating.] Wherefore I respectfully beg your paternity that by the promptings of divine pity you may assist me, so that I can complete what I have well begun. For you must know that without Ceres and Bacchus, Apollo grows cold.

MEDICINE AND LAW

The chief medical school of medieval Europe was the University of Salerno. Here, in a land of vigorous cultural intermingling, scholars were able to draw from the medical heritage of Islam and Byzantium. In general, medieval medical scholarship was a bizarre medley of cautious observation, common sense, and gross superstition. In one instance we encounter the advise that a person should eat and drink in moderation, but we are also instructed that onions will cure baldness, that the urine of a dog is an admirable cure for warts, and that all one must do to prevent a woman from conceiving is to bind her head with a red ribbon. Yet in the midst of this nonsense, important progress was being made in medical science. The writings of the great second-century scientist Galen (see p. 12), which constituted a synthesis of classical medical knowledge, were studied and digested, as were the important works of Arab students of medicine. And to this invaluable body of knowledge European scholars were now making their own original contributions on such subjects as the curative properties of plants and the anatomy of the human body. It is probable that both animal and human dissections were performed by the scholars of twelfth-century Salerno. These doctors, their crude and primitive methods notwithstanding, were laying the foundations on which Western European medical science was to rise.

Medieval legal scholarship addressed itself to two distinct bodies of material—canon law and civil law. The study of canon law or Church law was enormously stimulated by the Investiture Controversy and subsequent Church-state struggles. Drawing their precedents from the Bible, from the writings of the Latin Church Fathers, and from papal and conciliar decrees, the canon lawyers of Bologna and elsewhere elaborated difficult points of law, struggled to reconcile discordant canons, and assembled a series of great canonical collections. Many canon lawyers were enthusiastic supporters of the papal cause and devoted their scholarship to the task of providing a powerful legal foundation for the sweeping claims of the twelfth- and thirteenth-century papacy. Indeed, as we have seen, many of the popes were themselves canon lawyers.

Civil lawyers, on the other hand, tended to exalt the emperor and the kings under whom so many of them served. The science of civil law was built on the framework of Justinian's *Corpus Juris Civilis* (see p. 70), which was first studied seriously in the West in late-eleventh-century Bologna. Roman law appealed to the legal scholars of the High Middle Ages as a uniquely comprehensive and rational body of jurisprudence. Although it contained a strong element of constitutionalism, it inherited from Justinian's age a tendency toward imperial absolutism which was put to effective use by the court lawyers of the rising monarchies. Roman law became the basis of most of the legal systems of continental Europe, where it served to make government at once more systematic and more autocratic. Thus the civil lawyers played a significant role in the evolution of France from the limited Germanic monarchy of the earlier Capetians toward the absolutism of later times. And the development and durability of a parliamentary regime in England owed much to the fact that a strong monarchy, based on the principles of Germanic law, was already well established before Europe felt the full impact of the Roman law revival.

PHILOSOPHY AND SCIENCE

It is only to be expected that an age that witnessed such sweeping economic and political developments and such vigorous creativity in religious and artistic expression would also achieve notable success in the realm of abstract thought. Medieval philosophy is exceedingly variegated and is marked by boundless curiosity and heated controversy. Among the diverse investigations and conflicting opinions of the medieval thinkers, three central issues deserve particular attention: (1) the degree of interrelationship between faith and reason, (2) the relative merits of the Platonic-Augustinian and the Aristotelian intellectual traditions, and (3) the reality of the Platonic archetypes or "universals." The issue of faith versus reason was perhaps the most far-reaching of the three. Ever since Tertullian in the third century, there had been Christians who insisted that God so transcended reason that any attempt to approach Him through logic was not only useless but blasphemous. It was the mystic who knew God, not the theologian. Against this view, medieval philosophers such as Anselm and Thomas Aquinas maintained that faith and reason were dual avenues to truth, that they often led to the same conclusions, and that in no case were their conclusions contradictory.

The conflict between the systems of thought of Plato-Augustine and Aristotle did not emerge clearly until the thirteenth century when the full body of Aristotle's writings came into the West in Latin translations from Greek and Arabic. Until then most efforts at applying reason to faith were based on the Platonic tradition transmuted and transmitted by Augustine into the medieval West. Many philosophers of the more conservative type were deeply suspicious of the newly recovered Aristotelian writings, regarding them as pagan in viewpoint and dangerous to the Faith. Others, such as St. Thomas Aquinas, were much too devoted to the goal of reconciling faith and reason to ignore the works of a man whom they regarded as antiquity's greatest philosopher. St. Thomas sought to Christianize Aristotle as Augustine had Christianized Plato. In the middle decades of the thirteenth century, as high medieval philosophy was reaching its climax, the Platonic and Aristotelian traditions flourished side by side, and in the works of certain English thinkers of the age they achieved a singularly fruitful fusion.

The contest between medieval Platonism-Augustinianism and medieval Aristotelianism carried the seeds of still another controversy: the problem of archetypes or universals. Plato had taught that terms such as "dog," "man," or "cat" not only described certain creatures but also had reality in themselves—that individual cats are imperfect reflections of a model cat, an archetypal or universal cat. Again, we call certain acts "good" because they partake of a universal good which exists in heaven. In short, these universals—cat, dog, beauty, goodness, etc.—exist apart from the multitude of individual cats, dogs, and beautiful and good things in this world. And the person who seeks knowledge ought to meditate on these universals rather than study the world of phenomena in which they are reflected only imperfectly. St. Augustine accepted Plato's theory of universals with one amendment: that the archetypes existed in the mind of God rather than in some abstract realm, and that God put a knowledge of universals directly into our minds by a process which Augustine called "divine illumination." Both Plato and Augustine agreed that the universal existed apart from the particular and, indeed, that the universal was *more real* than the particular. In the High Middle Ages those who followed the Platonic-Augustinian approach to the universals were known as *realists*—they believed that universals were *real*.

The Aristotelian tradition brought with it another viewpoint on universals: that they existed, to be sure, but only in the particular—only by studying particular things in the world of phenomena could men gain knowledge of universals. The universals were real, but in a sense less real than Plato and Augustine believed. Accordingly, medieval philosophers who inclined toward the Aristotelian position have been called *moderate realists*.

But medieval philosophers were by no means confined to a choice between these two positions. Several worked out subtle solutions of their own. As early as the eleventh century the philosopher

Roscellinus declared that universals were not real at all. They were mere names that humans gave to arbitrary classes of individual things. Reality was not to be found in universals but rather in the multiplicity and variety of objects which we can see, touch, and smell in the world around us. Those who followed Roscellinus in this view were known as *nominalists*—for them, the universals were *nomina,* the Latin for "names." Nominalism lurked in the intellectual background during the twelfth and thirteenth centuries but was revived in the fourteenth. Many churchmen regarded it as a dangerous doctrine, for its emphasis on the particular over the general or universal seemed to suggest that the Catholic Church was not, as good churchmen believed, a single universal body but rather a vast accumulation of individual believers.

Having examined briefly three important issues of high medieval philosophy—reason versus revelation, Plato-Augustine versus Aristotle, and the problem of universals—we shall now see how these issues developed in the minds of individual philosophers between the eleventh and fourteenth centuries.

The philosophers of this period were known as "scholastics" because nearly all of them were connected with schools—monastic schools, cathedral schools, or universities. They first appeared in the later eleventh century as a product of the reawakening that Europe was just then beginning to undergo. The first great figure in scholastic philosophy was St. Anselm, an Italian who taught for many years in the vigorous monastic school of Bec in Normandy. In time he was appointed abbot of Bec, and in the 1090s he became archbishop of Canterbury. As archbishop he struggled vigorously against the Norman kings of England over the issue of lay investiture, and shortly after agreeing to a compromise settlement of the controversy he died in 1109. During his eventful career he found time to think and write profoundly on such subjects as the atonement of mankind through Christ's crucifixion, the possibility of a rational proof of God, and the relationship between faith and reason. Anselm stood solidly in the Platonic-Augustinian tradition and was singularly important in the development of medieval thought because of his confidence that reason was not incompatible with faith. He taught that faith must precede reason but that reason could serve to illuminate faith. His emphasis on reason, employed within the framework of a firm Christian conviction, set the stage for the significant philosophical developments of the following generations, and his keen analytical mind made him the most notable Western philosopher since Augustine. With Anselm, Western Christendom regained at last the intellectual level of the fourth-century Latin Doctors.

The twelfth-century philosophers, intoxicated by the seemingly limitless possibilities of reason and logic, advanced boldly across new intellectual frontiers at the very time when their contemporaries were pushing forward the geographical frontiers of Europe. The most brilliant and audacious of these twelfth-century Christian rationalists was Peter Abelard (1079–1142), an immensely popular teacher, dazzling and egotistical, whose meteoric career ended in tragedy and defeat.

Abelard is perhaps best known for his love affair with the young Heloise, an affair that ended with Abelard's castration at the hands of thugs hired by Heloise's enraged uncle. The lovers were then separated permanently, both taking monastic vows, and in later years Abelard wrote regretfully of the affair in his autobiographical *History of My Calamities*. There followed a touching correspondence between the two lovers in which Heloise, now an abbess, confessed her enduring love and Abelard, writing almost as a father confessor, offered her spiritual consolation but nothing more. Abelard's autobiography and the correspondence with Heloise survive to this day, providing modern students with a singularly intimate and tender picture of romance and pathos in a society far removed from our own.

Abelard was the supreme logician of the twelfth century. Writing several decades prior to the great influx of Aristotelian thought in Latin translation, he anticipated Aristotle's position on the question of universals by advocating a theory of moderate realism. Universals, Abelard believed, had no separate existence but were derived from particular things by a process of abstraction. In a famous work entitled *Sic et Non* (*Yes and No*), Abelard collected opinions from the Bible, the Latin Doctors, the councils of the Church, and the decrees of the papacy on a great variety of theological issues, demonstrating that these hallowed authorities very often disagreed on important religious matters. Others before Abelard had collected authoritative opinions on various legal and theological issues but never so thoroughly or systematically. Abe-

246 The High Middle Ages

lard, in his *Sic et Non*, employed a method of inquiry that was developed and perfected by canon lawyers and philosophers over the next several generations. But his successors sought to reconcile the contradictions and arrive at conclusions, whereas Abelard left many of the issues unresolved and thereby earned the enmity of his conservative contemporaries. Abelard was a devoted Christian, if something of an intellectual show-off, but many regarded him as a dangerous skeptic. Thus he left himself open to bitter attacks by men such as St. Bernard who were deeply hostile to his merger of faith and reason. The brilliant teacher was hounded from one place to another and finally condemned for heresy in 1141. He died at Cluny, on his way to Rome to appeal the condemnation.

But twelfth-century rationalism was far more than a one-man affair, and the persecution of Abelard failed to halt its growth. In the later twelfth and early thirteenth centuries the movement was powerfully reinforced by the arrival of vast quantities of Greek and Arabic writings in Latin translation. Significant portions of the philosophical and scientific legacy of ancient Greece now became available to European scholars. Above all, the full Aristotelian corpus now came into the West through the labors of translators in Spain and Sicily

These translations were by no means fortuitous. They came in answer to a deep hunger on the part of Western thinkers for a fuller knowledge of the classical heritage in philosophy and science. Still, the introduction of certain new Aristotelian works created a profound intellectual crisis in Christendom, for they contained implications which seemed hostile to the Faith. The apparent incompatibility between these new Aristotelian writings and Christianity was heightened by the fact that they came into the West accompanied by the commentaries of a great heterodox Spanish Moslem philosopher, Averroes. This brilliant skeptic emphasized Aristotle's doctrine that the world had always existed and was therefore uncreated. He also interpreted Aristotle in such a way as to deny personal immortality. Averroes reconciled these views with orthodox Islam by a curious intellectual device known as the "doctrine of the twofold truth." He maintained that certain things could be true philosophically yet false from the standpoint of revealed religion. The importation of this twofold-truth doctrine into the West had two important consequences, (1) the development of a group of "Latin Averroists," who insisted on the philosophical validity of Aristotle's heterodox opinions yet defended the Christian Faith as ultimately true, even though at variance with reason, and (2) the condemnation of certain of Aristotle's writings by the Church.

Against this background there emerged in the mid-thirteenth century a bold group of men dedicated to the reconciliation of reason and faith and therefore to the fusion of Aristotle and Christianity. They sought to confound the Latin Averroists by demonstrating that reason and revelation pointed to one truth, not two. The greatest figures in this tradition were the German philosopher Albertus Magnus (Albert the Great) and his remarkable Italian pupil, Thomas Aquinas. Both men were Dominicans; both taught at the University of Paris, concurrently with the great Franciscan philosopher Bonaventure who was the thirteenth century's greatest exponent of the Platonic-Augustinian tradition. The confluence of men such as these made mid-thirteenth century Paris one of history's most notable intellectual centers.

St. Thomas Aquinas created medieval Europe's consummate synthesis of reason and revelation. In his elaborate *Summa Theologica*, St. Thomas explored all the great questions of philosophy and theology, political science and morality, using Aristotle's logical method and Aristotle's categories of thought but arriving at conclusions that were in complete harmony with the Christian Faith. A moderate realist on the problem of universals, St. Thomas reasoned from sense experience rather than divine illumination. Like Abelard, he assembled every possible argument, pro and con, on every subject that he discussed, but unlike Abelard, he drew conclusions. Few philosophers before or since have been so generous in presenting and exploring opinions contrary to their own, and none has been so systematic and exhaustive. St. Thomas created a vast, unified intellectual system, ranging from God to the natural world, logically supported at every step. As the Gothic cathedral was the artistic embodiment of the high medieval world, so the philosophy of Aquinas was its supreme intellectual expression. It is not without reason that the *Summa Theologica* has been called a cathedral of thought.

To this day there are those who subscribe essentially to the philosophy of Aquinas. But on the other hand, many of his own thirteenth-century contemporaries rejected it in whole or in part. Franciscan intellectuals such as Bonaventure were particularly suspicious of the *tour de force* of this gifted Dominican. In England a profoundly un-Thomistic point of view was gradually emerging in the thirteenth century—a point of view that combined the mathematical tradition of Plato with the experimental tradition of Aristotle and directed them toward the investigation of the physical world. It was in thirteenth-century England that Western European science was born. The great English scholar Robert Grosseteste (d. 1253) was on intimate terms with neo-Platonic philosophy, Aristotelian physics, and the rich scientific legacy of Islam. He pioneered in the development of scientific method by outlining a procedure of observation, hypothesis, and experiment, and by urging the use of mathematical analysis whenever possible. Like other pioneers, Grosseteste followed many false paths—his explanations of such phenomena as colors, heat, and rainbows, were rejected in later centuries—but the experimental methods which he advocated were developed by his successors into an exceedingly powerful intellectual tool. Grosseteste's disciple, the Franciscan Roger Bacon (*c.* 1214–1294), produced a fascinating body of scientific sense and nonsense. Roger Bacon was more an advocate of experimental science than a consistent practitioner of it, but at his best he was almost prophetic:

> Experimental science controls the conclusions of all other sciences. It reveals truths which reasoning from general principles [the method of Abelard and St. Thomas] would never have discovered. Finally, it starts us on the way to marvelous inventions which will change the face of the world.

Hence the intense intellectual activity of the thirteenth century produced both the supreme synthesis of Christian rationalism and the genesis of a new method of scientific inquiry. In the realm of thought, as in so many other areas, the thirteenth century was both synthetic and creative. As the century drew to its close the intellectual synthesis of St. Thomas was being eroded by the doubts of his successors, who began to suspect that in seeking to reconcile reason and revelation he was attempting the impossible. Subsequent philosophers tended more and more to separate the two realms, many of them reverting to the Averroistic notion of the "twofold truth."

Universal systems such as that of St. Thomas have seldom been lasting, but for a few brief years Thomism represented, for many, the perfect merger of intellect and belief—of mind and soul. As such, it takes its place alongside the Gothic cathedral, the *Divine Comedy* of Dante, and the piety of St. Francis as a supreme and mature expression of the dynamic resurgence of high medieval Europe.

The world of the High Middle Ages is described in some outworn textbooks as stagnant, gloomy, and monolithic. At the other extreme, it has been portrayed as an ideally constituted society, free of modern fears and tensions, where men of all classes could live happily and creatively. In reality, it was an age of vitality, of striking contrasts, of dark fears and high hopes, of poverty that was often brutal yet gradually diminishing. Above all, it was an age in which Europeans awoke to the rich variety of possibilities that lay before them. A thirteenth-century poet, in his celebration of Springtime, captured perfectly the spirit of this reawakening:

> The earth's ablaze again
> With lustrous flowers
> The fields are green again
> The shadows deep.
> Woods are in leaf again
> And all the world
> Is filled with joy again.
> This long-dead land
> Now flames with life again.
> The passions surge,
> Love is reborn,
> And beauty wakes from sleep.

Suggested Readings

The asterisk indicates a paperback edition.

GENERAL WORKS

R. W. Southern, *The Making of the Middle Ages* (*Yale). A brilliant, sympathetic interpretation of the eleventh and twelfth centuries.
Frederick Heer, *The Medieval World* (*Mentor). Heer contrasts twelfth-century expansion with thirteenth-century stabilization.

ECONOMIC HISTORY AND THE FRONTIERS

Henri Pirenne, *Economic and Social History of Medieval Europe* (*Harvest). A compact, richly interpretive survey by a great scholar.
Henri Pirenne, *Medieval Cities* (*Anchor). Brief, lucid, and highly original.
Sidney Painter, *Medieval Society* (*Cornell). A short, introductory essay.
Steven Runciman, *A History of the Crusades* (3 vols., Cambridge University Press; Vol I: *Harper). Comprehensive and authoritative.

EMPIRE AND PAPACY

Geoffrey Barraclough, *Medieval Germany, 911–1250* (2 vols., Blackwell). Volume I is a valuable introductory essay; Volume II consists of specialized studies by German scholars in English translation.
Gerd Tellenbach, *Church, State and Christian Society* (Blackwell). The finest analysis of the Investiture Controversy in English.
Walter Ullmann, *The Growth of Papal Government in the Middle Ages* (Methuen). An intellectual history of the medieval papal ideology.
Ernst Kantorowicz, *Frederick II*. An excellent biography. Kantorowicz's conclusions should be compared with those of Barraclough in his *Origins of Modern Germany* (*Capricorn).
Innocent III, Vicar of Christ or Lord of the World?, J. M. Powell (Ed.), (*Heath). Essays by historians representing diverse viewpoints.

250

ENGLAND AND FRANCE

For high medieval England, the appropriate volumes of the monumental Oxford History are authoritative but rather heavy:
A. L. Poole, *From Domesday Book to Magna Carta*.
F. M. Powicke, *The Thirteenth Century*.
For a lighter treatment of the period see especially:
Christopher Brooke, *From Alfred to Henry III* (Thomas Nelson).
Helen M. Cam, *England Before Elizabeth* (*Harper). Very brief but excellent.
Robert Fawtier, *The Capetian Kings of France* (*St. Martin's). A short, masterful treatment, highly recommended.
Amy Kelly, *Eleanor of Aquitaine* (*Vintage). Sound and entertaining.

CHRISTIANITY IN THE HIGH MIDDLE AGES

Norman F. Cantor, *Medieval History* (Macmillan). A recent, highly interpretive textbook, particularly strong on matters ecclesiastical.
Summerfield Baldwin, *The Organization of Medieval Christianity* (Holt). A short introductory essay.
Steven Runciman, *The Medieval Manichee* (*Compass Books). A penetrating investigation of medieval heresy.
Paul Sabatier, *St. Francis of Assisi* (Scribners). A masterly older study, deeply sympathetic to St. Francis.

THOUGHT, LETTERS, AND THE ARTS

F. C. Copleston, *Medieval Philosophy* (*Harper). A popular introduction by a leading scholar.
Gordon Leff, *Medieval Thought* (*Penguin). A survey which emphasizes the development of metaphysics.
C. H. Haskins, *The Rise of the Universities* (*Cornell). Short and highly competent; a pleasure to read.
C. H. Haskins, *The Renaissance of the Twelfth Century* (*Meridian). An epoch-making book, particularly strong in the area of Latin literature.
Erwin Panofsky, *Gothic Architecture and Scholasticism* (*Meridian). A challenging study which endeavors to demonstrate lines of connection between these two great medieval enterprises.
C. H. McIlwain, *The Growth of Political Thought in the West* (Macmillan). The preferred, one-volume account of medieval political theory.

SOURCES

The Portable Medieval Reader, tr. J. B. Ross and M. M. McLaughlin
(*Viking). Like Cantor's *Medieval World,* a useful, well-chosen
selection of medieval sources in translation.

Documents of the Christian Church, tr. Henry Bettenson (Oxford). A
useful collection running from antiquity to the present.

The Little Flowers of St. Francis, tr. L. Sherley-Price (*Penguin). A
fascinating collection of sources relating to the life of St. Francis.

Otto of Freising, *The Deeds of Frederick Barbarossa,* tr. C. C. Mierow
and R. Emery (Columbia). A good example of medieval historical
writing.

Memoirs of the Crusades: Villehardouin and de Joinville, tr. Sir Frank
Marzials (Everyman). Excellent contemporary accounts of the
Fourth Crusade and the crusading adventures of St. Louis.

The Portable Dante, tr. Paolo Milano (*Viking). Good translations of
the *Divine Comedy* and other works.

Introduction to St. Thomas Aquinas, tr. Anton C. Pegis (Modern
Library). Intelligently-chosen selections together with a stimulating
introduction.

Index

254 Index